PENGUIN BOOKS

PIE FIDELITY

'Britain on a plate . . . examines a series of traditional British meals with Hornby's geeky obsessiveness and Orwell's incisive class observation . . . His prose is engaging, his storytelling effortless' Tim Hayward, *Financial Times*

'Brilliant, funny . . . loving every page' Dave Myers, The Hairy Bikers

'Maybe it's okay for us to be proud of what we do really well whether it's a perfectly baked scone with a lick of jam and a dollop of clotted cream or proper farmhouse cheddar cheese with chutney on granary bread. And in reading *Pie Fidelity*, it's clear we've got a lot to be proud of' Julia Platt Leonard, *Independent*

'An erudite, personal apologia for our much-mocked British cuisine . . . Brown evokes the emotionalism of eating' William Skidelsky, *Guardian*

'As much as his book is a reflection of his experiences, reading it inevitably leads the reader to examine their own past, and how food defines who we are, or used to be' *Waitrose Weekend Magazine*

'He builds a picture not just of the grub itself but of the people who put themselves outside it . . . In the end, notes Brown, our favourite food is often the food we remember from our childhoods. "We are," as he says, "what we ate."' Mark Mason, *Spectator*

D1639013

Pete Brown is a middle-class north London foodie, who grew up working-class in Barnsley. He may well now speak fluent ramen and conversational kimchi, but he does so with a thick fish-and-chips accent.

He has written several books on food and drink, including *Man Walks into a Pub*, *Three Sheets to the Wind*, and *The Apple Orchard*. His discriminating palate has led him to be a judge in the Great Taste Awards and the Radio 4 Food and Farming Awards, and a frequent contributor to Radio 4's *Food Programme*.

Pie Fidelity

In Defence of British Food

PETE BROWN

PENGUIN BOOKS

PENGUIN BOOKS

UK | USA | Canada | Ireland | Australia
India | New Zealand | South Africa

Penguin Books is part of the Penguin Random House group of companies
whose addresses can be found at global.penguinrandomhouse.com.

First published by Allen Lane 2019
Published in Penguin Books 2020
001

Set in 11.8/14.6 pt Baskerville MT Std
Typeset by Jouve (UK), Milton Keynes
Printed in Great Britain by Clays Ltd, Elcograf S.p.A.

A CIP catalogue record for this book is available from the British Library

978-0-141-98673-9

www.greenpenguin.co.uk

For Liz,
who eats

'Tell me what you eat and I will tell you who you are.'

– Jean-Anthelme Brillat-Savarin,
The Physiology of Taste, 1825

'The only thing the British have ever done for European agriculture is mad cow disease. You can't trust people who cook as badly as that. After Finland, it's the country with the worst food . . . That's where our problems with NATO come from.'

– Jacques Chirac, G8 Summit, Gleneagles, 2005

'Food is everything we are. It's an extension of nationalist feeling, ethnic feeling, your personal history, your province, your region, your tribe, your grandma. It's inseparable from those from the get-go.'

– Anthony Bourdain (1956–2018)

Contents

1. Pie and Peas   1

2. A Cheese Sandwich   42

3. Fish and Chips   83

4. Spag Bol   131

5. Devonshire Cream Tea   167

6. Going for a Curry   194

7. The Full English   233

8. The Main Event   279

9. Crumble   321

Acknowledgements   337
Select Bibliography   339

1.

Pie and Peas

'Britain is the only country in the world where the food is more dangerous than the sex.'

– Jackie Mason

1.

'Blimey, you really know how to treat a girl.'

Liz and I have been together for six months. Two years from now, we'll be happily married, but we don't know that yet. There are stages we must go through first, things to get out of the way. One of these is, of course, the first visit to each other's home town to meet the families. We got her side out of the way fairly quickly. For various reasons, mine has taken a little longer.

Barnsley is one of those towns people feel comfortable mocking, even if they've never set foot in the place. Now she finally has, Liz is being kind. She's joking. I think. But we're not yet at the stage where I can take that for granted. She seems to be laughing it off, but maybe I've screwed up.

My relationship status with my home town is . . . it's complicated. I remain fiercely proud of having been born and brought up there, and I believe I'm a better person for it. After spending more than half my life in London, I've kept enough of my accent for many people to assume I still live up north. But when I go back home – is it still home? – people hear a posh, neutral accent that encourages the more gregarious of them to ask where I'm from and disbelieve my reply.

Back in London – is this now home? – people tend to say. 'Oh, I've been past Barnsley on the M1, but we didn't actually go there.'

My reply, which I always pitch as conciliatory but which sometimes comes out terser than I intended, is 'Why would you?'

The only people I ever meet who did come off the motorway (or take the slow branch lines between Sheffield and Leeds or Huddersfield) are those who were visiting relatives, or people who 'went out with a girl/boy from Barnsley' while they were at university, and I joke, 'What? I thought I was the only one who made it out alive!' and then immediately feel disloyal.

For most of my adult life, southerners have been unable to distinguish Barnsley from Burnley, its near-twin on the other side of the Pennines. But then Burnley FC started doing well in the Premiership, and everyone knows Barnsley do not do well in the Premiership. And so, most people I meet take the piss out of my home town, aping my pronunciation of its name and making enquiries about whippets or pigeons, even when they've never visited it and can't describe it or find it on a map.

I'm proud of having come from Barnsley. I'm also proud of having escaped its confines. I still love the place; I just sometimes don't like it very much, and I doubt I'd ever move back there. I experienced it as an insular town where everyone knew their place, where the role of the schools was to churn out sixteen-year-old miners and the wives who would look after them when they were married by twenty. Even some of the teachers at my school would ask why the hell you wanted to stay on and do A levels when you could get a job at the pit and have 200 quid in your hand by the end of next week. And then all the pits were closed down, with no thought given to what would replace them, and the town lost its purpose. People who had only ever wanted to work no longer could. The heart and fight went out of the place. Why did I want to stay on at school and do A levels? So I could go to university and get out of there.

Barnsley has never been a pretty town – although it could have been. It sits on the edge of the Pennines and, before the scarring of the Industrial Revolution, the landscape shared the desolate beauty of the hills to the south. You can still see its charm in places, on roads that crest valleys which open up unexpectedly. If you can mentally undress these valleys of industrial estates, they can stir the soul.

Barnsley town centre sits on top of one of the hills. In 2003, architect Will Alsop drew up plans to remodel it along the lines of a Tuscan hill village. The suggestion was ridiculed not only by the kind of people who sneer at Barnsley from afar but also by residents who had long grown accustomed to the town's brutal functionality and militant unpretentiousness.

The architectural critic Ian Nairn made a short film about Barnsley in 1969, and his frustration with the place was palpable and – to me, when I finally saw it a few years ago – familiar. Standing among buildings half ruined, just before work was about to start on a massive new concrete development, Nairn observed that it 'looks as if Russian troops have been through'. He decried the scene as a perfect example of how civic planners 'let something run down till it's completely hopeless, scrap it then start again instead of trying to keep it alive'. Barnsley was 'a colossal puzzle' to him, characterized by 'the contrast of a lot of human vitality and no vitality in the style of the town'.

Coming from Barnsley but not spending much time there any more feels similar to having a close friend or family member who has gone off the rails and become the subject of gossip. I'm allowed to criticize them, but if you do I'll defend them with a vestigial fierce pride. Despite feeling ambivalence, frustration and sometimes sadness about the town I grew up in, I still want people to respect it.

That's why, on our first visit, I take Liz to stately Cannon Hall and the beautiful country park that surrounds it, just five miles from the centre of town.* We stroll through the kitchen gardens, photographing espaliered pear trees and giant rhododendron bushes whose twisted frames, to me, look like entrances to magical caves; many years ago, I'd fantasize about escaping into them. We go to perfect pubs in the nearby village of Cawthorne, which is always a contender for Britain in Bloom. I impress upon her how

* 'You wouldn't think we were just five miles outside industrial Barnsley' is said by someone every single time a group of people from Barnsley visits Cannon Hall. It became such a cliché among my friends that we would battle to be the first to say it when we saw any vision of outstanding natural beauty, including, but not limited to the Lake District, the Cornish coast, the central massif of Mont Blanc in the French Alps, and – my proudest moment – a safari lodge overlooking herds of wildebeest sweeping majestically across the plains of the Masai Mara.

close we are to the Peak District, and how Leeds and Shef-field, bracketing Barnsley half an hour's drive north and south, could shock southern visitors with how cool and cosmopolitan they have recently become.

But I avoid Barnsley town centre – known simply as 'the town' or 't'Tarn' in the local dialect because there are no towns other than Barnsley if you live here – for as long as I can. Until one day, with a perverse sense of pride (or so I thought at the time) I decide, to hell with it, I'm going to take Liz for pork pie and mushy peas at one of the cafés in Barns-ley Market – a meal she still refers to as 'our first date'.

Nairn called this 'one of the best and biggest markets in Yorkshire'. Looking at a model of the proposed develop-ment in 1969, he said he simply couldn't tell what it was going to be like. I suspect he had a hunch. It went up when I was a toddler, and it was a vast, preposterously ugly urban ocean of rough, pebble-dashed concrete that swamped the entire town centre, which now looked as if the Russian troops hadn't just been through but had settled down and built somewhere that reminded them of home. It became a regular feature in all those novelty gift books from the early 2000s with names like *Crap Towns* and *Boring Post-cards*. But Barnsley market overcame its disfigurement at the hands of the council and remained popular, the vitality of the people obscuring the anaemic failure of their sur-roundings. I remember it for the vibrant colours of Sailor Sid's Sweets and Sid's jaunty nautical cap, and, a few years later, for the grotto-like textile stall that sold badges embla-zoned with 'The Jam' and 'Yorkshire Mods'. But most of all, I remember the smell, a composite aroma I've never encountered anywhere else, whose constituent parts were new wool, fresh meat and hot pastry, commingling in the eternally damp, heavy air. Despite the ugliness, and despite the fact that austerity has been a way of life around here for decades rather than years, despite the town centre being full of shops with slogans like 'Cheaper than Lidl!' in their windows, the market remains something Barnsley can be genuinely proud of. The cafés and the chip shops in the nearby alleyways are so plentiful and popular that when McDonald's opened a big new 'restaurant' around the corner from the market it couldn't compete and closed a few years later.

Our 'first date' takes place fifteen years after I left home, and I haven't been back very much since, so I choose a café for Liz at random. If I ever had a favourite, I can no longer remember where it was. And while I recall walls of yellowed tiles and partitions up to waist height separating the cafés from the main market space, they now all seem to have been rehomed in clean, discrete, glass-walled retail units. Hoping it's only their outward appearance that's changed, I usher Liz through the door and order two helpings of a dish I regard as the food of the gods.

For about £2, you get a pork pie sitting in the middle of a shallow bowl filled to the brim with mushy peas. This is garnished with mint sauce and served with a cup of tea – the kind you only get in cafés where the coffee offering doesn't extend beyond Nescafé, because who would want coffee when you can get tea like this? When I order, the woman behind the counter asks me if I would like it weak, medium or strong. There's only one acceptable answer.

The pork pie itself is served piping hot, a detail that causes Liz to raise her eyebrows into an expression that says,

'Whatever you people choose to do behind closed doors is your own business, but why do you have to involve me in it?'

It doesn't exactly look like the nicest food you'll ever eat, and I'll admit that up to the point where we raise our forks, there's a streak of self-effacing irony in my insistence that we're about to try a local delicacy. Thinking of it in such high regard suddenly feels like part of the same protective mood that caused Barnsley fans, back in the team's glorious 1996–7 promotion season and subsequent brief, never-to-be-repeated Premiership campaign, to sing the words 'It's just like watching Brazil' to the tune of 'Blue Moon', in such a deadpan way that sports journalists actually believed we meant it and felt the need to make serious, rational comparisons between the two sides and point out in national newspapers that even though Neil Redfearn was on fire he didn't actually possess the same skill or flair as Ronaldo. As if we were somehow so blinded by our sudden success that we couldn't tell.

But when the fork comes down and the brittle pastry lid crumbles and the aroma and warmth rise up, revealing the meat inside to be pink and fresh rather than the zombie-grey of cellophane-wrapped supermarket wannabes, and the jelly surrounding the meat has melted, coating the pork in a slick, salty sheen, any sense of irony on my part falls away. I know. And I remember.

This is the best pork pie in the world.

And it's not just the pie: the whole dish is perfectly judged. The mushy peas are a deliberate foil, sweet but also lending some dryness, which contrasts perfectly with the vividness of the meat and tempers it. The vinegary punch of the mint sauce feels wrong but tastes absolutely right.

As Liz scrapes together the last morsels of pea and pastry and finally accepts that the only way she's going to get anything else out of the bowl is to lick it clean, she says, 'OK, fine, that was incredible. But don't you dare tell anyone I said that. Ever.'

2.

Eighteen years later, Liz still tells this story as a way of illustrating my distinctly northern style of what people in Barnsley still refer to as 'courting'. Every time she brings it up I protest that it wasn't our first date because we'd been together for six months by then and, anyway, she bloody loved it. But she tells it this way, and I play my part in responding as I do, because in the polite, middle-class milieu we now inhabit, the idea that I took my future wife for a meal in Barnsley Market, and that this meal consisted of a hot pork pie in a bowl of mushy peas topped with mint sauce, is funny. Sometimes when I protest I'm merely playing the role of the comedy northerner. But other times, given just the right amount of condescension, I immediately revert to the defensive posture prompted by an attack on my family/ football team/home town. Yes, the story sounds funny, but why do you think it's ridiculous? Would you be laughing so hard if, for that 'first date', I'd taken Liz to a street food festival in Shoreditch and bought her banh xeo from a little stall run by a Vietnamese family? I didn't think so.

Am I comparing like with like here? To a great extent, I believe I am. This crispy crêpe filled with pork, shrimp and bean sprouts is eaten by the locals in cities like Hanoi and

Ho Chi Minh City in cheap cafés, markets and in the street. Read about it on any blog or in any newspaper travel feature and, as with so many street-food dishes, the writer will invariably insist that it's important to find the little cafés that cater to locals rather than tourists and enjoy the dish in the same way they do. That's exactly what I showed Liz in Barnsley. We seek out street food – generally understood to be the food of the poor – because it symbolizes authenticity, integrity and unpretentiousness – all desirable traits in an age that's overloaded with artificial gloss. But translate all this from Vietnam to the north of England and, for some reason, these qualities lose their aspirational appeal.

Why?

I'll concede on one point.

It's pie, isn't it? Britain does pies better than anyone else in the world and has done since pastry was first perfected by chefs working for the Tudor monarchs. Shepherd's pie, cottage pie, steak-and-ale pie, steak-and-kidney pie, and their cousin the Cornish pasty are famous representatives of our culinary tradition. The debate over whether a stew with a pastry lid on it qualifies as a pie or not, or whether a true pie must be encased in pastry, is the second-most divisive topic in our current national discourse. In my choice of pork pie, I hadn't even gone for one of the Premiership varieties.

The very strength of a pie is that it's functional and reassuring. Pies are cosy and familiar rather than exotic. A pie is not romantic. It's not mysterious. Well, it can be, but not with the kind of mystery that lends itself to romance, and the humour of Liz's story comes from the fact that it was meant to be a romantic meal. Food and courtship are intrinsically linked – the first date invariably revolves around a meal.

It's an opportunity to show our prospective mates our best selves, to establish shared tastes at the same time as demonstrating just the right degree of sophistication. In its home, Vietnamese street food may be exactly the same to the Vietnamese as pie and peas is to people in Barnsley, but bring Vietnamese food to Britain and it sparks the imagination.

I realize now that in Barnsley, having impressed and, somehow, attracted Liz, I was now revealing to her something deeper about myself. She'd already told me she loved me, and I felt ready to open up. By showing her Barnsley, I was showing her where I came from and who I had been. And that's why it was so important for me to take her for pie and peas.

It may have presented itself in the café as the most ordinary meal imaginable, as visually off-putting as the town centre itself, but this was one of the meals I'd grown up with, and not just a meal but an occasion, a ritual, a part of who we were. The pie-and-pea supper was served at events in every school hall, church hall and working men's club, at every eighteenth and twenty-first birthday party, at wedding receptions and Christmas discos and golden wedding anniversaries. As a child, it was the highlight of the boring grown-up parties I was dragged along to. When it was served at school, it was a naughty, adult thrill. When we were old enough for our own grown-up parties, it was an acknowledgement that, while we might be forming our own, broader tastes and some of us were even preparing to leave t'Tarn for the outside world, this was the continuity that linked us to parents who no longer understood us. This wasn't just the best pork pie in the world. It was far more important than that – if anything can be.

*

'Come on, then, you've piqued us curiosity. Why are you takin' pictures on us?'

'I'm writing a book about food, and one of the things is pork pies.'

As soon as the word 'book' leaves my mouth, the woman's face falls and she turns away before I've finished my sentence. Given that she left her station behind the counter of Kay's Café and followed me around a corner to ask me what I was doing, she was obviously hoping for something far more exciting.

Forty-odd years after it was finished, the giant concrete bunker of Barnsley's market complex is being pulled down and, in some boozy afterlife, Ian Nairn is smiling. The market stalls and cafés have been moved again, to temporary accommodation. Most of the cafés surround a makeshift food court where shoppers pause for what they'd no doubt refer to as 'brunch' if we were a hundred miles or so further south.

Outside, the hoardings shielding the demolition work are covered in computer-generated simulations of what the new market space will supposedly look like. They show an attractive square full of stylish young people who look very different from anyone sitting in the food court today. Because the tenants of these new spaces haven't yet signed up, the restaurants in the picture have names like 'Magamama' and 'Bryon'. As far as the architects are concerned, this is clearly their vision of a Better Barnsley.

Somehow, I can't see it coming to fruition.

I was trying to be discreet when I took the photo of Kay's Café but when I examine it everyone behind the counter is glaring at me suspiciously. I wasn't even trying to photograph them: I was taking a picture of the menu boards above the stall. The three main ones are titled 'Hot Dinners', 'Yorkshire Puds' and 'Burgers', and it's the first of these I find most compelling. The options it lists are: chips; chips and gravy; chips and beans or peas; chips and cheese; chip butty; chips and egg; chips, egg and beans; chips and sausage; chips, sausage and beans; chicken, chips and gravy; meat, chips and gravy;* pie and peas; pie and gravy; pie and chips; and pie, chips, peas and gravy.

At the time of writing, a Byron (or 'Bryon') burger costs £9.50, and if you want chips (sorry, 'French fries') that's an additional £3. The burger at Kay's costs £2.95.

This would all be hilarious if the food were poor or tasted horrible. But just like in Ho Chi Minh City or, say, Knoxville, Tennessee, or Thiviers in the Dordogne, when the focus on the local dish is so narrow you have to be good at it because the competition is so intense.

I eventually choose Hilton's on the other side of the food court for my pie and peas, partly because I'm now scared of the women at Kay's and partly because Hilton's sign reading 'TRY OUR PROPER MUSHY PEAS' forces me to obey.

Pie and peas costs £2.90 these days. The crust is still crumbly and fresh, the meat gently spiced and generously seasoned. Without meaning to, I moan on the first bite. After eighteen years, it tastes as good as it always did. I feel a warming numbness, enlivening morphine for the soul.

* 'Meat' is sometimes generic in Barnsley. I once took Liz to Oakwell to watch Barnsley FC lose at home to Port Vale, and at half-time she went to the pie stall. 'What kind of pies do you have?' she asked. 'Meat,' came the reply. She just had some chips.

Looking at the market with fresh eyes and a full but not yet bloated stomach, I realize there's a very well-developed local cuisine here. The grocer's stalls are plentiful and their produce looks as fresh and inviting as you'd expect from any decent market. But the bakery stalls are on another level, like nothing I've seen anywhere else. In 2016, John Foster, who runs Foster's Bakery at the bottom of the street where I grew up, was the head baker on the BBC2 series *Victorian Bakers*, such is his stature in the world of flour and eggs these days. And he's not alone. Today the market stalls are crammed with a variety of freshly baked loaves, tea cakes and bread cakes. There are macaroons, coffee buns, flapjacks, currant slices, Viennese mince pies, fresh scones (plain and fruity), cream buns, lemon-curd tarts and egg custards, and I remember for the first time in decades how I used to love lemon-curd tarts when I was very small. These displays make London's recent cupcake obsession look sad and tawdry.

And then there are the butchers. There's a strong tradition of butchery in Barnsley. In the small satellite village of Mapplewell, where I grew up, there were five butcher's shops orbiting Foster's Bakery – far more than any other kind of shop in the village. In the centre of Barnsley there's still an area of the market that's devoted entirely to meat and fish. Returning now, I'm struck by the richness and variety on the stalls. As well as all the cuts I'd expect to see in a decent butcher's shop anywhere in the country, there are ham shanks and pig's trotters, piles of tripe and mounds of sliced brawn, not hidden away apologetically but centre stage. There's no attempt to sugar-coat the fact of where all this comes from. Pretty much every part of the animal – or 'beast', as the butchers say around here – is prepared for sale. When Fergus Henderson champions nose-to-tail eating in Smithfield, it's an important contribution to Britain's gastronomic conversation. Here, they just get on with it, like they always have, since Fergus were a lad and throughout the period of his entire life so far. Walking through the market as a middle-class North Londoner, I fall in love with my home town all over again.

Many of these butchers make their own pork pies. There are arguments over whose is best. Some say it's Percy Turner. Others are wrong.

Percy Turner, now in his sixties, still makes pork pies every day at his small butcher's shop in the village of Jump. Jump is another typical satellite village orbiting t'Tarn, clinging to the side of a hill overlooking a once-beautiful valley. Despite what its name might imply, not much happens in Jump. What passes for its centre consists of a post office, a hairdresser's and a convenience store, and next door to Jump Chippy there's a butcher's shop that doesn't even have a sign outside.

Most people who have been to Melton Mowbray are shocked to discover there is little or no evidence there of the town's pork-pie fame. People I know who judge the British Pie Awards (yes, it's a real and very serious competition) say that Melton Mowbray pork pies aren't all they're cracked up to be. I always ask them if they've tasted the pork pies from Percy Turner's in Jump, and they invariably suspect I'm taking the piss. I'm not. Some mornings, before the shop opens, there are queues down the street waiting for the day's fresh batch.

Percy Turner is too busy making pies to bother with a website or any kind of promotional activity. What you might call 'promotion' or 'marketing' is known in Barnsley as 'showing off', and you just don't. But then, Percy Turner doesn't have to. He doesn't need awards or TV chefs turning up to boost his business. There's a Percy Turner's Pork Pie Appreciation page on Facebook, unaffiliated with the butcher's itself, with 4,000 likes. There's a spoof M&S ad that a Percy Turner's superfan posted on YouTube. But I've failed to find any official recognition for what I truly believe to be the best pork pies in the world.

Following our Barnsley-style brunch in the market, my friend Chris and I arrive in Jump after the morning rush, when the queues have gone. There are no certificates or awards in Percy's shop, no photos of the man himself – who is standing with his back to the counter now, chopping meat – with local dignitaries or celebrities. There's not even a notice outside saying 'Home of Percy Turner's famous pork pie' or anything like that. In fact, there's not much of anything at all – none of the extraneous stuffings or condiments many 'artisanal' butcher's sell – just a few chops and a couple of trays of liver and diced steak. And on cooling racks in the corner, two half-trays of individual-portion pork pies. I buy half a dozen: they cost 75 pence each. Chris and I head back to his car, and before we open the door we're tucking into meat that is almost gamey, jelly that's still moist and crust that holds on to a faint, residual warmth. We stand there in the street, grinning and grunting as we demolish our second pie of the morning, unable to move until we've finished.

There's as much difference between a petrol-station Ginster's and a fresh, hot growler from Percy Turner's as there is between a cheap supermarket ready-meal and a curry cooked fresh on the streets of Delhi. I genuinely believe that if Percy Turner's hot pork pie and peas with mint sauce had emerged on the streets of Shanghai, Bangkok or Memphis, Tennessee, it would be widely available in fashionable eateries in London, New York and Paris as well as in Barnsley.

The fact that it isn't – and that the mere suggestion it might be sounds to most ears like a joke – obviously says something about the north and whatever place it holds in our national consciousness. And it probably has something to do with the comfortable, self-deprecating, distinctly working-class notion of the pie itself.

But I think there's more to it than that. It's not just about Barnsley – or pies. I suspect that if 'our first date' had been fish and chips in Whitby, haggis in Dumfries or farmhouse cider in Somerset, it would have got a similar reaction, whereas a glass of natural wine, a masala dosa, or even a pizza in any of these places would not. I suspect the ambivalence I feel about Barnsley – my tendency to be simultaneously critical and defensive of it – echoes aspects of how many of us feel about Britain more generally, particularly with regard to our traditional cuisine.

Every loving couple tells the stories that define them, which become part of the fabric of the relationship. The eighteen-year-old story of mine and Liz's first date was more than that. It was a loose thread in the fabric of Britain's rich tapestry, and I found myself pulling on it.

3.

At the end of the nineteenth century rural France was angry. Across the country, in isolated pockets, food and drink producers had been working with their *terroir* for centuries to create products whose reputations travelled further than many of the products ever did. Names like Champagne, Roquefort, cognac and Camembert became revered – if you were visiting a region where one of them was made you simply had to try them, because there was nothing quite like them anywhere else. And then, the world changed. The near-simultaneous arrival of refrigeration and railways meant that food and drink could be stored for far longer and transported more easily, quickly and cheaply over far greater distances than ever before. Soon, France's finest wines and cheeses were being served in the best restaurants and hotels across Europe and beyond.

Such was their fame that the stars of French regional agricultural produce began attracting imitators. The word 'Champagne' started to be used to describe any sparkling wine, or even cider produced using similar methods. Over the border in Switzerland, there was a warning of what the market could do when 'Gruyère' went from being the name of a cheese produced specifically in the canton of Fribourg to become a generic term encompassing many yellow, nutty, earthy hard cheeses, regardless of where they were made.

Led by the wine producers, French artisans demanded a system of *appellations d'origine*: state-sanctioned control of the use of names that implied a specific geographic origin.

This system evolved into the *appellation d'origine controlée* (AOC) laws in the 1930s, which in turn provided the basis for the European Union's Protected Geographical Indication (PGI) and Protected Designation of Origin (PDO) in 1992. Historian Kolleen Guy suggests that 'this ruralist and protectionist discourse elevated the land and its products to a central part of every Frenchman's legacy', that cheeses and wines and the special *terroir* that created them were part of 'a construction of Frenchness' at a time when what it meant to be French was being redefined, and when mass consumer culture was starting to have a widespread influence on the very notion of identity.

The obvious consequence of enshrining *terroir* into law was that these treasured regions now had to be strictly demarcated: you were either making your sparkling wine inside the region of Champagne or you were not, so a line had to be drawn somewhere in the chalky limestone subsoil. The precise placement of this border created bitter battles between the owners of the new *appellation d'origine* and those a few hundred yards away who argued they'd been making better champagne for longer than their nearby rivals. The conflict grew so heated it was characterized by the press at the time as civil war.

French producers weren't the only ones suffering from the problem of dishonest imitations. At the same time as Champagne was being feted as the world's best wine, Bass Ale, brewed in Burton-on-Trent, was the most famous and widely drunk beer on the planet. It first found fame in India so became widely known as India Pale Ale (IPA) and was subsequently exported across the British Empire and beyond, its distinctive red triangle instantly recognizable.

And while beer struggles to claim *terroir* in the same way wine has – Bass was brewed with barley from Norfolk and hops from Kent, Germany and the United States* – Bass was the best pale ale in the world because the high mineral content in the water drawn from Burton's wells, particularly the astonishing levels of gypsum, united these diverse ingredients and enhanced their flavour in a way no other water could. Such was the town's fame, and such was the quality of its beer, that reputable London brewers were forced to open satellite breweries in Burton to brew their own pale ales. Other, less reputable breweries simply called their vastly inferior beers 'Bass' and copied the logo. This was such a widespread problem that when the Patent Office acquired the responsibility for registering trade marks in 1876 a clerk from Bass was sitting waiting on the steps outside on New Year's Day, having spent the night there. The Bass red triangle became Britain's first-ever trade mark, narrowly missing out to German steel company Krupp in being the world's first.

Kolleen Guy argues that the French *appellation d'origine* legislation was 'not based on economic logic but on claims of authenticity, history and patrimony'. The protection of regional agricultural specialities was part of a broader exploration of the very idea of what it meant to be French. By contrast, in Britain, the pioneering of trademark legislation was based entirely on economic logic and nothing else. There was no legislation to protect the recipe for Bass, the terms 'pale ale', 'India Pale Ale' or even 'Burton Ale',

* Each of which, individually, has its own *terroir*, which has just as much impact in its contribution to the finished beer as the grapes in wine.

19

or the chemical composition of the water (which, as soon as it was successfully analysed, was artificially re-created by ale brewers around the world, adding salts via a process that is still used and is known as 'Burtonization'). The commercial mark – the brand – was the only aspect of the world's most famous beer deemed worth protecting.

Today, Champagne is still ruthlessly protected and remains the world's most famous and admired wine. Bass Ale still exists too, and its trademark is protected as robustly as ever by its present owners, global brewing giant Anheuser Bush-Inbev. But it has negligible market share, has had its recipe and production methods changed almost beyond recognition and is no longer considered to be an India Pale Ale.

I don't believe that the fortunes of champagne and Bass diverged so dramatically because Bass in the nineteenth century was of poor quality while champagne was wonderful. In fact, when it was finally drunk in India after its six-month sea journey from Burton, Bass was often celebrated for its champagne-like qualities.* Its demise did not happen because of something intrinsic to the beer itself.

Imagine if the French made beer instead of wine, if grapes didn't grow so well in France but certain regions excelled in the cultivation of hops and barley. Every decent restaurant in the world would now have a beer sommelier

* I re-created this journey, with a barrel of beer brewed to a nineteenth-century Bass recipe in tow, for my 2009 book *Hops & Glory*. The voyage transforms the beer. When I opened some at a trade show in Delhi, it went down a storm with everyone, apart from one man, who stormed up to me and said, 'Why are you trying to trick us? You claim this is beer, but it is obviously wine!' before asking for a refill.

and a cellar full of aged Old Ales and Barley Wines. Every TV food show would be debating whether this week's dish went better with a Parisian-style best bitter or a Burgundian stout. Perhaps the hard water of Hérault in the south of the country would have given rise to a beer that matured and ripened on its journey to the French colonies so, instead of India Pale Ale from Burton-on-Trent, the darling of what would now be a century-old craft-beer movement would be Senegal Pale Ale. But you'd only be able to call it Senegal Pale Ale if – rather confusingly – it was brewed in the Hérault area, using only local ingredients. If craft brewers in Portland, Oregon, wanted to create something similar, they would have to call it 'French-African-style Pale Ale'. They face no such difficulties with American IPA.

The logical conclusion to draw from this comparative case study would be that the identification of French food and drink is, for the French, a defining part of their national identity whereas, for the British, it's simply about commerce and consumption – we just don't care as much about the quality of the food and drink themselves.

But such a seemingly obvious conclusion would be wrong. This difference in our attitudes towards our respective national cuisines is more complex than that.

4.

In 2012, the market research firm YouGov asked 60,000 Britons what they loved most about their country. It could be anything: the BBC, Big Ben and 'the countryside' all featured in the top ten. Buckingham Palace made it in at number seven, with 'Queen' in fifteenth place – which turned out to be Queen, the band, rather than the monarch. The top three were: the bacon sandwich, a cup of tea and roast dinners. Fish and chips and Yorkshire pudding ensured that five of the top-ten best things about Britain were its food or drink. Fourteen different examples of food and drink made it into the top fifty – over a quarter of all the entries – and twelve of those were in the top twenty-five.

According to this survey – and many others like it – our traditional food and drink are more important than the monarchy and at least as significant as our landscape and national monuments in defining a collective notion of who we are.

For anyone who spends time thinking about food rather than just eating it, this is probably not all that surprising. Food is more than fuel to keep us alive. All animals must eat, but humans 'dine', and there's more to the notion of dining than simply ingesting food. Dining is bound up in notions of etiquette, manners and behaviour, and these principles vary significantly from one group or society of humans to another. There's scarcely a book about food that doesn't quote Jean Anthelme Brillat-Savarin's famous aphorism 'Tell me what you eat and I will tell you who you are', which has since been abbreviated around the world to 'You are what you eat.' Most of us probably have pretty similar ideas of the age and social class of the bloke who eats a full English breakfast in a greasy spoon every morning, the person preparing smashed avocado on sourdough toast in a well-appointed kitchen and the Ritz patron tucking into their famous Platinum Sturgeon Caviar Breakfast.

But the cultural meaning of food runs even deeper; so deep, in fact, that it even defines our ideas of what 'food' actually is. Stripped of any cultural reference points, 'food' is anything you can eat without it killing you or making you ill; ideally, it also contains some nutritional value. Most of us narrow this definition beyond that. What some people consider to be 'food' is not food to others. The difference – the vast majority of the time – doesn't rest on biological or genetic differences between nations and groups. It comes from how we and others see ourselves in relation to what's on our plate and the world at large.

French social scientist Claude Fischler believes that food is so central to our sense of identity because in the act of eating (or drinking), food crosses the boundary between 'outside' and 'inside'. We literally make it part of ourselves. This 'principle of incorporation' is fundamental in defining differences between our particular group and other groups of humans, which is why kosher, halal and the prohibition of eating pork are central to particular religions and why many Catholics still refrain from eating meat on Fridays. It's why many immigrant populations hold on to their native cuisines and food cultures long after they've assimilated other aspects of their new homes, such as language and dress. It's why vegetarianism and veganism often come as part of a broader ideological view and are used by people to define themselves against others – particularly by teenagers seeking to create the first separation between themselves and their parents. So, just as there's a difference between feeding and dining, this is the difference between 'food' and 'cuisine'.

Cuisine makes value judgements about which foods are

culturally, ideologically or morally acceptable to eat; which are the most prized; which should be eaten with which others and on what occasions. Both aborted duck foetuses and rotten-milk by-products are, strictly speaking, *food* if we want them to be, but *cuisine* stretches to include judgements on whether or not it's acceptable to eat one, both or neither; how they should be prepared,* whether they're a treat or for every day, suitable for breakfast, lunch, dinner or tea, and whether you should have either with ketchup or brown sauce.

Food-studies text books describe a 'food system' of cuisine that depends on three main variables: identity, responsibility and convenience. Every choice we make about what we eat is a combination – not necessarily in equal parts – of what's available, affordable and easy; what's acceptable morally, ethically and societally; and who we are and how we see ourselves.

In *Cooked*, Michael Pollan writes about the idea of 'disgust' in food and drink. He ties this to fermentation and argues that, in any given culture, the most prized food and drink is that which has been fermented, which includes chocolate, coffee, cured meats and all sorts of other foods, as well as alcoholic drinks, bread and cheese. But fermented foods are also the most culturally specific, the foods that are often most important in defining who we are and who we are not. The flavours and foods that one culture prizes above all others are those most likely to cause

---

* Your aborted duck foetus should always be boiled, dipped in salt and eaten whole, washed down with cold beer, according to the Filipinos who consider it an everyday delicacy.

disgust among other people. So, while the smell of mildewed tofu in Shaoxing may be enough to make a Western European vomit, the people who adore it are just as likely to be revolted by the curdled, bacteria-laced milk we call cheese. We can see that these foods aren't poisonous because we can watch each other eating them without dying or becoming sick. We know the 'Bush Tucker Trials' on *I'm a Celebrity Get Me Out of Here* are not an attempt to kill the contestants (even if we sometimes wish they were), but the whole point of them is to arouse disgust and nausea. It may well be food. But it's not *our* food.

This is why food helps to define even nations. We call the French Frogs and they call us Rosbifs. Americans call us Limeys because of the fruit English sailors used to ward off scurvy. In the First and Second World Wars, both the Limeys and the Hot-dog Eaters referred to the Germans as Krauts while the Frogs called them Boche, both names deriving from the German fondness for pickled cabbage. Wealthy northern Italians used to refer to Sicilians as Macaroni Eaters in the sixteenth century and, in the nineteenth, the English dubbed the Irish Potato Eaters.

Often these names are pejorative. To me as an Englishman, Rosbif doesn't particularly feel like a racial slur, but I'd think twice about calling a French person 'Frog' to their face.* 'Dogeater' is clearly meant to be offensive when applied to Southeast Asians because it contains a moral judgement about their supposed dietary habits. With frog's

---

* The term was originally applied to Jesuits and to the Dutch and was affixed specifically to the French only during the Napoleonic Wars.

legs, bush tucker or sauerkraut, there may be some genuine disgust at the thought of eating such things – in Japanese, *bata-kusai* is an old phrase referring to Caucasians that means 'stinking of butter'. But other times, from the outside at least, these differences can seem arbitrary. The Parakanã people of the Amazon rainforest absolutely adore roasted tapir, as much as they absolutely despise the very thought of eating monkey meat. Their neighbours the Arara feel just as strongly, but in reverse. Another example is an old American joke, or rather pair of competing jokes: How do they dispose of garbage in Italian (or Polish) restaurants? They put it on the menu in Polish (or Italian) restaurants.

Whether they're intended to be hostile or affectionate, food-based nicknames are meant to firmly separate 'Us' from 'Them', even if the foods we actually eat most of the time do not. Calling Mexicans Beaners (common among American racists) or South Asians Curry Munchers (popular among British racists) is deemed and intended to be offensive, which is curious, given that the kinds of people who would use these terms are often likely to be big fans of these foods too.

So if food is about representation, what does British food say about British people?

The first thing it seems to say, if we listen to folklore and gossip, is that we're not very good cooks and, what's more, we seem to be perfectly OK with that. British food has long had an awful reputation around the world, especially in Europe. Jacques Chirac's offensive remark about British food, repeated at the front of this book, is outrageous, especially as he was being hosted by top British chefs at the time. Chirac's spokesperson did not deny the remarks, instead saying merely that they did 'not reflect the tone or content' of the overall meeting where they took place.

Normally, if the French say something about anything, the British want to think the opposite, but on this particular issue we seem happy to acquiesce. In 1946, George Orwell wrote an essay titled 'In Defence of English Cooking', in which he noted, 'It is commonly said, even by the English themselves, that English cooking is the worst in the world.' In some respects, that doesn't seem to have changed. Prince Philip once praised the nation that feeds and clothes him by asserting that 'British women can't cook.' When I started to tell friends and colleagues that I was writing a book about British food, the instant replies from Brits and foreigners alike were usually along the lines of 'You mean about how bad it is?' Belgian food writer and Anglophile Regula Ysewijn told me she had a similar reaction when telling British people she was planning a book on the best of British food, invariably receiving the reply, 'That'll be a very thin book.' In our self-deprecating manner, we seem happy to accept the idea of British cuisine as a bit of a joke. In his book *How We Eat*, psychologist Leon Rappoport asks rhetorically, 'Is there any well-defined social group sharing a culture that does not believe its own cuisine is better tasting and healthier than any other?' As a Brit, I feel I have to raise my hand on behalf of my nation.

There's no structural reason why our food is supposedly so bad. We've always had excellent pasture and a temperate climate which helps it yield incredibly high-quality meat and produce. And if we can't grow it here, we've been world leaders in international trade for centuries. Exotic fruits, meats, herbs and spices first came to Britain with the Romans. The food enjoyed by the rich during the Middle Ages wasn't too different from the spicy food eaten in India at the time, and the British Empire was founded on our quest to control the trade in exotic spices. So the raw ingredients aren't the problem. Today we have excellent chefs and cooks with more than their fair share of Michelin stars. And some of us are noted for our discerning palates: few nations have elevated the appreciation and criticism of food and drink as highly as the British.

So how did Britain get such an awful reputation for food? And why are many of us happy to accept it?

If you're one of the 66 per cent of Britons who describe themselves as being passionate about food and drink, you're probably reading this and shaking your head, thinking, 'No, you're wrong! We're in the middle of a food revolution now! Britain has an amazing food culture.'

This is true: the last twenty years have seen a gastronomic rebirth sweep the country. Recipe books written by TV chefs top the charts every Christmas, and there's at least one cookery show on primetime TV every night during the week, all year round. Whether you look at the range of ingredients available in supermarkets, the number of different cuisines available in high-street restaurants or the number of food magazines on sale in the newsagent's, there's no doubt that Britain is developing an enthusiastic, creative interest in food. Particularly if you're under thirty-five and came of age while the foodie revolution was already happening, according to 2018 research by digital publisher GreatBritishChefs.com, you're more likely than not to agree with statements such as 'I enjoy talking about food and planning what I am going to eat' and 'I like to try out new recipes.'

But the foodie revolution is happening as a reaction against traditional British food. The Great British Chefs research segments food into 'simple', 'homely' and 'traditional' on one hand, and 'experimental', 'international', 'adventurous' and 'modern' on the other. Even the most hardcore foodies are no more likely to cook the former than anyone else. They're at least twice as likely as the national average to cook the latter.

People seeking to champion Britain's exciting culinary scene today invariably do so by comparing it to how awful British food used to be. When people rave about London as the best place in the world to eat, they do so by pointing out how many different international cuisines are available in one city. If traditional dishes such as fish and chips or the humble cheese sandwich are celebrated, it's with a spirit of putting a new (and invariably expensive) twist on them, reinventing them and presenting them in a way that means many people can no longer afford to buy them. Even if you want to praise British food, it seems you have to take it away from its roots to do so rather than celebrating them.

This does reveal a few more interesting aspects of Britishness. One is that, despite how some loud and ugly voices come across, as a whole we're more receptive to foreign influence than any other nation on earth. Cuisines such as Italian and Chinese travelled widely around the world thanks to large population migrations, diasporas who may have wanted a new life but wanted their traditional cuisine to remain part of it. More recently, American burgers spread with the wider globalization of American culture and entertainment. But Britain goes further in its absorption of other food cultures. Before the influences of successive waves of immigration of European Jews, Germans, Italians, South Asians and people from across the former empire, we had been aping French food in high society arguably since the Norman invasion, and bringing back exotic food from ships that traversed the globe. We continue to have a remarkably open attitude to new cuisines today: market researchers Mintel, in their 2017 report 'Attitudes towards World Cuisines', showed that 70 per cent of us regularly eat Chinese and Indian food. When you include other cuisines such as Thai, Mexican, Japanese and Middle Eastern, 60 per cent of us eat three or more different national cuisines over a three-month period. There's always a longer queue in a branch of McDonald's than there is in most chip shops, and there are far more pasta and pizza restaurants in any town than restaurants that serve traditional British food.

When the foodie revolution really got under way in the late 1990s, in the wake of Britpop, Cool Britannia and Tony Blair (before the messy war-crimes stuff), it felt like Britain was comfortable with its multicultural past, present and future and confident enough to look outwards. There was a surge in the popularity of exciting new ethnic food styles, each one arriving more quickly than the last. Thai was followed by sushi was followed by ramen was followed by Mexican, whether you were looking at restaurants, 'world cuisine' ready-meals in supermarkets or popular cookbooks. In 1998, when Fat Les sang of their fondness for vindaloo in a song supporting England's World Cup campaign, it didn't feel wrong. Well, OK, it might have done, but it didn't feel *incongruous*. Three years later, the now-late Robin Cook declared chicken tikka masala to be our 'true British national dish . . . a perfect illustration of the way Britain absorbs and adapts external influences'.

In 2003, this sentiment was confirmed by 'The Nation's Favourite Food', a massive online poll conducted by the BBC for a subsequent TV series and book. Venerable classics such as roast dinners and toad-in-the-hole were up near the top, but they were competing with spaghetti bolognese, lasagne, pizza, Chinese stir-fry, macaroni cheese, chilli con carne and curry, all of which seemed as British as roast beef, supporting Cook's assertion.

We do more than eat foreign cuisines: we adopt them and assimilate them. One generation's 'foreign muck' is the next generation's traditional British. Dig into history a little and even some of the finest bastions of traditional British cooking began life as visitors to these shores, just as all our ancestors did.

My only frustration with our remarkable openness to the food of other cultures is that it can sometimes be at the expense of defending our own. I adore getting the Eurostar to Paris, exiting the station and revelling in the sheer *Frenchness* of it all. It's hard to resist diving into one of the many brasseries on the other side of the station square and ordering a plate of snails and a glass of wine. This is what's so great about being abroad – the otherness, the reality of it, the heightened awareness in all your senses. But if I were a French person coming the other way, hoping for an equal but opposite experience, I'd feel somewhat cheated. Exiting the Eurostar terminal into the shopping mall that was once St Pancras station, you're immediately faced with French patisseries and boulangeries, a champagne bar and a sandwich chain called Pret A Manger. Look further afield and you'll find a sushi bar, an American burger joint and an Italian restaurant. When you eventually do find the Betjeman Arms pub, finally there's a range of high-quality classic British dishes, but they're served in an environment that feels much more like a French brasserie than a traditional British pub.

If we are proud of our national dishes – as the 2012 YouGov survey suggests we are – we love them quietly, privately. Seventy-two per cent of Brits say, when they cook at home, 'British' food accounts for more than half of what they make. On the day I'm writing this, yet another survey is released. This one, commissioned on behalf of Young's Seafood, reveals that, when asked, 70 per cent of British people would choose British products if given a choice, and 60 per cent believe British food is the best in the world. The survey claims Britishness is a 'growing trend' in food choices, thanks to a sense of patriotism, memories of childhood and, for 60 per cent of respondents, its 'traditional and comforting' nature. This is certainly consistent with other surveys stretching back at least a decade. But compared with our actual behaviour, research respondents seem to be lying to the researchers, or to themselves. Where are the big branded chains of British restaurants to rival the burger joints, pizza and pasta restaurants and Italian-inspired coffee shops that have colonized every high street?

In the years following Robin Cook's famous speech, the world became a much scarier, less certain place. It's been well documented that in times of economic crisis people yearn for the reassurance of the past, for tradition and continuity and an age that hindsight presents as safer and more understandable. While we still have far more curry restaurants than fish-and-chip shops, and global-cuisine ready-meals are still on sale in every supermarket, they've been joined by new ranges of 'traditional pub classics' packaged in a palate of dull, dependable browns.

We see it as well in the steady wave of polls and surveys. Almost every traditional food you can think of now has a 'national week', from Real Bread Week in February and British Pie Week in March through a very busy May that somehow manages to cram National Doughnut Week, International Hummus Day, National Vegetarian Week, Coeliac Awareness Week, National Barbecue Week, British Sandwich Week and British Tomato Week into its thirty-one days, to National Fish and Chips day in June, Afternoon Tea Week in August and UK Sausage Week in October, to name but a few. The better-run weeks will invariably commission some kind of survey on our eating habits, and their results are remarkably consistent. Although they jockey for position from poll to poll, the bacon sandwich, the roast dinner, fish and chips and the full English breakfast are invincible. While we may eat pizza and pasta more often than anything else, when asked, we celebrate pies and puddings. Orwell knew this in 1946, when he wrote, 'It must be remembered that in talking about "British cookery" one is referring to the characteristic native diet of the British Isles and not necessarily to the food that the average British citizen eats at this moment.'

We have an emotional fondness for our favourite meals that far outweighs their actual role in our diet. We don't think of ourselves as Burger Eaters or Pizza Munchers – in terms of identity, we're still Rosbifs and resolute Full English Breakfasters.

Foodie academics explain this partly with the notion of 'cultural superfoods'. Thinking back to the food-systems triangle, the convenience point shapes dominant cuisines in different parts of the world: tortilla in Mexico, pasta in Italy and rice and soy in Asia can become so dominant, thanks to their ready availability, that they almost define the places and the people who live there.

Over the last seventy years or so, as a result of ethnic migration and the globalization of food supplies, many of these cultural superfoods, once particular to one part of the world, have become more general. Today in Britain you might have potatoes with one meal, rice and soy sauce with the next and tortilla the following day. But even if we eat some of these foods really often, they're not cultural superfoods to us because they're not the meals that define us. We might eat burgers, pizzas and breakfast cereal more than any other foods, but so do lots of other people all around the world. These foods don't distinguish us from anyone else, whereas fish and chips, the full English breakfast and roast dinners do. People in other countries don't eat these like we do. 'They' recognize these meals as setting us apart, and eating the 'proper' version of them is part of the cultural experience of visiting Britain. 'We', too, recognize that they make us different.

I decide to dig into as many of these surveys as I can find, looking for the meals that crop up again and again. I'm looking for what marketers call the category killers – a list of meals that collectively can explain our strange relationship with our national cuisine, maybe even the nation itself. I'll need to explore their history, how and why they came to be our cultural superfoods, the basis of our national cuisine. But to truly understand them I'll also need to explore them in their natural environments. It's tempting, with a list of Britain's favourite meals, to find the very best versions of them and, in so doing, defiantly stand up for traditional British cuisine and argue for its place alongside the greatest cuisines in the world. I hope to be able to make that argument, but based on the norm rather than the exception. It's easy, albeit expensive, to find someone who has reinvented 'posh' fish and chips or a 'gourmet' English breakfast. And sometimes, I'm glad that people do. But for an honest picture of our food culture, I need to try the *typical* rather than the *best* versions of these meals. If 'typical' happens to coincide with 'best', as it does on Barnsley Market's pie-and-peas stalls, then that's great. But the most important thing for me now is to explore each meal in its archetypal location.

I quickly get to a list of twelve or fifteen meals culled from the surveys, but that's too many. Eventually, I whittle it down to eight, just about manageable for a project that properly does justice to each. But it's a painful process and

I lose some national treasures along the way. If it were you compiling this list, then your mum's steak-and-kidney pie, strawberries and cream at Wimbledon or steak and chips in your local boozer may well have made the cut. For me, each fell at the final hurdle.

Pie and peas was the meal that gave birth to the whole idea, so it's first to make the cut. I've already been back to Barnsley to check it still stands up, and it forms the beginning of my culinary journey not just in its own right as one of the most criminally underrated meals in the world but also as a nod to all the other pies and puddings that Britain looks to when we need our food to embrace us and tell us everything is going to be OK.

The Holy Trinity, jostling for top position in every survey, are fish and chips, Sunday roast dinner and the full English breakfast. Each of these has, at different times, stated its claim to be Britain's national dish, and all three remain meals for which the British are famous around the world. The full English, of course, must be eaten in a greasy-spoon café. Fish and chips is, for me, synonymous with my childhood but, for many of us, its strongest association is with the seaside. The Sunday roast, in the early twenty-first century, has become synonymous with the pub, and a nice country pub feels like the most appropriate kind.

To these, I add the cream tea. It's a bastion of Englishness, a meal based around our national drink (or rather, one of them), and it gives an insight into our national obsession with etiquette. In choosing where to have it, I have no choice but to piss off half the West Country. I decide to annoy the Cornish, as they're further away from me, and opt for the Devon cream tea on its home turf.

Next, I decide to broaden the palate. I need to explore Britain's adoption and appropriation of other cuisines, and so curry – probably in the shape of the chicken tikka masala – is an obvious choice. The dish was allegedly invented in Glasgow, so it's tempting to go there, but I want to hedge my bets and look at curry more widely. Tikka masala has been replaced as Britain's favourite curry by the spicier jalfrezi and has a rival as an Anglo-Indian creation in the rotund shape of the balti. I decide to go to Birmingham and the Balti Triangle, where I know I will have an expert guide.

Also a relatively recent arrival to these shores is spaghetti Bolognese. Since the 1960s, it's become one of our favourite comfort meals and the dish we choose to cook at home more than any other. This is a meal that I have to have someone cook for me, ideally as we stand in their kitchen on a wet, dark Tuesday night after work, the windows damp with rain outside and condensation within. Finally, I choose the cheese sandwich. It doesn't feature in all that many surveys but, like my pork pie, it represents a much bigger constituency. Britain is the home of the sandwich. As a nation, it's our favourite choice for lunch and, while the variety of fillings expands eternally outwards from our foodie big bang, cheese of some sort, in combination with various other ingredients, is our most popular choice. But it's so ubiquitous, as I compile my list I fail to come up with the quintessential place to enjoy it. It should be a typical lunchtime that most of us will recognize, but there's so much scope to that, I need to think further about it.

It's a good list of meals, an interesting agenda for an exploration of Britain.

'You haven't got any desserts,' says Liz.

I don't really eat dessert. But she's right. Sweet puddings, pies and cakes are a vital part of British cuisine. As befits a good meal, I'll come back to this right at the end. And get Liz, who used to be known as 'The Crumble Lady' in certain parts of Stoke Newington, to make it for me – the ninth and final dish.

I'm just about ready to go. And then, perusing the list one more time, I realize with some consternation that, with one notable exception, this is a list of my personal favourite meals. I really didn't think that's what I was doing when I was compiling it. I thought I was being objective, data driven. But this can't be a coincidence. The other thing I notice about it is that, by today's standards, it seems to be a very working-class diet.

Like the majority of the British population (according to yet more surveys), I like to think of myself as working class. Undoubtedly, I was born and brought up as working class, but now, by any objective measure, I'm a middle-class cliché, and I have been accused, inevitably and more than once, of being part of the metropolitan liberal media elite that supposedly runs everything. I do tick some boxes: I'm degree-educated, internationalist, a staunch advocate of multiculturalism and a foodie to the core. Ask me what my favourite food is and I'll instantly say sushi. Half a dozen oysters and a glass of crisp Chablis. A whole fresh shellfish (sorry, *fruits de mer*) platter – now you're talking. A bowl of ramen (the proper stuff with real stock, not the crap you get from chains) is my version of an indulgent treat, and two years ago I almost burned the house down trying to make authentic stock by leaving pork bones on a rolling boil for far too long. I cook a lot at home and have an entire bookcase full of cookbooks in the kitchen. Lately, I've been working my way through a book of Korean recipes and have several pots of home-made kimchi on the go. I bake my own sourdough bread. I've even had a go at making my own cheese.

And on top of all that, over the past few years I've somehow become part of the nebulous cloud of commentators that surrounds the world of food and drink. My first three books were all about beer. They did well enough that, at a time when beer was still considered somehow inferior to other forms of food and drink, I became 'the beer guy' on the broader gastronomic scene. I've done a bit of beer stuff on TV, quite a lot on the radio, got to know Hairy Bikers and *Masterchef* judges and been patronized by restaurant critics. I've judged awards for food and drink, and entered, won and subsequently even judged awards for writing about it. In the middle of writing this book I was invited to take part in a Christmas edition of BBC Radio 4's *Food Programme* and sat down to a festive lunch with Sheila Dillon, Giorgio Locatelli, Yotam Ottolenghi and Angela Hartnett, among others, with lines from Talking Heads' 'Once in a Lifetime' looping around my brain throughout the whole meal.

But when I look at a list of meals that contains fish and chips, curry, Sunday roast and the mighty fry-up, I no longer feel like this person. Sushi and ramen and all the rest of them are meals I like the experience of eating and meals I like intellectually – they appeal for their flavour, and also for what I know to be their nutritional value, their stories, and, yes, the fact that I feel discerning and sophisticated for liking them. These meals say something about the person I am, or at least the person I want to be. But fish and chips, bacon and curry, in particular – these meals cut through the crap. My adoration for them runs very deep and comes from the heart.

Anthropologists Peter Farb and George Armelagos propose that a cuisine is like a language, a system of communication that you learn from birth and is difficult to change when you get older. Even if you migrate from one culture or cuisine to another – literally, from one country to another that has very different food or, more commonly, from one class or group to another that has different ideas and habits around food – the argument goes that, while you can learn to speak the new language and eat the new food, you will take an accent of your native cuisine with you. So, as a middle-class north London foodie who grew up working class in Barnsley, I may well now speak fluent ramen and conversational kimchi, but I do so with a thick fish-and-chips accent.

As well as delving into the history of British cuisine and travelling the country to explore it, I realize I need to explore my own life to this point too, and the role of food within it. All my life I've used food – along with newspapers, books, clothes and music – to help separate myself from my upbringing and my background, to stand apart from it. Now, I want to use food to reconnect with it. The meals in this book – and we'll explore further why they might be perceived to be working class – include those that truly make my heart sing. And according to survey after survey, I'm not the only person who feels this way. It seems a great many of us do, even if we admit it only to researchers with clipboards or in online surveys. These meals are more than food – more even than *good* food. They're soul, heart, comfort, home. They're who I really am. And possibly, who many of us really are.

2.

A Cheese Sandwich

'There is a feeling which persists in England that making a sandwich interesting, attractive, or in any way pleasant to eat is something sinful that only foreigners do.'

– Douglas Adams, *So Long, and Thanks for All the Fish*

1.

The first item of food that I can remember preparing for myself was a cheese sandwich. Its humble simplicity means the sandwich is the kind of meal kids can easily make: it doesn't involve turning the oven on and, if you're the kind of family whose diet contains a significant proportion of processed foods and shop-bought industrially produced bread, it doesn't even have to involve sharp knives. Today, pretty much any meal I prepare begins with my sharpening a kitchen knife. Back then, we had cheap, blunt knives that were almost childish in design.

For such a seemingly simple concept, the cheese sandwich is ripe (sorry) for constant reinterpretation. We all think we know what it is, what it looks and tastes like. But each of us has a different idea of what a perfect or even a typical cheese sandwich is. When I start talking to friends about this book, the first question they ask is what meals I've chosen. Every single time I say 'cheese sandwich' the other person always smiles and nods, and then says something completely different from the last.

'Ah, you mean a ploughman's lunch?'

'Ah, you mean a cheese toastie?'

'Ah, you mean cheese and pickle?'

'Ah, you mean cheese and onion?'

'Ah, you mean cheese and tomato?'

'Ah, you mean a ham-and-cheese baguette?'

'Ah, you mean Brie and grape?'

Brie and grape?

Someone really did say that, and I think they were being serious. But this particular iteration of our favourite sandwich is regarded with deep suspicion by some.

I know of no better evocation of Britain's struggles around food than the fussy-eaters sketch that appeared regularly on *The Catherine Tate Show* between 2004 and 2007. Janice and Ray are a Yorkshire couple who are continually outraged by the pretentiousness and naked greed of restaurants and cafés that charge ten quid for dishes such as tempura – which, as they tell the camera in tones of uncontrollable disgust, is no more than 'battered veg'.

In one sketch, they save particular scorn for the café in Harrogate that serves all its sandwiches on French bread. ('It were all they had.') Despite this, they order two cheese sandwiches. 'How far wrong can you go with a sandwich?' they ask rhetorically, before revealing the horror of a Brie-and-grape baguette in the wrong place.

JANICE: 'They've put grapes in a cheese sandwich. In French bread. The dirty bastards.'

RAY: 'Five pound sixty and we had to pick the grapes out ourselves.'

JANICE: 'The dirty, robbing bastards.'

What is considered to be pretentious varies from culture to culture and from one era to another. That first cheese sandwich I made when I got home from school aged nine or ten was none of the above: it consisted of two slices of Mother's Pride smeared thickly with Blue Band margarine, the foundation for the sheer delight of squeezing brilliant-white Primula cheese spread from its star-shaped nozzle, holding the soft metal tube high above the kitchen counter and gleefully crushing it until I had a mound of processed cheese that resembled a worm cast on a beach, before spreading it in a fat layer, popping on the top slice and cutting my creation in two.

Like all normal people, we always used to cut our sandwiches horizontally. Then, one day, it occurred to me that the sandwich might be more pleasant to eat, a little neater, if I cut it diagonally, into triangles rather than rectangles, like I'd seen it done in shops and cafés.

'Look at you, cutting your sandwich all posh,' sneered my little brother. 'You think you're good just 'cos you were confirmed yesterday.'

And the thing is, he was right. I did. And my posh sandwich-cutting habits stayed in place far longer than my church attendance.

There's a moral dimension to the idea of cuisine. Our attachment to our own cuisine goes so deep that, often, it's not just that 'ours' and 'theirs' are different: if this is true, then 'ours' must be right while 'theirs' is wrong. Leaving aside big cultural differences such as whether or not you eat dogs or horses, even the way in which we eat foods that are common to us but are prepared in different ways can be used to pass moral judgement. Janice and Ray often complain in their sketches about being ripped off, but their bigger, more constant grievance is that food from or inspired by other cultures is 'dirty'. The sketch works so well because the punchline of 'dirty bastards' is something few of us would say out loud, especially people like Janice and Ray, who clearly consider themselves superior and respectable. But their attitudes ring true – and not just of people from their background, age and social status. Both we and the Japanese eat vegetables, and we both eat things in batter. But 'battered veg' is wrong. Similarly, it's perfectly fine to have grapes garnishing a cheese plate but abhorrent to put them in a cheese sandwich. It's just not what 'we' do.

Or maybe you disagree. You might think the humour in the sketch comes from Ray and Janice's ignorance, the fact that they've never seen these foods before and are horrified by them, while you and I regard them as typical of what's out there today. They see themselves as superior to others, but in their puffed-up outrage they're revealing their parochial ignorance.

That's true as well – but only if you possess a particular kind of social aspiration. When certain food rules are so strong that they unify and define a culture, breaking those rules can be a way of showing you're outgrowing it, that you're more worldly, knowledgeable and sophisticated than those around you. That's why I first tried sushi. It's why New Yorkers with European ancestry first started eating Chinese food, and why people in China started eating McDonald's. In the 1970s, Liz's Auntie Angela and Uncle Gerry used to tell everyone who would listen in the town of Cwmbran how much they enjoyed red wine and blue cheese because they'd been to France, mainly because they believed no one else in Cwmbran was anything other than deeply suspicious of both red wine and blue cheese because they'd probably never been to France.

When we're more affluent and cosmopolitan, when we travel more and meet people from backgrounds increasingly different from our own, our new experiences can make our established, familiar culture feel more old-fashioned, less aspirational and, in many cases, more associated with lower social classes. There are no sushi restaurants or ramen joints in Barnsley. There will be one day, possibly soon, but the new always filters in through the middle classes, keen to better themselves, while the upper classes are often perfectly happy in the belief that they already have the best. When there are sushi restaurants in Barnsley, weekend-newspaper style supplements will no doubt be declaring sushi to be 'over'.

When I cut my sandwich diagonally, I was saying it was a superior way of cutting sandwiches to the way my family had always done it, that I now knew better. I could have gone even posher and cut the vulgar crusts off; then they would have been really sophisticated. If I'd gone completely mental, cut off the crusts first and then my Primula sandwich into rectangular fingers about an inch wide and four inches long, they'd have looked very similar to the sandwiches I was served at Fortnum & Mason when I was a judge for their Food and Drink Awards. The cheese sandwich is our favourite lunch because it is at once constant and mutable. You can have a posh one, a fashionable one, a traditional one or a Primula on Mother's Pride one. It's still a cheese sandwich.

There are over 700 named cheeses produced in the UK, so diverse in flavour and texture that they pair well with many other ingredients and need to be broken down into different types to be examined properly. In her indispensable *Flavour Thesaurus* Niki Segnit separates out hard cheese, goat's cheese, blue cheese, soft cheese and washed-rind cheese, all of which vary somewhat in their many ideal pairings. Hard cheese – which in Britain is by far the most likely candidate for a sarnie – is listed as a perfect match with over thirty other foods, including the obvious ones such as apple, onion and tomato or, if you fancy something a bit different, anchovy, globe artichoke or fig. A soft cheese such as Brie does indeed form a perfect marriage with grape, and also loves avocado, blackcurrant, pineapple and smoked fish.

Across the country, the bread these cheeses and pairings might be served on could be called a stottie in the northeast of England, a cob in the Midlands, a bap in Scotland or Ireland, a barm cake in Lancashire, a tea cake in Yorkshire, or a roll pretty much anywhere. Cut from a loaf, in any region it might be white, brown, wholemeal or sourdough. Sourdough, in particular, could be seen as either a symbol of hipster fecklessness, a complete rip-off or a nutritious natural fightback against corporate garbage, depending on your point of view. In many cuisines the quality of bread you're able to afford has long been a symbol of affluence and sophistication. Until the last few decades, white bread was considered to be quality without equal in a cuisine where white foods were considered superior while darker foods were felt to be cruder and more primitive. This has now reversed: think about the way we still use 'refined' in the context of manners and polite company in a fairly positive way versus the connotations it now has in many foods. Dark 'peasant' and 'farmhouse' breads, the more rustic the better, now cost far more than a 'refined' white loaf – although in some cases the fact that they're foreign in origin helps, because they're not part of our core system of food and are therefore exotic and interesting.

While it may appal Ray and Janice with its dangerous sense of otherness, on its home turf a fresh baguette with Brie is a simple and emphatic example of how the very best foods can be for everyone. Locally made bread and cheese have been standard peasant fare in much of Western Europe for centuries. Like pretty much any fermented food, cheese was first made as a way of extending the life of milk. Milk is highly nutritious but goes off after a few days, whereas cheese can last for weeks, months or even years in some cases. And like any other fermented food, the transformation from milk into something more characterful makes it more valuable and prized – at least among those who live where it's made.

A Brie-and-grape baguette eaten in the town of Brie in northern France is the exact equivalent of Cheddar on white bread in Somerset, and yet Janice and Ray are not the only people who think of one as posh (or disgusting) and the other as everyday (or normal). The cheese sandwich can be made to stand for and mean anything. Like any other widespread phenomenon, the differences in how it's treated around the world reveal the local wrinkles in our identities and attitudes.

2.

One of my favourite pubs in the world is the Blue Bell, in the tiny North Wales hamlet of Halkyn. The pub has no kitchen, but its owners at the time of my first visit – Steve Marquis and his wife, Ness – made up for that in inventiveness and kindness. Every few months, Saturday night at the Blue Bell was Cheese and Pickled Night. Guests were invited to bring along a piece of cheese and the pub provided bread, crackers and plates. Each person handed over their cheese on arrival and Ness took it into the back room and arranged it on to large serving plates with little flags indicating the name of each variety. Anyone in the pub could then help themselves to as much cheese as they liked. There was no admission charge or fee for a plate.

When I turned up with my friend and occasional co-author Bill Bradshaw we sensed that our contribution would be scrutinized and had to be interesting. 'Don't worry,' said Steve, 'There's a cheese man at the market this afternoon in Mold. He's got all sorts.'

Bill and I were in the area visiting some pubs for a book we were working on. It was a long, gruelling afternoon, and by the time we reached the small market town, the Cheese Man of Mold had packed up and gone home. The only place we could go for cheese was the big Tesco on the outskirts.

We headed straight for the deli counter, ignoring the packaged stuff on the shelves. At five thirty on a Saturday afternoon, it was staffed by a single teenage girl whose body language seethed with hostile boredom.

'Hmm . . . What can you recommend that's good?' asked Bill, because he's friendly like that.

'Dunno,' glowered the girl. 'I only eat normal cheese.'

'*Normal cheese?*' said Bill. 'Do you mean Cheddar?'

She nodded slowly, clearly thinking Bill was an idiot for even having to ask.

The girl's 'normal cheese', in its various guises, sells more by volume in the UK than all other cheeses put together. It takes its name from the village and gorge in Somerset where it was first made. Once, there were 400 cheesemakers in the area and it was commonly agreed that, to be called Cheddar, the cheese had to be made within thirty miles of Wells Cathedral, which stands just a few miles away from Cheddar Gorge.

Since ancient times, cheese has been made by straining sour milk through a cloth. The curdling solids – simply, curds – could be kept while the liquid whey was drained off. The earliest cheeses would have been soft and creamy, but when the Romans arrived in northern Europe they brought with them the art of using rennet, which they'd learned from the Egyptians. Rennet makes the curd solidify into a soft block, which allows more whey to be removed, leaving a firmer, more solid cheese that's better suited to ageing.

The west of Britain shares the same maritime climate as northern France and has always had excellent pasture for dairy cattle. When you compare the *terroir* of western

England and north-west France, the rich pasture common to both is perfect for soft, creamy cheeses such as Camembert, Livarot and Pont-l'Évêque. Cheeses in this style were once common in Britain.

The climate and terrain across the whole of France is more varied than ours, however, which is one reason why French cheeses are more diverse in style than English cheeses. One of France's most celebrated cheeses is produced in Roquefort-sur-Soulzon in the south of the country. The town's cheesy fame allegedly dates back to Pliny the Elder, who supposedly lauded it in his CE79 work, *Natural History*.

Pliny was certainly a fan of cheese generally, writing, 'It is a remarkable circumstance, that the barbarous nations which subsist on milk have been for so many ages either ignorant of the merits of cheese, or else have totally disregarded it.' But what fans of Roquefort don't tell you is that Pliny's mention was ambiguous and not exactly complementary. In a chapter where he details all the fine cheeses available in Rome, 'where the various good things of all nations are to be judged of by comparison', he says, '[g]oats also produce a cheese which has been of late held in the highest esteem, its flavour being heightened by smoking it. The cheese of this kind which is made at Rome is considered preferable to any other; for that which is made in Gaul has a strong taste, like that of medicine.'

What we now understand to be Roquefort cheese is not smoked and is not made from goat's milk. When Pliny says this cheese was made in Gaul, that could mean anywhere in a region that today encompasses France, Luxembourg, Belgium, most of Switzerland, northern Italy, as well as the parts of the Netherlands and Germany on the west bank of the Rhine. And anyway, Pliny didn't like it that much because it tasted of medicine. This could mean he's referring to the chemical hit of a ripe blue cheese but, even if that's the case, it's doubtful that Roquefort cheese was unique in this. But never mind all that: if you're marketing a food icon, when the legend becomes fact we invariably print the legend.

Prehistoric cheese-making colanders have allegedly been discovered near the town of Roquefort-sur-Soulzon, and what is undeniable is that it has the perfect conditions to make great cheese. The region is honeycombed with caves formed by faults in the mountain cliffs, and these faults channel a gentle flow of air into the caves that creates a fairly constant temperature of between eight and twelve degrees Celsius and keeps the humidity high. These are perfect conditions for the growth of a mould known as *Penicillium roqueforti*. This mould, plus reliable access to salt from the Mediterranean, led to the evolution of the soft, blue, salty, cave-aged cheese we now know as Roquefort.

The cheese was popularized by local Benedictine monks from the eleventh century on, and soon other monasteries in the area were buying caves to make their own. In 1411, Charles VI of France granted the town of Roquefort a monopoly for the ripening of the cheese in these caves – the first ever *appellation d'origine* – meaning only producers in the town could use its name. In 1961, a landmark ruling decreed that while similar maturation methods could be used across southern France, only those whose ripening occurred in the natural caves of Mont Combalou were permitted to bear the name Roquefort. On top of that, the milk must be whole and raw, the sheep it comes from must be Lacaune dairy sheep, and they must be fed on pasture.

Today, much of the economic activity in the region centres on the production and distribution of the cheese. A visitor's centre run by the Caves de Roquefort Société illustrates the process of making Roquefort cheese, gives a guided tour of the caves and offers guests free samples and a chance to buy cheese. Despite still only being produced locally, Roquefort is enjoyed around the world and considered one of the best blue cheeses ever made.

It's a great story, a fantastic cheese and a symbol of how food and drink can come to define a region, or even a nation. Now let's compare that story to the history of 'normal cheese'.

From the Middle Ages, regions in England such as Cheddar and Cheshire gained fine reputations for their cheeses – Cheshire cheese is even mentioned in the Domesday Book. Records of cheese being made around the village of Cheddar date back to at least the 1100s, although that cheese was probably very different from what we now know as Cheddar. Like most agricultural produce, for a long time cheeses from Cheddar were only eaten close to where they were made. But steadily people began to realize that hard cheeses were more stable and travelled better than softer ones. Cheddar's fame spread and, in 1170, King Henry II declared it to be the best in Britain and bought 4.6 tons of it. During the reign of Charles I (1625–49), all the cheese made in Cheddar was sold before it was even made and was available exclusively to the royal court.

Cheddar cheese-makers developed a unique method which became known as 'cheddaring'. In all hard-cheese making, as the curd sets it is sliced or 'milled' to release more of the whey. Cheddaring ramps up this process by turning the curds, pressing them together and stacking them in blocks, cutting them again and repeating the process to squeeze out even more of the whey and leave a crumbly, layered, dense texture. After cheddaring, the cheese is pressed into large rounds or wheels, and historically was wrapped in cloth and left to mature in the caves of Cheddar Gorge, which – just like those in the Combalou Mountains – give the perfect stable temperature and humidity for the bacteria that mature and ripen the cheese.*

Until the early eighteenth century, cheese-making was common practice in farms around the country. Farmers supplied fresh milk to neighbouring villages and made any surplus into cheese because, before refrigeration, that was the only way to preserve it. Then, the world's first Industrial Revolution created seismic population shifts. By the mid-nineteenth century, most people in England lived in towns and cities. When the railways arrived it was easy to deliver fresh milk to large, concentrated populations who needed it. The economic necessity of making cheese disappeared – even if the appetite for it never did.

Industrialized Britain was a powerhouse, the most advanced country in the world. Its three founding principles were mechanization, science and trade, a dream combination that no other country could match in any one aspect, let alone the force of all three together. If we think

* Elsewhere in Britain, where there are no caves, heavy stone farmhouses and barns designed to withstand British weather were a fine substitute for other styles of cheese.

back to the contrasting stories of champagne and Bass Ale, it must have seemed blatantly obvious at the time that the only thing worth protecting was the commercial marque. Drunk on progress, people believed anything offered by nature could be improved upon. If there were local quirks and advantages in growing produce or raising livestock in one region rather than another, this wasn't celebrated as *terroir* but seen as a challenge that could be overcome.

And so, inevitably, technology transformed the cheese-making process too.

In the 1850s, Cheshire was still by far the most popular British cheese, both at home and as an export. Then, in 1856, Joseph Harding, the son of a Somerset farmer, went public with his new scientific method of Cheddar-making and changed the world of cheese.

There were many different parts to Harding's new method but one overriding principle: the primacy of hygiene and scientific rigour over traditional farmhouse rule of thumb. We may now be rediscovering the romance of *terroir*, the communion with nature that honest, artisanal produce gives us, but Harding had known nothing else and the results were inconsistent and, occasionally, poisonous. As far as he was concerned, 'Cheese is not made in the field, nor in the byre, nor even in the cow, it is made in the dairy.' His innovations included the use of a consistent starter culture, control and measurement of the acidifying process, strict temperature control and, perhaps most importantly of all at the time, an obsession with hygiene throughout the whole process. He described a good Cheddar as 'close and firm in texture, yet mellow in character or quality; it is rich with a tendency to melt in the mouth, the flavour full and fine, approaching to that of a hazelnut', which remains close to the style guide of a good Cheddar today and makes me want a sizeable chunk of it in my face right now.

Harding's method made Cheddar taste better than it had, and more consistent and more stable so it could last longer and travel further. It meant that Somerset Cheddar suddenly had the potential to become the tastiest, safest, most commercially attractive cheese in the world. So Harding did what anyone would do: he gave his secrets away for free, teaching anyone who was interested how to make perfect Cheddar cheese. He didn't even charge for his time. Cheese-makers in the United States, Canada and Australia took his methods, made Cheddar on a larger scale, more cheaply than Somerset producers could, and began selling it back to Britain. While the French were busy protecting their cheeses with *appellations controlée d'origine*, Britain's revolutionary cheese was given away to the world with no protection, no guideline, no definition whatsoever. By 1913, over 80 per cent of the cheese eaten in Britain was imported and Britain's farmhouse cheese-making culture was almost destroyed – almost, but not quite. It took the British government to finish it off completely.

Their motives were understandable. At the outbreak of the First World War, Britain was importing most of its food. This almost led to defeat at the hands of German U-boats – and probably would have if they hadn't got so carried away they started sinking American ships carrying food, thereby bringing the United States into the war.

In the 1930s, as Hitler rose to power, Britain realized that if there was to be another war the country had to be more self-sufficient in its food supply. One of the measures to help achieve this was the creation of the Milk Marketing Board (MMB) in 1933, to regulate and control the supply of milk to feed the nation. The MMB guaranteed a good price to farmers for their milk and even collected it from the farm. There was simply no longer any economic rationale for farmers to make cheese. The MMB also took control over what to do with any surplus milk, so it licensed certain dairies to produce a select range of cheeses, including what became known as 'government Cheddar'. This was not great cheese but, once cheese and milk were rationed in 1941, it was all you could get. Before the First World War, there were 3,500 farmhouse cheese-makers in the UK. By 1945, there were just a hundred.

Rationing lasted until 1954, at which time legendary food writer Dorothy Hartley, in *Food in England*, wrote simply, 'Our cheeses are lost to England.'

In a post-war climate that still championed efficiency and economy above all else, the Milk Marketing Board endured. The value placed on consistency meant they weren't keen on identifying individual farms, so farms were given numbers instead. Consumers got around this by figuring out that, for example, Montgomery's was 'farm 744' and Kirkham's was 'farm 34' and seeking out these numbers. The MMB also acquired control of the use of the term 'farmhouse cheese', so if someone like Montgomery's were to try to sell their own produce as 'traditional farmhouse Cheddar', which is what it was, they weren't allowed to call it that.

Britain's reputation for food that was awful, rather than merely plain, had been well and truly established by this point. So it's no surprise, looking at it from this perspective, that when we became more exposed to foreign food – by being part of the European single market, by witnessing more multicultural immigration and by taking newly affordable foreign holidays – we tended to think that anything foreign was better than what we had. At the same time as my Primula sandwiches were being displaced by American-style, fluorescent orange, indestructible Kraft 'Cheddar cheese' spread at home, people eating in decent restaurants were being offered cheese boards that were exclusively French.

In 1990, the Milk Marketing Board was finally dissolved and farmers were no longer guaranteed a good price for their milk. The bad news was that over half of Britain's dairy farmers went out of business. The good news was that those who survived did so by diversifying and British farmhouse cheese began a steady revival that continues today.

But many British people aren't aware of this. Most of us still buy Cheddar in pre-wrapped blocks from supermarkets, just like we did when things were run by the MMB. That might have something to do with the fact that the market-leading brand of Cheddar in the UK is Cathedral City. Dairy Crest was the new name given to the MMB's milk-processing division when it was separated off from the board in 1980. It was floated on the stock exchange in 1996. By the time of its flotation, Dairy Crest was a business with a broad portfolio of dairy-based products, with little place for historical tradition and local *terroir* in its brand marketing save for imagery and loose claims that focus-grouped well. Its Cheddar cheese, which is not made using traditional methods, is produced in Davidstow, Cornwall, which is neither a city, nor does it have a cathedral. Davidstow is 120 miles away from Wells in Somerset, but this doesn't stop Dairy Crest from featuring an illustration of Wells Cathedral on every packet of Cathedral City, implying a link with Cheddar's birthplace that the brand no longer has.

The European system of geographic protection for foods came into operation in 1993. This means that within the area in which the scheme operates (and in countries with mutual agreements) regionally produced food and drink is protected from competitors passing themselves off as the same thing. At the time of writing in 2018, Britain has a total of 65 products with protected status. France has 217, Italy 267, and Portugal 125. Breaking that down, Britain has 16 protected cheeses, the French 52, the Italians 47. To be fair, this is a slight improvement from 2010, when France had more cheeses enjoying protected status than Britain had for all its products combined. Roquefort is of course one of those protected cheeses. It's too late to do anything for Cheddar, which had become a worldwide commodity a hundred years before the legislation was introduced. But Cheddar producers have retrenched and rethought: in 2007, producers in the West Country gained a European Protected Designation of Origin (PDO) for 'West Country Farmhouse Cheddar', which means that any cheese bearing this name within the EU must be made using traditional cheddaring methods and local milk from Somerset, Dorset, Devon or Cornwall.

But now, that might not count for anything. The rules that protect Britain's iconic foods are part of the European

Union's regulatory framework. With Britain out of the EU, West Country Farmhouse Cheddar, along with Yorkshire Wensleydale (it, too, had to be specific, long after the simple 'Wensleydale' horse had bolted), Stilton, Melton Mowbray pork pies, Stornoway black pudding, Cumberland black sausage and Cornish pasties, lose the European-wide protection that means no one else can falsely claim theirs to be the real thing. I wrote to the Department of the Environment, Food and Rural Affairs (Defra) to ask what was going to happen to our protected foods after Brexit. Their reply, in full, was:

> The Government is planning to use the EU (Withdrawal) Bill to transfer into domestic law the EU schemes that currently protect our GIs. This will ensure that UK GIs remain protected in the UK after we leave the EU. Defra officials are working closely with officials from other government departments, the devolved administrations, and the Crown Dependencies on this.
>
> Douglas Potter
> Ministerial Contact Unit

In other words, foods that currently enjoy protection across the whole of Europe, as well as in the parts of the world with which the EU has reciprocal agreements on food protection, will from now on be protected in Britain only, meaning anyone outside the country will be free to imitate our products so long as they don't try to sell them here.

3.

Despite all the wrongs that have been visited upon it, Cheddar remains my favourite cheese, and it didn't become the world's favourite for no reason. I have a palate that loves strong flavours so, for me, an extra-mature supermarket block is a delight. Of course, I know that this isn't proper, artisanal farmhouse Cheddar and, when I can get my hands on an almost Parmesan-like Montgomery or a cracked, blue-veined Mrs Keen's, you can give me a bottle of Worthington White Shield ale or a glass of Somerset farmhouse cider to go with it and I'm happy for the rest of the day.*

'Mature' is by far Britain's favourite style of Cheddar, even if what Cathedral City regards as 'mature' still comes across like an infant to fans of the massive, almost chemical flavour of a real extra-mature farmhouse Cheddar. But Cheddar can also be mild and creamy, or anywhere between there and extra mature. Having enjoyed cheeses so blue they give you a hit of methane at the back of the throat, and French cheeses so ripe you have to pin them to the board with a knife to prevent them from making a run for it, every now and again there's nothing wrong with 'normal'. As American cheesemonger and writer Gordon

---

* It's a popular myth that wine and cheese are natural bedfellows, but even some wine writers grudgingly concede that it's a struggle to find a pairing that enables both to shine. In Normandy and in Somerset – both famous cheese regions – cider is considered a superior match. Beer, too, with its carbonation, counteracts the fatty build-up of cheese, refreshing the palate and keeping the flavours alive. In the best pairings, they entwine around each other until you can't tell where one ends and the other begins, each greater than it is on its own.

dgar says in *Cheddar*, 'A cheese that is used in Big Macs, mousetraps and mac and cheese, yet is still served in mansions, is a cheese that calls out for more attention.' In its place, there's a case to be made for this cheese as a rival to any other. And its place, surely, is Cheddar Gorge in Somerset.

Cheddar Gorge today is not what I expect. It's an otherworldly place that resembles an out-of-season Swiss Alpine ski resort more than any other place I've been in Britain. It looks nothing like a seaside town but it somehow *feels* like one, all light and airy, the kind of place you would only ever come if you were on holiday. It's full of squat one- and two-storey buildings of ancient stone that house gift shops selling woollen jumpers, cheap drinking games, plastic Union Jack shopping bags on wheels and all sorts of ephemera that you neither see nor need in everyday life.

The gorge itself seems incongruous in a county not really celebrated for mountainous terrain. The road rises up and twists sharply to the left, then switches back to the right and suddenly you're twisting between massive slabs of rock whose aspects suggest they're ever so slowly trying to amble off, sliding and crawling in different directions when no one's looking.

Because this is a place of obvious natural interest, it's part run by the National Trust. Just down the road from the gorge, sandwiched between two tea shops in the low stone buildings leading up to it, is a National Trust shop. Given that the Trust describes itself as 'a charity that works to preserve and protect historic places and spaces', this is obviously the place to discover something about the history of the gorge and cheese-making within it.

The gorge is the only reason this shop is here but, once you're inside, it could be anywhere in the UK: apart from one guidebook of local walks, the rest of it is entirely generic. There are no books, not so much as a leaflet, that says anything at all about Cheddar Gorge itself, as if the organization charged with protecting and celebrating Britain's natural history is entirely oblivious to the extraordinary feature rising above it and just happens to have opened a shop here by coincidence. The bookshelves have a small selection on food and drink which includes a gluten-free cookbook but has nothing on Cheddar or any other cheese, and nothing at all about cider, this area's other famous contribution to Britain's gastronomic life. It's as if they've tried extraordinarily hard to completely ignore anything that makes the local area fascinating or unique.

Just up the road, spread out on the first bend that twists up into the rocks, is the Cheddar Gorge Visitor's Centre, which is run by the same people who do Longleat Safari Park; they share with the National Trust the responsibility for managing the gorge. It's a characterless, concrete building with a Costa Coffee and a gift shop that sells fluffy dinosaurs. I look for an exhibit, a book – Christ, even a leaflet – that hints at the connection of the gorge and caves to cheese-making, but there's nothing. They do sell a bit of Cheddar cheese in the gift shop, but there's no fanfare around it. If you were running a shop and you stocked cheese and wanted to sell more of it, to make money, because that's what shops do, wouldn't you put up a little sign next to it telling you a bit about the story of it? Am I really the only person who has ever come to Cheddar because of its cheese connection? Here, where the cheese was born, there's less acknowledgement of it or information about it than you'd find in a half-decent delicatessen anywhere else in the world. The Costa sells what Costa sells, the chain as unwilling or unable to deviate from its corporate template here as it is anywhere else.

This bizarre determination to avoid any celebration of the cheese that made the word 'Cheddar' world famous is making me feel rather glum, so I cheer a little when we spot The Original Cheddar Cheese Co. This pretty shop proudly states that it was the first shop built in Cheddar Gorge and is now the world's oldest Cheddar cheese shop, dating back to 1870. The company makes its own cheese, some of which is matured in caves, but it's not made or matured here in Cheddar, so if you want to apply the same standards to Cheddar as the French would, they're stretching their claim to be 'the home of Cheddar cheese'.

Thank goodness, then, for the similarly named but completely different Cheddar Gorge Cheese Co. just a bit further down the road. This is a relatively new addition to Cheddar Gorge so it can't claim any long-standing tradition, apart from being the only cheese-maker in the world that makes Cheddar cheese in Cheddar and matures some of it in the caves of Cheddar Gorge. It's a business that was in seemingly terminal decline when John and Katherine Spencer took it over in 2003, deciding that there might be a market for Cheddar made in its rightful location using the traditional process and ingredients. They source all their milk from one local farm and stick to the traditional, back-breaking tradition of cheddaring. This is it: the only place in Cheddar that doesn't just sell cheese but *celebrates* it. The shop sells loads of cheeses, which, after the rest of

Cheddar Gorge, is a relief rather than the obvious statement it should be. It sells cheese knives, cheese boards, cheese biscuits, chutneys and pickles to go with cheese and hampers containing combinations of all of these which would make the perfect present for the cheese lover in your life. There are two big tasting counters staffed by people who may well think of Cheddar as 'normal cheese' but can tell you anything you want to know about it.

Behind the shop are the rooms where they make Cheddar, with glass walls that allow you to see in from the corridor that runs around them. For a couple of quid you can read and see exhibits about the history and production of Cheddar and watch people leaning over big steel baths cutting and stacking in the traditional cheddaring process.

Back out in the tasting room there are two versions of the mature cheese. One was matured in Gough's Cave, the star of the complex at the foot of the Gorge. The other was matured here, in rooms with a temperature and humidity which match those in the caves. Despite all measurable conditions being identical, the cave-aged cheese is softer, mellower, yet fuller in flavour than the one matured here, which is slightly sharper. I had been wondering whether my growing obsession with *terroir* and cave-ageing was mostly sentimental. But here's proof that this stuff makes a real difference to the world's favourite cheese. And yet this small company is the only one on the planet that seems to think it's important enough to take a commercial interest in.

I'm glad that Britain is not a boastful nation, but sometimes everyone needs to stand up and give an account of themselves. There's no doubt we love the cheese we donated to the world, but sometimes our modest refusal to shout about it looks less like humility and more like we just don't care.

4.

If, for whatever reason, you're looking for the ordinariness in British food, the traditional sandwich is the perfectly mundane expression of how we treat our 'normal' cheese.

It's often said that the idea of eating food between two slices of bread was first had by John Montagu, the 4th Earl of Sandwich, in the late eighteenth century. We'd been eating bread, and putting things on it, for thousands of years by this point, and the idea that no one else had ever considered putting an extra slice on top before Montagu is ludicrous. In fact, this concept was already ancient by the time Montagu was born, and spanned several different cultures. But Montagu was fashionable at a time when food fads were coming so thick and fast they made Instagramming your smashed avocado seem distinctly old hat. Montagu allegedly asked his valet to bring him cold meat between two slices of bread so that he could eat with one hand without having to interrupt his card game by using a fork, or getting his hands greasy. When he did so, other gentlemen quickly began to ask for 'the same as Sandwich', and the name stuck.

The only source for this origin story is Pierre-Jean Grosley, a French historian and travel writer who published a series of not entirely serious portraits of London life in 1770, including the passage:

> A minister of state passed four and twenty hours at a public gaming-table, so absorpt in play that, during the whole time, he had no subsistence but a bit of beef, between two slices of toasted bread, which he eat without ever quitting the game. This new dish grew highly in vogue, during my residence in London: it was called by the name of the minister who invented it.

In 1993, Nicholas Rodger, in his biography *The Insatiable Earl: A Life of John Montagu, Fourth Earl of Sandwich*, suggested that with his various responsibilities, including Postmaster General, First Lord of the Admiralty and Secretary of State for the Northern Department (later to become the Home Office), it was more likely that Montagu wanted the convenience of the sandwich so he could continue working at his desk.

Whichever version is true, it's undeniable that Montagu's influence meant his title was conferred upon what was previously known simply as 'bread and meat' or 'bread and cheese' – which, curiously, is how my dad referred to sandwiches all his life (he was never a fan of nobility in any form). Its practicality, neatness and portability are the reasons the sandwich has stuck around ever since, even as it has broadened in scope in terms of fillings and expression.

Certainly most of us today would identify more with Rodger's explanation than Grosley's. Sandwiches are synonymous with lunch, a relatively recent arrival in our culinary landscape and one which has become intimately linked with work and is eaten briskly at a desk, from a tray in a damp, busy sandwich shop, or on a bench in a utilitarian works canteen.

These are often soulless places, even the upmarket sandwich chains, so it's not surprising that for many of us the packed lunch occupies a special place in our memories. When someone lovingly prepared it for you it could often be the source of a warm, tender surprise. Or not. It was like a quiz show, opening the box to see if you'd won or lost. My dad used to make me the cheapest sandwiches he could, using a kind of reconstituted ham that had unidentifiable bits of green-and-red vegetable in it. With hindsight, I think the green bits might have been gherkin but at the time my disdain for it was such that I christened it 'spewmeat', both for what it looked like and how it made me feel. Sandwich boxes were one of those items that twelve- and thirteen-year-olds somehow always contrive to lose, so often I just had them wrapped in cellophane, finding my sandwiches sweaty and squashed in the bottom of my schoolbag each lunchtime, the ugly filling pressed against the cellophane like the distorted features of a bank robber inside a stocking mask.

By contrast, a few years ago I went on a short walking holiday in the Peak District. I was staying in a B&B in the tiny village of Edale, at the southern end of the Pennine Way, and for a few pounds extra the owner would make you up a packed lunch in a Tupperware box to take out walking. One of the best meals I've ever eaten was sitting alone on a hillside, opening the box to discover cheese-and-pickle sandwiches on fresh granary bread, an apple and a Breakaway biscuit. I didn't even know they still made Breakaway biscuits, but they're the perfect biscuits for a packed lunch, and when you're alone on a hillside they make you feel like the master of all you survey. I may have even cried out to the hills in triumph.

You don't see too many adults having packed lunches any more. Many parents still make them up for their kids to take to school, but googling the term 'packed lunch' brings up page after page of features on children's lunch boxes and little else, usually focusing on how unhealthy they are and how schools should ban poor children from bringing them in (rather than offering any constructive help on how they might make better packed lunches). Grown-ups in our consumer society are expected to buy their lunch rather than bring it from home. If you see someone at a desk or in the canteen with a lunch box, chances are they're either on an economy drive or a special diet. So, whenever I see someone bring a packed lunch on to a train (usually an elderly couple), I want to give them a little fist-bump of solidarity. They've looked after their pennies and, whatever they've brought, it'll be nicer than whatever I have to settle for from a buffet car that will be almost bare even as the train sets off. Sometimes it can be better to stick with simple than take a risk on something that's supposed to be special but isn't.

The cultural norm today is that we're expected to buy our sandwiches pre-made and pre-packaged. Marks & Spencer began selling packaged sandwiches from seven of its stores as an experiment in 1980. Few believed the idea would work – why would people pay money for something that even a child could make at home? The speed with which they took off astonished everyone. Soon, packaged sandwiches – diagonally cut, of course – were being sold in every branch, and this led directly to the creation of the entire M&S food empire. Every supermarket copied the idea, then the specialist high-street sandwich retailers and coffee shops arrived, and now the packaged-sandwich industry is worth £8 billion a year.

The main attraction is, of course, convenience. A sandwich is never going to be as thrilling as a decent cooked meal, but we're forever busy, forever distracted, and lunch as an 'occasion' – as the sandwich industry calls it – is actually disappearing. We may mark the time in the day, and it may still be rigid in workplace canteens, schools and institutions, but for people who work flexibly it's less about stopping and enjoying a meal than it is about grabbing something to refuel while you carry on working. In her 2010 book *Sandwich: A Global History*, Bee Wilson wrote, 'Sandwiches freed us from the fork, the dinner table, the fixed meal-time. In a way, they freed us from society itself.'

It's a beautifully weighted description of an accidental freedom. Britain is way ahead of other countries in the packaged sandwich, and the advice of British sandwich-makers on everything from packaging to cress is sought by companies from Russia to the Middle East. The head of the British Sandwich Association, Jim Winship, told journalist Sam Knight in an interview for the *Guardian* that the British sandwich industry is the most advanced in Europe, 'light years ahead of the rest of the world'. Towards the end of his long article Knight observes that this is a 'very British' success story, a 'national pastime of modest expectations, remorselessly fulfilled'.

One way to raise expectations – and one of the key reasons the industry has succeeded in getting us to buy sandwiches rather than make them – is the dread of monotony versus the thrill of novelty. Daring new fillings are devised obsessively by the sandwich industry to win ever more 'occasions' in every 'day part' (they never refer to 'meal times'). Keep track of sandwich innovation, and the Brie-and-grape baguette suddenly looks as reassuringly dull as a horizontal-cut Primula and marge.

But the modern desire for innovation eventually starts to undermine the whole point of the sandwich, which is to be a convenient food the eating of which doesn't interrupt other activities. I recently had a croque monsieur on a train, pre-toasted then packaged in cellophane and microwaved on demand. I suppose it must be someone's idea of luxury to have melted cheese on top of the sandwich as well as inside, but the idea doesn't translate well to situations where the sandwich's core benefit of convenience is most important, such as on a moving, rocking train. A microwaved croque monsieur train-style, with its cellophane wrapper glued to the cheese and made brittle by the microwave so that it must be painstakingly peeled and chipped away, has the mouthfeel and flavour of a damp flannel, but you can only find that out after getting third-degree burns and needing a change of clothes. If they just put the filling inside, where it's meant to be, we wouldn't have this problem.

And yet impracticality seems to be a growing trend in sandwiches, especially at the premium end of the market, where the very idea of the sandwich is being 're-imagined'. If you consider the burger to be a type of hot meat sandwich, 'gourmet' burgers have long since passed the point where anyone without a detachable jaw can even think of eating them without disassembling them, so what was the point of assembling them in the first place? Why make a plate of food look like a bloated, grotesque parody of a sandwich if it can't be eaten as one? Type 'cheese sandwich' into a Google image search and you get roughly what you'd expect: a variety of sandwiches, mostly toasted, mostly made from two slices of diagonally cut bread. But type 'cheese sandwich competition' and you get multi-layered behemoths with filling spilling out of the sides, slices of bread that would be too thick to eat on their own, never mind with the five inches of whatever they contain, and some that look like they have been intentionally designed to cause injury. If these people were instead 're-imagining' the boring, humdrum motor car, they'd no doubt revolutionize it by ingeniously putting the seats on the outside and the wheels on the roof, so it's probably just as well they're interested in sandwiches instead, where they can do less harm.

The dirty bastards.

5.

I struggle with deciding where to go and eat my typical cheese sandwich more than I do with any other meal in this book. It's lunch. It's probably out of the home. It is, to use that dreadful marketing phrase, often eaten 'on the go'. I consider trying to go to an office or workplace canteen and then rule this out: I'd either have to sit in the corner looking weird or do some kind of focus group with the people who work there, pestering them about their favourite fillings while they're trying to enjoy a brief respite from the daily grind. I should probably go to a Pret A Manger or a Greggs, to reflect the modern experience of the packaged sandwich. I could do that anywhere in the country, but the idea of just sitting in a Pret watching people queue up to be upsold feels faintly depressing. And then I find myself in Deal on the Kent coast and realize that the town of Sandwich is a mere five miles away.

The title 'Earl of Sandwich' was created by Charles II in 1660 for the fourth Earl's great-great-grandfather. But in the quirky manner of nobility, the dynasty never really had any connection with the town of Sandwich at all, being based in Cambridgeshire and, more recently, Dorset. So, in fact, there's no reason to associate the town of Sandwich with anything remotely interesting or noteworthy about sandwiches whatsoever. But I do anyway. *Because it's called Sandwich.* And that seems a good enough reason to go and eat a sandwich there rather than anywhere else.

Sandwich describes itself as 'England's most complete medieval town'. It bases this claim on a street plan that has changed little since the days of the Domesday Book, and it has the highest concentration of listed buildings per head of population of any town or city in the country. It's certainly very pretty: the road from the station into the centre of town is lined with tiny cottages and a little brook runs alongside the path, overhung by ancient willows. Sections of the medieval town wall are still largely intact and now the route of a pleasant walk overlooking the centre. The streets – all strangely empty today – twist and bend and quickly rob me of my sense of direction, and somehow I've missed the commercial centre and come out on the other side, on to The

Butts, a field that was originally designed for archery practice in the fourteenth century and was allegedly where Henry V's archers practised before setting sail for France for their famous victory at Agincourt. Thoughtfully, the sign telling this story, like all the other signs on the tourist route around town, is given in French as well as English. An elegant cricket pavilion now stands where the archery butts used to be. Sandwich couldn't be more quintessentially Home Counties – a phrase that, as a northerner, has to me always symbolized the North–South divide, as if our homes in Yorkshire or Lancashire somehow don't count or aren't as important, which, as far as most politicians of any era are concerned, is quite true of course.

But Sandwich looks beautiful under the low wintry sun, the air blue and crisp – and if I can only find the centre of town, I'll hopefully discover a cheese sandwich that transcends differences of class and region.

Reassuringly, there are lots of cafés in Sandwich, but a Trip Advisor search a few days before my visit makes me worry. I can find many mentions of baguettes, toasties and paninis [*sic*] but can't find anyone reviewing a simple, straightforward sandwich. I've found that Trip Advisor is never a completely reliable tool to plan a visit anywhere (unless you use one-star reviews of Mediterranean holiday destinations that complain of the TVs not being big enough and the food being too foreign to find your perfect break) but on a straw poll of reviews it seems sandwiches in Sandwich are mainly of the breakfast variety. Burgers and baked potatoes – along with the toasties, baguette and panini – seem to prevail much more at lunchtime.

As I finally find the centre of Sandwich, my hopes rise.

There are some lovely-looking cafés and shops and the well-heeled residents obviously enjoy their food. On the corner of No Name Street stands the No Name Shop, a place my friends told me I simply had to visit. Needing no further encouragement, I do.

The No Name Shop is a French delicatessen, with a café – Le Bistro – upstairs. There's also a branch back in Deal, although that one doesn't have a café. As French delis go, it's very good indeed – you'd be delighted to find a place like this on the streets of Bordeaux or Dijon. Its main feature is a large fridge featuring the best selection of French cheeses I can remember seeing for a very long time.

I have no problem with this shop being here, nor with its sister branch in Deal – the amount of money I spend in both is proof of that – but I feel frustrated that there isn't also an English deli in Sandwich with a wide array of English cheeses.

With the exception of the superb Neal's Yard Dairy and Paxton & Whitfield, the vast majority of upmarket cheese selections I see still focuses far more on French and Italian cheeses than British. Some even make it a point of pride that they stock only French cheeses. They either seem unaware of any of the 700 produced in Britain or assume that British cheeses can't possibly be as good because, well, they're British. Even when you find a place that does have pride in British cheese, I don't think I've ever seen a cheese shop that proudly boasts that it *only* sells British cheese. On the one hand, why would you? You'd be missing out on some excellent French and Italian cheeses, and that would be bizarre. So why is it not equally bizarre that a shop in England, run by English people and patronized by English customers rather than French expats, would *boast* that it sells only

French cheeses? Where I live in Stoke Newington there's a stunning Italian deli selling products exclusively imported from Italy run by a descendant of Italian immigrants. I'm delighted it's there and am a regular customer. But in my particularly affluent and foodie part of trendy North London, where people are always talking about how important it is to celebrate local produce and reduce food miles, there is no English deli proudly championing English produce.

This attitude is not confined to retailers. I've heard several friends moan about how Brexit will mean we'll find it harder to come by Brie, Roquefort and Camembert and will have to make do with 'rubbish' British cheeses. In fact, cheeses such as Stilton, Red Leicester and Stinking Bishop have great reputations around the world. Since the farmhouse cheese revival, British cheeses fare just as well as their counterparts in international competitions. In 2017, Cornish Kern was named best cheese in the world at the World Cheese Awards, beating off competition from 3,000 rivals from 34 other countries. British cheeses also won the top prize here in 2014 and 2010. Each time at least one British media outlet reporting the results said that the humble British cheese had 'even' beaten cheeses from France, Italy or Switzerland, as if we're some cheesy San Marino playing these countries in the football World Cup.

The No Name Shop sells an impressive array of filled baguettes, including Brie and bacon; Brie and quince jelly; mozzarella, pesto and tomato; and ham and Emmental. But that's not quite what I'm looking for just now, and obviously there's no Cheddar – let alone Cheshire, Yarg or Wensleydale – to be seen. I buy a ripe mini-Camembert for later and, as I leave the shop, I'm not sure which of the many variations on the cheese sandwich I'm in pursuit of for today's lunch, other than that it needs to be something ordinary, something Janice and Ray would accept, not because they're right, but because this is a test now to see if our supposed favourite workday lunch still exists in a recognizable form. It has to be Cheddar between two slices of bread – any other additional feature or ingredient is up for grabs.

Just across from the No Name Shop is the cobbled medieval market square, open to the street at the near end, with the elegant council building facing from the back, the Sandwich Guildhall Museum lining the right-hand side and a lower, older-looking building flanking on the left. And there it is.

Somehow my Trip Advisor search missed the Sandwich Shop in Sandwich, which is bizarre because a sandwich shop called the Sandwich Shop in Sandwich is obviously the place I was looking to eat my sandwich all along.

Apparently, the building dates back to the sixteenth century, but it looks much newer, other than its less-than-even roof. The big, friendly windows are full of posters advertising local theatre productions and concerts. Lettering across the top of the nearest window advertises 'freshly made sandwiches using local ingredients' and 'delicious home-made cakes'.

Inside, there are more people than I've seen in the whole town of Sandwich so far. The shop is staffed by two women in their thirties. 'Hello! I'll be with you in just a minute!' calls one of them as she sorts out the order of the elderly gentleman in front of me. Apart from the servers, I'm the youngest person in here by about fifteen to twenty years.

It's a bright, airy space that belies its antiquity, with a

laminated floor and Scandinavian-style furniture. Plump cushions are scattered on the wide window ledge. Paintings of beach huts and summer flowers by a local artist hang for sale on the walls. In the disused fireplace on the far wall from the door there's a wicker basket full of books and, next to it, a laminated newspaper cutting reading, 'Determined teenager raises trek cycle total'. Typed across the bottom is 'Please put in a minimum donation of 50p per book' and wedged in one corner of the basket is a collecting tin for Cancer Research.

It's January and the menu leads with warm food. But below the range of jacket potatoes and toasted sandwiches most of the space is given over to a range of 'sandwich platters'. These are sandwiches which come with salad and coleslaw on the side and each has its own title as well as a functional description of its ingredients. As soon as I spot it, I order the 'Classic Farmhouse': Cheddar, chutney and 'mild onion', for £3.85.

'White, brown or granary?'

Oh, this is brilliant. Definitely granary.

'Take a seat and we'll bring it over to you.'

A couple of women in their seventies come in and settle at the table next to mine, put on their specs and analyse the menu. 'Ooh-*ooh*-ooh,' says the first one, the middle *ooh* rising to indicate something interesting. 'Toasted sandwiches *and* baked potatoes!'

They consult for a few minutes before their purses come out and money changes hands. The *ooh*ing woman heads to the counter to place their order.

'Roast beef and horseradish, and I'll have it on white if she asks,' says the one at the table, loud enough for all to hear.

'With the salad, or just the sandwich?' says the other one.

'Ooh no, just the sandwich.'

As her friend places the order, choosing a special toasted ham and cheese for herself, my tea arrives and, two minutes later, so does my sandwich. It is, of course, cut diagonally, with the narrow end of one half placed artfully over that of the other, which makes it look way more interesting and far classier than if the two halves had just been cut and left next to each other. The arrangement also leaves more space for the small salad of baby leaves, cherry tomatoes, sweetcorn, red onion and red pepper, and the coleslaw on the other side of the plate. A tiny bowl of vinaigrette dressing sits neatly in the middle.

The sandwich contains a thick seam of grated Cheddar. This sits on a firm layer of chutney which has the chopped mild onions firmly embedded within it. The whole thing has a nice cohesion to it, straightforward and practical, and yet at the same time the abundance of grated-cheese flakes spilling out of the sides give it a sense of opulence.

I open the sandwich to check: there is no mayonnaise. They didn't even ask me if I wanted any. Because as they and I both know, it doesn't belong on a sandwich like this. It never has.

I take a bite. And then, immediately, uncontrollably, take another. The bread has the flavour and feel of bread, malty and sweet and savoury, a player in its own right rather than merely a carrier for the filling. The cheese is soft, creamy and rich, and just a little spicy. The ratio of pickle and onion is perfectly judged, offering a sharp, slightly acidic foil without dominating, keeping the palate fresh and making the whole thing moreish. It's just a

79

humble cheese-and-chutney sandwich, no more or less than it should be. And it's honest, and plain, and balanced, and satisfying, and bloody wonderful. I love it, mostly because it has neither insecurities nor delusions of grandeur. It's not trying to be anything other than a nice cheese sandwich. I feel like I'm having a genuine Proustian moment, a rush of memories of all the nicest cheese sandwiches I've ever eaten all rolled up and tied in a bow, because it's so long since I've had a cheese sandwich that tastes like this.

I suspect I'm like many middle-class people in that, until a few years ago, if anyone ever mentioned Proust I nodded along, roughly familiar with the reference without ever actually having read him, because I once saw a new, unabridged translation of *À la recherche du temps perdu* in Waterstones, regarded its heft, and resolved that if I were to live long enough to reach an era when organ replacement and cellular regeneration were to extend the average human's fit, healthy, active lifespan to, say, 150 years, I would totally give it a go, but not before then. And then, eventually, for a project in which I used neuro-scientific theory to pair different beer styles with different music, I needed to delve into what 'Proustian' really meant.

The poignancy of the passage is that when Marcel tucked into his madeleine it prompted an involuntary sense memory well before what we might call an 'intelligence' memory. He was overcome with feelings of pure joy prompted by the flavour which weren't initially attached to anything he could place. It took his brain a while to catch up and link the euphoria to the long-forgotten memory of his aunt feeding him madeleines dipped in her tea. The memory of the flavour and how it made him feel were far more immediate and visceral than where he was, or who he was with. And this is what happens to me now. The taste and texture of grated Cheddar, chutney and granary bread makes me feel happy, excited and elevated to a degree that the Sandwich Shop in Sandwich, lovely though it is, cannot take full credit for. There's something posh about it, something rarefied, something about other occasions where sandwiches were cut diagonally, maybe even into quarters. There are flashing sensations of indistinct older relatives, church halls on bright afternoons and crisply ironed shirts that were kept for best. I wait for them to resolve into a long-forgotten Proustian recollection. But instead they blow away again like autumn leaves.

At the next table, the ladies' sandwiches have arrived.

'I think it might be home-made coleslaw, don't you?'

'Mmm, yes . . . It's not as good as mine.'

'. . . No.'

I've finished the first half of my sandwich, and I hesitate before picking up the second. I don't want the experience to end, so I eat this one more slowly, because if I ordered another one such vulgarity would probably shatter the moment. Despite my pacing, it ends too soon. Inevitably, some of the grated-cheese flakes fall out and, once I've finally finished the sandwich itself, I spend a few delightful minutes dabbing these from the plate with my fingers.

At the next table there's some consternation over the tea.

'We ordered two pots of tea and we only got one.'

'No, it's OK, that's a pot of tea for two.'

Turning to me, the server says, 'Excuse me a moment, sir. May I?'

'We do it by volume. This is a pot of tea for one,' she says, holding my empty teapot aloft. 'The one you have there is twice as big. We serve it like that because it saves on the washing-up. But if you'd rather have two small ones instead of one big one that's absolutely fine, just mention it next time you come in. And we never say no to topping the pot up with more hot water.'

The Costa Coffee two doors away, occupying the corner on the market square on the other side of the Age Concern charity shop, has about twice as many customers as the Sandwich Shop and the average age is at least thirty years younger. The pre-prepared, pre-packaged sandwiches in here are £3.95 each and don't come with a freshly chopped salad and coleslaw. I'm pleasantly full from my Sandwich Shop sandwich – not stuffed, but sated. Even if I were still hungry, none of these sandwiches look at all appetizing in their packaging. I order a large tea.

'It comes in one size, in a pot.'

'Yes, but can you just give me a large cup of tea in a cup instead?'

'I can give you a pot or a large takeaway paper cup.'

'But you can't give me a tea in one of those large drink-in coffee mugs stacked just there?'

'Do you want the pot or the large paper cup?'

After a brief journey to what felt like the twentieth century, I've just landed glumly back in the twenty-first, in an age where we have great-quality food if we know where to look for it but choose not to and don't celebrate it even when we do find it. As the man said, we have modest expectations, and we fulfil them, remorselessly.

3.

Fish and Chips

'It is quite likely that fish-and-chips, art-silk stockings,
tinned salmon, cut-price chocolate (five two-ounce
bars for sixpence), the movies, the radio, strong tea,
and the Football Pools have between them averted
revolution. Therefore we are sometimes told that the
whole thing is an astute manoeuvre by the governing
class – a sort of "bread and circuses" business – to
hold the unemployed down. What I have seen of
our governing class does not convince me that they
have that much intelligence.'

– George Orwell, *The Road to Wigan Pier*, 1937

1.

My fondest teenage snogs tasted of fried fish and chips.

Between the ages of seven and eighteen, many of my
happiest memories revolve around two fish-and-chip shops
in Mapplewell, the pit village about five miles outside
Barnsley where I grew up. Like most of the villages around
t'Tarn, it was built on and around the slopes of a steep
hill. Most of the shops and pubs were based around the

junction of main roads at the bottom of the hill, and the houses and the people who lived in them grew gradually posher as you went uphill. Teachers, clergymen and accountants lived at the top. My dad grew up in a Victorian cottage about halfway down.

We moved back there when my grandmother fell ill, when I was seven. As well as her cottage, my long-departed grandfather had also owned the cottage next door, which was rented to an elderly couple called – I promise – Granville and Lily Sidebottom, and a large yard with a row of garages and outbuildings on the other side, which ended with a tiny shop called New Road Fisheries. When my grandmother died, my dad inherited it all. We owned a chippy!

Dad rented the chip shop to a man I only ever knew as Greasy Graham, who loved the motorcyclist Barry Sheen, decorated the shop in pictures of his hero and sometimes pretended to be him. The rhythm laid down by the hours of the chippy set the pace of school holidays and weekends. As the road was quite busy my brother and I were only allowed to play in the yard, and we'd occasionally stray into the outhouse where the peeler and chipper were, staring at the sheer volume of peeled potatoes sitting in a deep drum of water. The shop opened between 12 and 2 p.m., and then again from 4 till 8 p.m., because you'd have to be some kind of freak to eat later than that in the evenings. We'd steer clear of the queues that snaked out of the shop and up around the corner, waiting until we had the yard to ourselves once more before continuing our re-enactment of *Thunderbirds*. My mum worked a few shifts behind the counter before she went back to full-time work, which meant we always got generous portions of chips when she finished.

My dad was no businessman and never that good with money. He sold the cottage next door to Mrs Sidebottom (Granville died not long after my grandmother) and later sold the chippy to Greasy Graham because he couldn't understand why he was responsible for all the repairs and maintenance but never saw any of the profit from what was always a busy shop. I don't think it ever occurred to him to put the rent up. A few years after that, we moved to a new house further down the hill which was more expensive than the old Victorian terrace. And so, in just under four years, we went from owning two houses and a shop outright to having one house with a mortgage which only grew rather than shrinking over the years.

Fish and chips, and its sportier counterpart, sausage and chips, remained my favourite meals. In comics like *The Beano* or *Beezer*, where the 1970s still looked an awful lot like the 1940s, fish and chips was the prize enjoyed by the scruffy, working-class kids at the end of the strips where they 'won', the happy opposite of the violent assault with a slipper by a father or policeman when they were less fortunate.

The size of the portions of the spoils of victory and the severity of the beatings of defeat were exaggerated in the comics compared to what went on at home. But like the comics themselves, both were roughly a weekly occurrence during the long summer holidays. In our new house I'd be sent down to the bottom end of the road by the school to pick up dinner (not lunch) from Ramsden's, a tiny fish-and-chip shop tacked on to the end of another Victorian terrace and the house where Gerald Ramsden (no relation to the famous Harry – at least as far as I know) lived with his family. At noon on a Friday, you usually queued for about half an hour. The line snaked around the inside of the shop, hugging each wall in turn, then out of the door into a small yard outside, round each side of that, then out on to the pavement and up the street.

If you wanted a fish 'putting in', you were supposed to order it when you reached the door of the shop or, at the very latest, when you were leaning against the front window inside. At this point, you were only about ten minutes from being served, so Mr Ramsden would take a fresh fillet of fish, dip it in a bowl of batter and toss it in the fryer so that it would be hot and freshly crisp right around the point at which you finally reached the front of the queue. Or somebody would do that, anyway – Mr Ramsden was usually too busy holding court to put the fish in himself.

I was always shy about speaking up and would often order my fish too late, when the fear of the telling-off I was going to get for not ordering earlier ultimately overcame the dread of becoming the new focus of Mr Ramsden's wit. If you've ever avoided sitting near the front at a comedy gig for fear of being singled out and ridiculed by the comic on stage, you might have some idea what it was like ordering a fish from Ramsden's.

'Er, could you put us a cod in, please, Mr Ramsden?'

'Eyup, Pete! As tha' got any more O levels yet?'

'No, Mr Ramsden, not yet.'

'What tha' doin? Tha' gerrin' lazy. 'Ow many's tha' got now?'

'Ten.'

'Ten? What tha' still doin' at school?'

'Me A levels.'

'A levels? 'Ow many o' them as tha' got, then?'

'None yet.'

'None? Tha's been doin' 'em six months! I dunno, all them O levels and no common sense to go wi' 'em.'

Thinking back, I'd rather have taken a slippering from Dennis the Menace's dad, given the choice. But that's because I wasn't yet able to tell the difference between cruel mockery and good-natured ribbing.

Stan Richards, who for many years played the popular character Seth Armstrong in *Emmerdale*, lived just up the road and would occasionally be in the queue with the rest of us. I think Mr Ramsden practised his banter on the rest of us so he could at least try to give Seth – I mean Stan – a square go when he came in. Barnsley humour is whip sharp and Stan/Seth was an old master. It was always a longer wait on these occasions. I don't think anyone actually wanted to get served, in case they missed the best bits.

It was worth the ribbing for the fish and chips. They were exquisite. The fish was piping hot, the batter crisp and brittle on the outside, with just the slightest hint of moisture remaining where it coated the fish. The fish was chunky rather than completely flaky, buttery and moist in the mouth, its softness contrasting beautifully with the crunch of the batter so that you had to have both together in every bite – each on its own was less than half the sum of the whole.

But by this time, fish itself was a rare treat for us kids: more often, I'd be ordering fish for my dad while, for me, it was sausage and chips, or maybe fishcake and chips. The latter was probably my favourite dish of all, served with a polystyrene cup of radioactive curry sauce that managed to be dangerous and exotic without being at all spicy. The fishcake led to confusion and upset once I left home and started going to chippies elsewhere. I'd see 'fishcake' on the menu and then be confused when I got a small disc that was luminous orange, dry and dead, and had something inside that had the consistency and mouthfeel of thick phlegm and tasted *fishy* instead of tasting *of fish*. I felt sorry for the rest of the world, all these people labouring under the impression that this is what a fishcake was, when people in Mapplewell knew that a real fishcake consisted of a slab of fresh fish sandwiched between two solid wedges of potato, dipped in batter and deep fried – in other words, it was like all the best bits of fish and chips together in every bite, the potato firm and soft, the fish juicy and urgent, the crunch of the batter announcing each mouthful. You could eat it with one greasy hand and it cost about half the price of a full fish.

When my friends and I reached pub age – that is, the age when we could get away with being served – we'd always drink up in time to catch the chippie before it closed. Ramsden's was still one of those family shops that opened at dinner time and teatime. It didn't cater for the pub crowd. Didn't need to. Gerald Ramsden did well enough in those six hours to be able to put his feet up at night. But by now Greasy Graham stayed open until about eleven, cannily catching the tipsy crowd strolling home with beer munchies but shutting in time to avoid the full-on drunks who lingered until chucking-out time. I was now friends with the sons and daughters of the teachers, accountants and clergymen at the top of the hill, having lost touch with the lads on my street near the bottom when I started studying for the O levels Mr Ramsden took such a keen interest in.

We took the piss out of Greasy Graham behind his back (until he 'slid off' down to the neighbouring village of Royston to expand his empire), but his shop was too important to us to risk pulling the funniest stunt in Barnsley, the joke we always talked of cracking, which was to pop your head around the door at ten to eleven and ask, 'Have you got any chips left?' and when receiving a positive reply, yelling, 'Well, it's your fault for making too many!' and running away. Instead, every Friday after the pub (and, er, every Wednesday after Scouts), a few beers to the good, we'd get our fishcake, chips and curry sauce and I'd wander further up the hill with my friends to the four-way junction, where we all lingered for as long as we dared before separating and heading home in different directions, me trudging back down the hill we'd just walked up.

In the two or three years before I left for university, after the worst of my acne had cleared up and I discovered the transformative power of bathing and washing my hair more than once a week, I went out with a couple of different girls from the group and had occasional dalliances with a couple more. Once the chip papers were discarded and those on their own had wandered off, the couples wiped greasy hands on jeans, drifted respectfully apart on the small patch of grass by the junction, and kissed in that way you only ever kiss when it's not a prelude to something else.

2.

Mapplewell is a long way from Knightsbridge. Years before I heard the term 'imposter syndrome', I felt it on a daily basis. In the late 1990s, I was working for Lowe Howard-Spink, an advertising agency in a building that straddled the entrance to Hyde Park from Knightsbridge itself. I had my own office, just opposite Harvey Nichols. The Horse Guards regimental barracks was just next door. I lived in a flat in Notting Hill, just on the other side of the park. When Princess Diana died, the traffic was jammed all around the area for two weeks. Between her death and the funeral, I mainly walked to work through the park, via the ever-widening ocean of floral tributes outside Kensington Palace. I'd lived in the flat since 1995 and, by this time, I no longer expected the knock on the door and a person with a clipboard saying, 'There seems to have been some mistake. I see from our records that you are Pete Brown from Barnsley. I'm afraid you need to vacate the premises immediately.'

My paranoia was mostly unfounded but never entirely without justification. And I felt it keenly on the day my career at Lowe's began to draw to a close.

As the strategic planner on the Heineken account, it had fallen to me to make a recommendation on whether the beer should continue with 'Refreshes the parts that other beers cannot reach' – the slogan that made it famous – or whether that line was now tired and should be replaced. After months of research, I suggested it was time to retire the line. This was a collective decision, but as soon as it had been made I found myself suddenly on my own, holding a telephone while the agency's founder, Sir Frank Lowe, was asking me why I had personally decided to bin the most successful, well-loved and famous advertising slogan of all time.*

When he refused to listen to any of the arguments I raised, interrupting me and closing me down at the start of every sentence, I realized the conversation was in itself a form of punishment and nothing I could say mattered. Deciding that my career was over and that, given this was the case, I needn't put up with his bullying bullshit any more, I said, 'Look, if you're not even going to listen to anything I say, how do you expect me to help you?'

'That's what I'd like you to tell me,' he said (in my imagination, wearing a grey Nehru-collar suit and stroking a fluffy white cat in his lap as he did so.) 'So can you go home and think about that tonight over your fish and chips?'

Frank Lowe had never met me in person and knew nothing about me. But he could hear my northern accent. Maybe it was something he said to everyone, but I doubt it – no one else in the agency said, 'Oh, he says that all the time.' If he'd said to an Asian member of staff, 'Can you go home tonight and think about that over your poppadoms?' I'm sure it would have been considered a racial slur. But as well as being used to label nations, certain foods are also used to signify class differences. Even today, Conservative

---

* To be fair to the mean old bastard, his argument was given credence when, in the week the new campaign launched, with a new line I can guarantee you do not remember, a new edition of the *Oxford Dictionary of Quotations* was published which included 'refreshes the parts', describing it in roughly the same way Sir Frank did in that phone call. Although, thinking about it now, he probably made that happen somehow, just to make a point.

politicians routinely make claims that 'people on benefits' 'waste' their money on fast food. These days, they're more likely to be thinking of burger-and-fried-chicken chains when they say this. But their forebears looked down on fish and chips in a very similar way.

When John Walton published his rigorously researched *Fish and Chips and the British Working Class* in 1992, he was derided by colleagues and reviewers alike. A friend of my wife spluttered, 'But surely even *you* can't pad out fish and chips to a whole book!' while *Private Eye* stuck him in Pseuds Corner, seemingly for merely considering it to be a subject worthy of academic study. Meanwhile, many histories of British food studiously avoided any mention of the dish.

Food history focuses on what the upper and, latterly, middle classes ate. Partly that's because this is where the best contemporary records were kept: we know in some level of detail what a succession of monarchs ate on a regular basis for at least the last 500 years. In-depth writing about the diet of the poor only really begins to appear around the time of philanthropic Victorians such as Charles Dickens and Henry Mayhew. But partly it's also because food history tends to be written and read by people who are interested in food, and there's an assumption that the diets of the poor must, by definition, be dull and boring. Clearly, fish and chips is not dull and boring. But while it has moved from being the food of the poor to being Britain's pre-eminent national dish, its lowly origins still cause discomfort.*

---

* Another time at Lowe, all the strategic planners went for a departmental away-day in Brighton. I suggested we went to the chippie on the pier for lunch.

Funnily enough, Dickens and Mayhew were writing just when fried fish was becoming a staple in the slums of London's East End and give us some of the earliest mentions of it. Before this point, the dish was a rare treat for anyone who didn't live on the coast. River fish had a muddier taste and have never been popular. By the end of the eighteenth century, ice was being used to transport fresh salmon from Scotland to London for those who could afford it. But while there are recipes in books from the sixteenth, seventeenth and eighteenth centuries for fish – some fried, some not – for most of our history, most people never got to taste fresh fish.

Just as they did with champagne, beer and fine cheeses, railways and refrigeration changed the picture. With an island coastline and abundant stocks, as soon as it could be frozen and transported fish became widely available and affordable. First in London's Billingsgate Market, and then in fish markets in cities across the country, fish went from being a luxury to an affordable working-class essential by the mid-nineteenth century.

It seems pretty certain that the idea of frying fish in batter was introduced by London's Sephardic Jewish population. Hannah Glasse, author of *The Art of Cookery Made Plain and Easy* – the most famous cookbook of the eighteenth century – included, 'The Jews way of preserving Salmon and all Sorts of Fish', which instruted:

It was only when we arrived there and I joined the queue that I realized several of my colleagues had assumed I was joking.

> Take either salmon, cod, or any large fish, cut off
> the head, wash it clean, and cut it in slices as crimp'd
> cod is, dry it very well in a cloth; then flour it, and
> dip it in yolks of eggs, and fry it in a great deal of
> oil, till it is of a fine brown, and well done; take it
> out and lay it to drain, till it is very dry and cold.

This is a pretty similar recipe to pescado frito, a dish from the southern coast of Spain, and it doesn't seem a huge leap away from modern fried fish, but Glasse then advised pickling this fried, floured fish so that it would 'go good to the East Indies'. In any case, its popularity seems to have spread. In 1823, M. Radcliffe's *Modern System of Domestic Cookery* described how to wet a fish with egg, then coat it in breadcrumbs, before frying in a thick-bottomed pan with 'a large quantity of dripping or lard . . . till the colour is of a fine brown yellow and it is judged ready'.

Court reports, coroner's reports and newspaper accounts from the 1820s onwards refer to various Jews making their living from frying and selling fish. Further evidence that fried fish was originally associated with London's Jewish population are the contemporary accounts of it being used to bolster anti-Semitism. Along with large, hooked noses and a reputation for meanness, the smell of fried fish about their person was a common trope of Victorian Jewish caricatures. Panikos Panayi recounts how, when he established the clear connection between Jews and the origins of fried fish in his 2008 book *Spicing Up Britain*, he was placed on a 'watch list' by the fascist group Stormfront, who shared his findings, as well as his address, phone number and email, saying, 'The news will not go down well with Britons who assumed the food was all theirs.' The irony that late-nineteenth-century racists used fried fish as an example of everything that was supposedly wrong with London's Jewish population is obviously lost on their modern equivalents.

The food of the Jews eventually became the food of the poor. Henry Mayhew, the lesser-known journalistic rival to Dickens when it came to atmospherically evoking the world of mid-nineteenth-century London, wrote in *London Labour and the London Poor*:

> The supply [of fish] is known in the trade as 'friers', and consist of the overplus of a fishmonger's store, of what he has not sold overnight, and does not care to offer for sale on the following morning, and therefore send to the costermongers, whose customers are chiefly among the poor . . . Many of the 'friers' are good . . . but some are very queer indeed, and they are consequently fried with a most liberal allowance of oil, which will conceal anything . . . A gin-drinking neighbourhood, one coster said, suits best, for people haven't their smell so correct there.

The origins of chips aren't as clear. Potatoes originated in the Andes and arrived in Europe in the sixteenth century, but they were initially regarded with suspicion, not least because many varieties were poisonous unless prepared correctly – and no one knew how to prepare them correctly – and also because, coming from the New World, they're mentioned nowhere in the Bible. But the potato steadily won Europe over. The continent was frequently ravaged by famine, and potatoes – most of the time – proved to be a sturdier alternative to wheat and barley, yielding much more nutritional value per acre. Potatoes spread from Spain and Portugal to become a staple across Europe and have been credited with fuelling the continent's population boom in the nineteenth century.

This is when they arrived in Britain, initially as food for the urban poor. Poor cereal harvests were compounded by the Industrial Revolution moving people away from land on which they could grow at least some of their own crops. Regular supplies of fresh bread became difficult because bread required an oven, which few households possessed; potatoes could be grown on urban allotments and cooked over any kind of fire. By the time fresh fish was available in inner cities, potatoes had become a working-class staple, with many street vendors selling baked potatoes from carts or trays.

The same people who are proud of already knowing that fried fish was introduced by European Jews are also often quick to claim that chips were invented by either the French or the Belgians, but they could have developed in Britain independently around the same time. There are two parts to the mystery of the birth of the chip: first, the frying of chopped potatoes, rather than boiling or baking them, and second, the shape of the potato pieces being fried. Potatoes were being fried rather than just boiled in Britain and Ireland from the moment they arrived. The association with France comes, ironically, from Charles Dickens, who, in *A Tale of Two Cities*, refers to 'husky chips of potato, fried with some reluctant drops of oil' in Revolutionary Paris. It's claimed that this is the earliest known use of the word 'chips' in relation to fried pieces of potato. But it's worth bearing in mind that Dickens wasn't yet born in the 1780s, let alone present in Paris. When he used the word 'chips' in this context, he was writing in England in 1859, using Thomas Carlyle's book on the French Revolution as his main historical source – a book that makes no mention of 'chips of potato, fried husky or otherwise'. Against that, French cookbooks give recipes for frying potatoes from the eighteenth century onwards, whereas they don't start appearing in British cookbooks until the nineteenth. However, contemporary accounts suggest fried potatoes emerged in both countries at roughly the same time. Wherever potatoes became a regular part of the diet, the frying of them was never far behind.

Sellers of fried-potato pieces and sellers of fried fish were operating independently before some genius brought the two together. Chips were more popular in industrial northern towns, particularly in Lancashire – which adopted the potato earlier than the rest of England (possibly due to closer links between the county and Ireland) – whereas fried fish was more popular in London. When the two finally came together, this preference remained in the relative portion sizes – for a while, in London, you got more fish than chips, while the reverse was true in the north.

The earliest known shop selling fish and chips together was founded by Joseph Malin in London's East End in 1860. But this was established by a survey from the National Federation of Fish Fryers over a hundred years later. Other shops, lost to history, may well have been in business before this. What's certain is that, during the 1860s, the appeal of fish and chips began to spread. This, then, was a meal of the late Industrial Revolution, made possible by refrigeration, artificial ice and rail transport, and made necessary by the appalling conditions faced by the working poor in industrial cities.

By the early twentieth century, there was barely a heavy industrial town or city without at least one fish-and-chip shop. In places where women worked outside the home, it was a quick and easy alternative to cooking. By the end of the nineteenth century, fish and chips was no longer just a street food and in London it was possible for poor people to sit down in a fish-and-chip restaurant with white table-cloths, cutlery and china plates and get a taste of how the other half lived.

The other half, of course, didn't like this. Middle-class commentators – who presumably had never been near a chippie in their lives – condemned fish and chips as indigestible, expensive and unwholesome. It was blamed for everything from transmitting typhoid to babies to causing 'secondary poverty' by, as Walton puts it, encouraging 'the incompetent or immoral misapplication of resources that would otherwise have been sufficient to sustain an adequate standard of living'.* What would later be summed up by Walton as 'the convivial, open, public nature of the purchase and often the eating of fish and chips' was seen as vulgar and uncouth, like showing your dirty laundry in public. There are accounts of middle-class people getting servants or tradesmen to go to the fish-and-chip shop for them rather than be known to eat such a common meal.

* Or, as Edwina Currie put it a hundred years later, 'I get very, very troubled at the number of people who are using food banks who think that it is fine to pay to feed their dog . . . but they never learn to cook, they never learn to manage and the moment they have got a bit of spare cash they are off getting another tattoo.'

The truth was that fish and chips represented a dramatic improvement on what had been available before. In 1879, a piece in *Chamber's Journal* – written by someone who had actually visited a fish-and-chip shop – said:

> Fried fish shops – and you must go to the East End to taste fried fish to perfection – where you can have a good fill for about twopence. There are thousands among the wretched classes who have no plates or knives, and who if they could not buy something ready cooked from such shops, would have nothing cooked at all.

For millions of people, the only alternative to fish and chips was not a meal home-cooked from scratch featuring some lean, grilled meat and plenty of fresh veg – it was bread and margarine and black tea. These people had no access to fresh vegetables, rarely saw a cut of meat and, even if they had good food to cook, were faced with the additional cost of cooking it. The extent of the malnutrition and food poverty facing the poor was brought home in 1914 when, during army recruitment at the outbreak of the First World War, it was discovered that former public schoolboys joining up were on average six inches taller than the rest of the male population.

Fish and chips may be fast food and it may be takeaway food, but it's not junk food. It's heavy in calories and fat, which may not be ideal for today's largely sedentary population, but those calories and fat were desperately needed by early-twentieth-century manual workers who didn't get enough of either. Fish and chips also contains vitamin C, vitamins B6 and B12, iron, zinc and calcium, as well as iodine, omega-3 fatty acids and some important dietary fibre. These are not just empty calories, and the many families who ate three or four times a week from the chip shop did well on them. As Orwell wrote in *The Road to Wigan Pier*, 'You can't get much meat for threepence, but you can get a lot of fish and chips.'

In terms of sheer numbers, fish-and-chips shops peaked around the time Orwell was writing, with about 35,000 shops across Britain. While they may have been in predominantly working-class areas, there were so many shops that they defined Britain. In 1928, an article in *The New York Times* claimed, 'England's hot dog is "fish and chips".' It was never rationed during the Second World War and, after the war ended, food in Britain began to change. Slowly, foreign cuisines permeated our national consciousness, and in response the idea of 'British cuisine' started to take shape in a way it hadn't before. The steady growth of Chinese, Italian and Indian restaurants forced people across all classes to consider what their British equivalent was. In his 1953 book *Traditional Dishes of Britain* Philip Harben, one of the first celebrity chefs, wrote:

> What is the national dish of Britain? . . . The teeming millions of Asia subsist mainly on rice. Macaroni in its various forms is the staple diet of Italy. Germany and sausages are almost synonymous. When you think of Scotland you think of porridge. What then, is the national dish of Britain? The Roast Beef of Old England? Not a bit of it! The answer is: Fried Fish and Chips.

As British kitchens improved, chips became a staple of home cooking too. One way to determine someone's age is to ask them if they know how to put out a chip-pan fire because, through the 1970s until sometime in the early 1980s, there were government information films in almost every commercial break showing you how to cover the pan with a wet tea towel, just before the ads for frying oil such as Crisp 'n Dry. When I was very small, my mum made her own chips, and they were the best we had ever had. But then she stopped. Trying to remember why this was, I realized it was the introduction of McCain's Oven Chips, which first launched in Britain in 1979 and were so successful the company is now the largest manufacturer of frozen potato products in the UK. Chip pans disappeared from the nation's homes, the fire-prevention ads from our screens.

The ease of oven chips – cooked straight from the freezer without a big pan of oil – dealt a blow to the chippie. And from the 1960s onwards, fish-and-chip shops were also facing intensifying competition from other kinds of takeaway. The number of fish-and-chips shops in Britain was now in long-term decline and, by 2003, it had shrunk to just 8,600. But compare that to the seeming ubiquity of Wetherspoon's pubs (900 across the UK), Costa Coffee branches (around 1,600) and McDonald's (around 1,200), and fish and chips is still by far our favourite takeaway. OK, maybe not just fish – it's now the most expensive item on the menu, and we might choose cheaper sausages, pies or fishcakes instead – but the chippie remains the fast-food option that differentiates Britain from the rest of the world.

3.

'You want to go down Chip Alley,' says Liz's cousin Martyn.

The parallels between South Yorkshire and South Wales are striking. It may seem obvious, as both were coal-mining areas, but it goes beyond what I expected. Liz and I first met just after her mother and my father had died, and in the early years of our relationship we kept surprising each other with archaic phrases that each of our late parents had used. I'd always believed them to be Yorkshire sayings, while Liz had always been convinced they were peculiar to South Wales. It created an imagined affinity between our lost parents.

Like Liz, Martyn was born and raised in Cwmbran, where he still lives and runs his own business as an electrician. While Martyn the electrician from Cwmbran and Pete the ad-exec-cum-writer from Barnsley may not seem to have much in common on paper, we bonded more strongly than I did with anyone else in Liz's extended family because we shared a curiosity and sense of wonder about the world that's not typically associated with working-class men. Martyn passed this on successfully to his kids. His wife, Trish, was a dinner lady who was part of Jamie Oliver's movement to inspire better food in schools. When they came up to London to stay with us when the kids were young, and when we asked what they would like to eat, young Lauren and Shane, then aged around nine and eleven, wouldn't say 'McDonald's' or 'Pizza'; they'd shout, 'Something we've never had before!' So each successive visit would mean venturing to a Turkish *ocakbaşi* around the corner, or a Vietnamese pho down the road in Shoreditch, then on to sushi or dim sum in Chinatown in the West End. Every time they were packing to leave, they'd nip to the Asian supermarket on the high street to stock up on big packets of spices they couldn't find at home. Now in his early twenties, Shane works long hours for not much more than minimum wage to support his wife, Jess, and their son, Mason. Some nights when he gets home, to relax he and Jess will fire up Google Earth and spend time virtually wandering the streets of famous barbecue towns in the American South. When they find a rib shack they like the look of, if there's a link available, they'll click through to the menu, analyse it, and then Shane will try to re-create the dishes at home.

But while it's great to wander, the Joneses also appreciate the value of what's close to home. Martyn can make going to his local pub for a couple of pints of cheap lager sound like the most inspiring, aspirational, noble and heroic idea anyone has ever had. Trish now runs her own worker's café, Café 77 on the Springvale industrial estate in Cwmbran, cooking up wholesome, home-made food from scratch every day, such as full English breakfasts, roast-beef dinners and shepherd's pies, all served in massive portions at un-believably low prices. And yes, you're damn right, that's me using my platform as a writer to shamelessly advertise a family member's business. If you ever find yourself any-where near the Springvale industrial estate in Cwmbran on a Monday to Saturday between 7.30 a.m. and 2.30 p.m., you simply can't afford to give it a miss. You won't eat better for less anywhere else outside your own home.

About ten years ago, when I mentioned to Martyn that

I was going to be in Cardiff overnight after a book event, he had no hesitation in recommending where I should go for dinner.

'What it is, right, it's a street in Cardiff, and it's full of chip shops. Chip Alley, it is. You can have anything with chips. Fish and chips. Sausage and chips. Pie and chips. Anything.'

'Sounds good. I'll have to check it out.'

'I mean: rissoles and chips. Curry and chips. Proper curry, mind, not just curry sauce. You can have anything with chips.'

'Cool.'

'Kebab and chips. Faggot and chips. Fishcake and chips. Burger and chips. You can have anything.'

'I think I get it, Martyn.'

'Beans and chips. Anything you want. Spare ribs and chips. Chip Alley, they call it.'

Chip Alley, or Chippy Lane (debate rages among locals as to which is the correct term), is how short, narrow Caroline Street in the heart of Cardiff city centre is better known. Local newspapers proclaim it 'the most famous street in Wales for late-night grub', and the earliest record of a chip shop being here among the fruiterers, watchmakers and fishmongers dates back to the 1870s, when a shop selling skate wing and chips for 2d won the reputation of having the cheapest chips in Cardiff. Dorothy's Café and Fish Bar opened in 1954 and is the oldest of the current businesses; it proved so popular that the whole street was soon colonized by chip shops and, later, kebab shops. In the heart of the nightlife, and only two minutes' walk from the Millennium Stadium, the shops stay open until 2 a.m., and around pub closing time it's the busiest street in the city. The bins quickly fill with chip papers and cartons, eventually becoming cairns of litter which then spill to carpet the entire street, such is its volume. Everyone is drunk and, while the Welsh can get drunker than any other nation I've seen while still remaining standing, there is in general more cheerfulness to it than I've seen among any of the other nations of the United Kingdom. Sure, there's the odd bit of trouble – such as when footballer Craig Bellamy was arrested for assaulting two men in Chip Alley in 2011 – but that's only because everyone who is still awake in Cardiff at this time is here. For the number of people crammed into the tiny street, it's remarkably good-natured. I had a lovely time all those years ago at Martyn's recommendation and, now, it's great to have an excuse to go back, and call it work.

The old Brains Brewery once flanked the western side of Caroline Street, but it's now long gone and the area has been redeveloped as 'the Brewery Quarter', one of those pedestrianized shopping precincts that have found their way into every big English city these days and use the word 'quarter' to justify rents that only big chains can afford. The pedestrianized heart of Cardiff is now indistinguishable from the pedestrianized heart of Birmingham, Liverpool or Sheffield. It's the same shops and the same restaurants in the same order: Jamie's Italian, Fat Face, Starbuck's, Karen Millen, Wagamama and White Stuff.

And Chip Alley has almost disappeared.

The Brewery Quarter opens directly on to Caroline Street and about a third of one side is taken up by the biggest branch of Five Guys I have ever seen. Across the alleyway from it is Le Bistrot Pierre. Across the road from that a branch of Tortilla. There are no chip shops at all left on that side of the street.

Mercifully, Dorothy's is still there, in the centre of the last remaining strip of chippies and kebab shops – maybe five or six in total, no more than a quarter or a fifth of the street they used to dominate entirely. Dorothy's is an institution now so, unlike most of its former neighbours, it can still afford to compete. It even has a plaque by the door:

Dorothy's Fish Bar . . .
. . . a traditional fish and chip shop with a difference.
The home of chicken curry off the bone
1st
To introduce chicken curry to Cardiff City centre
over 47 years ago
Our fresh chicken is spit roasted on the premises
on a daily basis
We still maintain the same successful recipe for a
home-made chicken curry using the finest ingredients
Why not try Dorothy's home-made
Rissoles
Fishcakes
Or Scotch eggs

I adore this on so many levels. That massive '1st' clearly tells a story. Right next door to Dorothy's, Tony's Fish and Chip Bar also advertises chicken curry off the bone as 'Tony's Special' in its window. And next door to that, The Red Onion gives chicken curry central billing. Chicken curry off the bone has obviously become such a big deal in the culinary microclimate of Chip Alley, it's important to ascertain whose idea it was.

I also love how important it is to establish that this is chicken curry 'off the bone'. Apart from in some cafés in Old Delhi, where whole chickens are simply chopped into pieces with a big cleaver before going into the pot, I don't think I've ever had chicken curry *on* the bone. Was there a time when chicken curry was served on the bone in Cardiff? It's doubtful, if Dorothy's really was the first to introduce the entire concept of chicken curry to Cardiff city centre. But perhaps it symbolizes something different here. Maybe it's part of making clear that this is proper chicken curry rather than mere curry sauce.

I'm almost saddened that, standing in Dorothy's, I'm duty bound to order fish and chips instead, because that is today's mission. I know it will be good, but my dedication to the cause almost breaks my heart when I gaze at the menu boards above the counter and think to myself, in the voice of the late Jim Bowen, 'Here's what you could have won.'

There's so much up there – Martyn really wasn't kidding, or even over-labouring his point. Near the middle of the board's dense type is a section with the subtitle 'The Usual'. This consists of chips, large chips, chicken curry and chips, chicken curry without chips (!), large cod and chips, ¼ piece of chicken and chips, and chip butty. On the other side of the board are sections titled 'Sausages', 'Pies', 'Pasties' and 'Cartons', the latter listing curry, gravy, beans, cheese and mushy peas; and a separate section of 'Extras', which is a broad category consisting of anything that doesn't fit under the main headings, such as home-made rissoles, Scotch eggs, fishcakes, burgers and, curiously, 'large cod'.

And then, in the centre of the board, some of the

possible combinations of these ingredients are presented in two innovative graphics:

The pain of having to choose just one meal is unbearable. I know I'm ordering fish and chips, but look: chicken curry and chips has a little gold crown on it.

'By the way, you're having chicken curry off the bone and chips,' I say to Liz.

'I know,' she says simply, and I feel a surge of love for her. She's saying this because she understands my sense of loss at not being able to order it for myself and knows she's going to have to give me some of hers to try. And she's also saying it because she really, really wants to eat chicken curry off the bone with chips on a chilly street in the middle of Cardiff, right now. There aren't many women in the world this special.

My fish and chips come in a golden polystyrene tray so full it barely closes. There are more chips than I could possibly eat – and I can get through a lot of chips. They don't look like the greatest chips ever – they're quite small and stumpy, spindlier than I prefer them. But they're incredibly tasty. Under the lashings of salt and vinegar there's an additional enticement about them – from the type of oil they're fried in, maybe? – and I seem to be getting hungrier the more of them I eat. The fish is perfect: too long for the box to close over it, it resembles a topographical scale model of Great Britain. The batter is light and crispy, quite crunchy but beautifully soft and yielding when I bite into it, the fish hot and soft and clean beneath. There's easily enough here for two people, and I have to leave an obscene amount so I still have space to try the chicken curry off the bone, big chunks of chicken breast sliding off the chips as its sauce spills from a tray that can't contain it, with a hybrid flavour that resembles, and probably is, the kind of gravy you get with a really good roast chicken with some sweet and fragrant spices stirred in, with just enough heat to make you notice.

It's a better meal by far than anything Five Guys has to offer, which is why Five Guys remains deserted as the queues start to stretch outside the doors of each of the last few survivors of Chip Alley. The changes here are not being driven by consumer demand. It's all about 'development' and a city's image of itself and the tacit agreement that smooth, shiny chain brands are implicitly better than small, slightly tatty independent businesses. As with sandwich shops, all these new restaurants and boutiques are far more expensive than the establishments they've replaced. Their slick uniformity tells us that these are the places we now really ought to be shopping in, even if our incomes have risen by nowhere near the level of prices on the city streets.

In 2011, the only chain business on Caroline Street was a branch of Greggs, which almost qualifies for honorary status anyway. That year, in a local story about the debate between Chip/Chippy Lane versus Chippy/Chip Alley, Hywel Thomas, PR manager for Cardiff & Co., a now-defunct company with a mission to 'promote Cardiff to the world', said of Chip Alley,* 'It's part of the city's character. The city would probably be dull without it, wouldn't it?'

Cardiff now has its answer to that question.

---

* 'I'm born and bred in the city and it's Caroline Street or Chip Alley, definitely not Chip Lane,' he added.

4.

The smell of vinegar evaporating from steaming-hot chips is one of the most rousing scents in the world. Those much-vaunted aromas of freshly baked bread and fresh coffee come nowhere near.

On 11 October 1997, I was in a pub in Notting Hill watching England play Italy in Rome. England needed just a point from the game to qualify for the 1998 World Cup, but they had to fight like gladiators to get it. Paul Ince, the England captain, played half the game with a thick bandage around his head from a wound that needed stiches. The cameras kept cutting from his blood-soaked shirt to the stands, where mobs of Italian riot police were surrounding and beating England fans to the ground, and beyond. I've never felt such tangible waves of hate and anger spill from a TV screen before or since. The pub was as packed as a stadium terrace with furious England fans. No one dared say a word – the atmosphere was too tense.

And into this pressure cooker stepped someone with a portion of chips in paper. People were hemmed in so tightly the chip-holder had to hoist them over their head to get through. I watched the chips floating along, as if on a magic carpet, the smell of hot vinegar permeating the room and adding a sense of longing to the atmosphere. As they swept along, I saw hands, almost as if of their own volition, start reaching and grabbing the chips. Suddenly, inevitably, the chips and their papers flew high into the air and a Wild West-style brawl ensued.

Any meal that wishes to stake its claim as a national dish

must have deep cultural resonance as well as tasting good and being popular. This moment, for me, was when fish and chips achieved that status.

The National Federation of Fish Friers (established in 1913) asserts on its website that 'Fish and chips are the undisputed National dish of Great Britain . . . a cultural and culinary symbol of our country, instantly recognized as British the world over.' Of course, they would say that. But few commentators on the subject these days seem inclined to disagree. Wayne Rooney served fish and chips at his wedding, while Michelle Obama treated her daughters to a fish supper during a visit to London in 2009. One London chippie – the Seashell in Lisson Grove – has in recent years hosted Denzel Washington, Michael Jackson, David Gest and Liza Minelli, Lady Gaga, Jimmy Page and the entire cast and crew of the Chinese edition of *Top Gear*. Some of this could be interpreted as an attempt to say, 'Look how normal and down to earth we are,' but there's too much at stake with an important visit or a celebrity wedding to virtue-signal in this way if there's a risk that the food is going to be poor. Fish and chips – done well – isn't.

The problem is, as with any meal, there are good and bad fish and chips. And as a nation, we're brilliant at selling knock-off versions of superior goods and convincing the gullible that they're the real thing.

When I went to university and first encountered pub 'fish and chips' I was horrified by the thin, bendy cod fillet coated in bright orange breadcrumbs, the skinny, gristly, mean-spirited oven chips and peas that tasted of paper towels. I was surprised to learn that some people really thought this was what fish and chips were like. Come to London as a tourist and head for a centrally located pub to try the national dish and, chances are, you're going to be disappointed. Never enter a hybrid kebab/fried-chicken/fish-and-chips shop (unless you're in Chip Alley) and expect good fish and chips, especially if there's no shiny silver hot box on top of the counter or deep fat fryer behind it. Even in a bona fide chippie, when you do see an array of battered and fried products glistening under the glowing bulbs, how do you know how long they've been there? Too often, the batter has gone chewy and the centre of the fish is lukewarm and dry. The chips are wizened and thin, curved and sharp as hawk's talons, with the consistency of old toffee and the taste of oxidized, dirty oil. If the shop is empty when you walk in, and you have to cough to draw the server's attention away from their smartphone, beware.

In the 1930s, anyone who ate fish and chips regularly knew this. Today, in the places the meal is still important, people still do.

I recently stayed for a week on a caravan park in west Wales. Down on the main road there was one chip shop that was part of the park complex and another, opposite, that belonged to a small supermarket. On my first night there, I went to the park chippie and found it deserted. I ordered fish and chips and, too late, as I was paying, I spotted a business card with a McCain's logo sitting on top of the till. When I started eating, I realized this hadn't just been a speculative sales call. Oven chips are what you cook at home when you can't or don't want to go to a chip shop or can't be bothered with the hassle of a deep fat fryer. A chip shop using McCain's oven chips is the equivalent of a restaurant heating up supermarket ready-meals in the microwave.

Days later, I went to the village chippie. We'd checked the opening times because we'd been foiled before. It opened at 5 p.m. and closed at eight. A sandwich board stood outside reading, 'Last orders 7.45'. I was there at seven twenty, queuing outside. By seven thirty-five, I was inside the shop and a yellow-haired matron in her fifties was at the door with the keys jingling in the lock. At seven forty the door was closed and a man rushed up, pointed at the sign reading seven forty-five and spread his arms in supplication. The manager sighed, swept open the door, said, 'OK, get in, you're the last one,' and locked it behind him, opening it again as swiftly as possible for each departing customer. Nothing stayed in the hot box for more than thirty seconds. The orders were of epic proportions – each customer in this packed shop was here to feed a family. Everything was fresh. It couldn't not be. As soon as your order was cooked it was in your hands. Oh, but the wait between ordering and receiving! The monotonous desire, punctuated every thirty seconds by another delighted soul having the door unlocked for them as they swept out with their treasure, was hell.

When I finally emerged triumphant, the door slamming shut and jangling behind me, the McCain's place across the road was still open, still empty.

If you've only ever tasted terrible or even average fish and chips in tourist traps or chain pubs, you have no idea how good they can be. And just as importantly, if your only experience of fish and chips is based on living near somewhere like Gerald Ramsden's or this seaside chippie

113

in west Wales, you simply think that's what fish and chips are like.

In its heartland, fish and chips has always hit peaks of excellence. In the 1930s, when there were chip shops on every street, and even some mid-terrace houses with front rooms converted with ranges and fryers, if the quality wasn't good even the poorest patrons would simply go somewhere else. John Walton shows how people were very particular about the details of the dish – be that the overwhelming preference for haddock in Glasgow rather than hake in Manchester, the universal agreement on the superiority of King Edward potatoes over all others, the particular choice of frying 'medium' (always beef dripping in Yorkshire) or the making of batter, which, as the *Fish Fryer's Review* commented in 1931, was a proud fish fryer's trademark:

> Almost every fryer has a pet method, the result of experience and experiment, in fact I may term it a secret process, to be jealously guarded and kept in the family.

When we were kids, my friends Al, Chris and Steve also got their fish and chips from Ramsden's. Their dad, George, was the local Methodist minister and the church he looked after was just across the road from the chip shop. Mr Ramsden never showed any interest in how many O levels George Gittner had. Instead, when it was George's turn to ask for a fish putting in, Mr Ramsden would ask, ''Ow many people 'as tha' married this week then, Reverend?' And from there, the conversation would follow a familiar tack.

Years later, George told Chris and Al that when Mr

Ramsden announced that he was finally selling the business, their conversation briefly grew more reflective. He confided to George that, while he may be selling the fixtures and fittings as well as the enormous goodwill the business had, the recipe for his batter was not part of the deal. 'I've never telled anybody what's in it, not even them that works here. All I'll tell thee is there's beer in it.' He was true to his word. According to Revd Gittner, Gerald Ramsden 'took the secret of his batter to his grave'.

Al, Chris and I talked for ages about how much beer Mr Ramsden must have got through, about the lightness that beer's carbonation gives a good batter, and wondered if he'd had a special deal with a local brewery. We'll never know. But in all the years I queued in his shop it never occurred to me that there might be anything special about his batter or that he might have been unusual in only cooking fresh fish to order. Why would it? It was all I knew. As with the pork pies in Barnsley Market, maybe one reason we don't shout too loudly about how great our food is is that we have absolutely no idea how much better it is than the stuff other people have to put up with.

In 2014, the *Daily Telegraph* noted, 'Not only did the Ivy in London feature fish and chips on its made-over menu when Chris Corbin and Jeremy King relaunched the place and made it chic in 1990, but so did its smarter sister, the Caprice . . . No longer the working man's nourishment, a fish supper is now classless, which somewhat increases its credibility as our national dish.'

It's to their credit that top restaurants such as the Ivy and the Savoy don't muck around too much with fish and chips. If you really know your food, you know there's not much that can be done to improve on a classic. But I doubt the fish and chips at the Ivy is any better than at Gerald Ramsden's. And if that sounds like a ridiculous thing to say, then recall a previous analogy: would you expect Vietnamese street food at the Ivy to be better than that served in Hanoi?

Of course, as the *Daily Telegraph* makes clear with its reassurance that the fish supper is 'no longer the working man's nourishment', for some people the food of the poor can never be a credible contender for our national dish – it must somehow gain an upmarket cachet if it wants to be taken seriously. This means that restaurants with less self-confidence than the Ivy or the Savoy are always trying to 'reinvent' it or do it 'with a twist', strategies which safely remove fish and chips from its roots and allow middle-class diners to enjoy some British tradition in the safe knowledge that the working-class people who once relied upon it will not be able to afford this version. Batter is replaced by panko breadcrumbs, fillets by goujons, ketchup by wasabi-flavoured tartare sauce. You might get eight enormous, uniform chips stacked in a Jenga block or, worse, your chips served in a cup or a miniature shopping trolley, while your goujons are delicately stacked on top of a bed of lightly crushed minted peas, all on a sheet of ironic fake newspaper which is in turn placed on a chopping board rather than a plate and you'll be charged £20 instead of £6.

It's not necessarily the experimentation I object to, it's the assumption that there was something wrong with the basic dish in the first place. 'Instead of questionable fried fish and soggy chips, expect Camden Hells-battered fish, Cornish shrimp burgers and smoked-haddock kedgeree, served with truffled chips or wilted spring greens, without a mushy pea in sight,' gushes one review of a (now closed) posh chippie in *Harper's Bazaar*, as if no one in a traditional chip shop ever thought of using beer in their batter and there's something wrong with mushy peas. Battered, a 'gourmet' fish shop at the Armoury Wharf in Leeds, made the newspapers in 2008 when it started charging for scraps – the leftover batter bits that are piled up in the corner of a north of England chippy hot box and traditionally offered as a free garnish to anyone who wants them. Battered charged £2 for them, which they justified by offering them 'zested and juiced with lemon, sprinkled with chilli flakes and mixed with rock pepper or nutmeg'. I feel ashamed that this establishment was in Yorkshire. But it, too, has now disappeared. Meanwhile, Google Earth shows me that Ramsden's is now called the Aqua Fish Bar and New Road Chippy is Whites Fisheries. While these names may be fancier, the photos suggest little else has changed.

Famously in gastronomic circles, Britain is pretty much the only maritime nation that doesn't have its own peasant seafood soup. If you've dined on bisque, bouillabaisse or buridda in a harbourside café in the Mediterranean, it can be dispiriting to approach a 'seafood restaurant' in Brighton or a coastal pub that advertises 'locally caught fish our speciality' only to discover it's a chippie with pretensions. Britain has 11,000 miles of coastline. Spain and France each have less than 5,000. So how do they have a more interesting and varied array of seafood and fish cooking than we do?

The answer is simple: *because we have fish and chips.* If you can make a really good battered fish, crisp and glistening, and chips that offer a little crunch of resistance before bursting with soft seduction, why the hell would you waste your time making anything else?

5.

'Where are you going for your fish and chips?'

It sounds like an innocent enough question. It's one I'm often asked, about each meal in this book.

Chip Alley was good. I had to do it and I'm glad I did. But in retrospect, it wasn't the typical experience of the meal, and that's what I'm looking for. Where am I going for my fish and chips? Where do the unlucky people who didn't grow up near Gerald Ramsden's think of when they think of fish and chips? They think of swooping gulls, the sound of the sea and the gentle stabbing of wooden forks in paper as they stroll along a beach or promenade.

'Well, it's got to be the seaside, hasn't it?' I reply to Professor Vanessa's question.

Vanessa Toulmin is Director of City and Cultural Engagement at the University of Sheffield and Research Director of the National Fairground Archive and Chair in Early Film and Popular Entertainment. She's an expert on traditional British working-class entertainment and knows more about fairgrounds and circuses than any other living person. I'm about to find out that her query is something more than polite interest.

'Mm-hmm, and which bit of the seaside exactly?'

I've been thinking a lot about A. A. Gill's final

restaurant review, the one in which he revealed he was about to die of cancer, chose fish and chips as his final (professional) meal and flew up to Whitby in Jimmy Carr's helicopter for fish that was 'generous, fresh off the boat, battered with loving authority', and 'thick, crunchy and floury' beef-dripping twice-fried chips.

'Yeah, Whitby, I think.' I smile, waiting for the expert's affirmation of my choice.

'No you're bloody well not.'

Sorry?

'You are not going to Whitby for your fish and chips. You can forget that right now. Fish and chips belongs to the north-west, and if you don't believe me I'll introduce you to my friend John Walton and he'll tell you. You're going to Blackpool. Certainly to Lancashire. Bloody *Whitby*,' she spits.

I decide to go to Blackpool for my fish and chips.

We used to go to Blackpool about once a year when I was a kid, rarely for a full week but often for a daytrip. Barnsley, nestling on the east side of the Pennines, is almost as far away from the sea as it's possible to get in Britain – try to stick a pin in the very centre of Great Britain and you'll be pretty close. It would take about an hour and three quarters for us to drive to the east coast, maybe half an hour longer to the west coast. The only reason we ever headed west was to go to Blackpool.

There are many coastal towns with football teams, but it's Blackpool FC that gets the nickname 'The Seasiders'. Because Blackpool *is* the seaside, as in, 'Oh, I do like to be beside the seaside.' It's the place you think of in that song.

During the 'wakes weeks', when entire northern towns would shut down for annual cleaning and maintenance of the mills and factories, whole populations would decamp to the resort en masse. These had to be scheduled, one a week, so they didn't clash. Every week from June to September, a different town would take over the guest houses, trams, pubs, arcades, piers, donkey-rides, promenade, fish-and-chips shops and beach. Between the wars, Blackpool had 8 million visitors a year – three times more than its nearest rival – and visitors peaked at 17 million a year in the 1950s.

By the time I was visiting in the 1980s, Blackpool's decline had set in. Mills and mines were closing across the north and the contrast of affordable package holidays had made everyone realize how cold, wet and windy Blackpool was most of the time. But this was a resort built on fronting it out, having an eye on the main chance and grabbing it with both hands. As a kid, I was hopelessly in love with the place and, if the cracks were beginning to show, if the paint was peeling and the carpets in the amusement arcades were looking threadbare, I made sure not to notice. My classmates started going on holiday to Spain and coming back with deep tans. My family never got on a single plane together. I wasn't really that bothered, so long as we could still go to Blackpool.

In 2009, I spent about five days in Blackpool researching a book on summer holidays that never got written. It was the first time I'd been back in twenty-five years and I found a resort in the middle of a civil war.

On one side were the stag and hen parties. The kiss-me-quick hats of my childhood had been replaced by shocking-pink cowboy hats and feather boas. Shops on the seafront sold giant inflatable dildos and sticks of rock with phrases like 'lager lout' and 'fat slag' written through them. Neon-covered pubs had two or three heavy-set bouncers on the door at midday and signs reading, 'It is a CONDITION OF ENTRY that you consent to being searched for ALCOHOL, DRUGS and WEAPONS (likely to cause harm)' – inviting debate as to the distinction between these and weapons unlikely to cause harm. By seven o'clock each night there was a strong police presence on the streets.

Facing off against the stags and hens were the guest houses, shops and cafés that advertised themselves with the words 'Families and couples welcome' – typically British code for saying stags and hens were not. About half the pubs advertised themselves with signs reading 'FAMILY PUB' in a way that somehow filled those two happy words with seething hostility. Inside the vast complex of the pirate-themed Coral Island amusement arcade Liz and I found the Buccaneer Family Pub and went in for a drink. As we were leaving, two young men were trying to come in. A bouncer stopped them and pointed to the sign on the door reading, 'Family Pub'.

'We've got kids wi' us,' said one of the blokes.

'You'd better go and gerrem, then,' replied the bouncer.

Defeated, off they went. This remains the only time where I've seen the presence of children stipulated as a criterion for entry into a pub rather than a reason to not be allowed in.

Blackpool was split in two, with every single commercial establishment declaring its allegiance to one side or the other. The chippies, open to all, were the only neutral ground along the whole seafront.

I interviewed Mike Chadwick, a marketing executive for Visit Blackpool. The resort's hopes of revival had been pinned on winning the contract for a new super-casino, which for some bizarre reason had been suggested as something that would bring economic prosperity, happiness and a reduction in crime rather than the opposite. To many outside observers Blackpool seemed like a natural fit; this, the next step in its shady evolution. But in the end Blackpool didn't get the contract and had to think again.

Mike told me all about the new initiatives they had planned instead to broaden Blackpool's appeal to a wider spectrum of people. Blackpool always had to be the biggest and best. Now it would spread to compete with other cities in areas such as conferences, theatre and short breaks. Promenades were designed for promenading, so the new promenade would be a people's playground. He had all the chutzpah and charisma of an end-of-the-pier comic and Petulengro gypsy fortune teller combined. While I was with him, I almost believed him.

Eight years later, I'm back. A gang of us have been brought here by our friend Nick, who also now lives in Stoke Newington, after being born and brought up in Blackpool, and whose mum – who, as far as any of us know, has the name 'Nick's Mum' written in her passport – still lives here. We've come to spend a day playing on the amusements, going up the tower, walking along the piers and, when it gets dark, seeing the illuminations.

Without thinking about it too deeply, I had assumed

that we would be doing all of this with a slightly detached and condescending air of North London-flavoured irony, enjoying Blackpool because it was so bad it was good. After my last visit I couldn't imagine how we might enjoy it any other way.

And then I get mugged: the entire town of Blackpool picks my snobbish pockets and robs me of my cynicism. The beachfront hotel we stay in, the Funny Girls dinner and cabaret show we attend, the Blackpool Tower Experience, the hours we spend in the great ballroom and walking across the new comedy carpet outside aren't so bad they're good. They're just good, by any standards, and by comparison with anywhere else. The promenade *has* been reimagined as a place to promenade, with modern-art installations to keep you walking to the next part, and the next. Coral Island, which I described in my 2009 notes as 'monstrously tattered, mired in the requisite gloom', is bright and clean and exciting. The 'family pub' signs are faded, the 'stags and hens' signs and midday bouncers have vanished altogether.

Mike Chadwick and his mates only went and bloody did it: they reinvented Blackpool.

After spending a morning in the tower – which really is, hand on heart, comparable with any family-entertainment experience this side of Disneyland – we stroll along the prom in a daze. You can't stand in a single spot along the Golden Mile – Blackpool's challenge to the Vegas Strip – without being able to see at least three or four fish-and-chip shops. Further inland, there are alternatives to fish and chips, but to explore those would be to miss the point of coming here on holiday. Fish and chips are Blackpool's fuel. A Mass Observation Survey on 'Holidays' in 1941 went to Blackpool and reported that 'fish and chips are easily the most popular meal partaken outside the boarding house. Out of nearly 300 meals observed in restaurants all over Blackpool a third included chips while more than a quarter included fish. Today, those figures seem modest.

After a while, you can start to acclimatize to the difference between various types and levels of chippy. At the bottom of the scale you have those who advertise themselves on price. Most of these hang around the ends of Blackpool's three piers like hustlers, their signs reading, 'Fish and chips £2.99!' the fonts, sizes and colours adding a silent, 'Aw, COME ON! I'm cutting my own throat here! What more do you want me to do? OK, OK, tell you what, I'll throw in a free diet Coke, too, but come on, you're breaking my heart, man. WHADDYA MEAN "I'M GOING OVER THERE?" THEY'RE A POUND MORE EXPENSIVE!'

Well, yes, they are, but they're the next tier up, the mainstream tier. Here, the signage is still very visible but it has a little more class. You can spot this because 'fish and chips' is always preceded by the word 'traditional'. Some enhance this with blown-up black-and-white photographs of Blackpool in its pomp; others balance it with witty names like 'The Northern Sole'. Most still advertise deals, because Blackpool is all about the deal, but they do so with fewer block capitals and starbursts.

Then there's the premium tier, the places that refer to themselves as restaurants and would likely wince if you called them 'chippies' to their face. They're cleaner, sleeker and more modern, focused on the dining experience. If you really must order takeaway, they have smartly branded cardboard boxes for that rather than mere paper.

We find ourselves standing idly outside a place called Blackpool's Fish Factory while we wait for Liz to complete the purchase of some scary 3-D lenticular pictures of cats, and some of the Little Baby Jesus, from a promenade souvenir stall. We have no plan, but it's nearly lunchtime and we're standing outside a fish-and-chip shop – obviously. The sky, which has been doing some interesting things since we got here, is grey with the shades of every one of Instagram's filters imposed on it all at once. It has depth and texture as well as colour. The temperature is somewhere between bracing and parky. If it gets much colder, it might even turn a bit nippy. This is not unfolding in the way I hoped my seaside fish and chips would: it looks like we may be forced to eat inside. From *plates*.

'Blackpool's Fish Factory' seems no better or worse than its scores of competitors, a firm level two, offering 'traditional fish and chips to eat in or take away', but with strong aspirations towards level three. The name is a giveaway: ambitious places such as this often tend to focus on the fish, now often the premium item on a chippy's menu, rather than celebrating the universal bedrock of chips. The words 'fish and chips' are studded with lightbulbs which will doubtless come on if the brooding sky gets much darker.

The glitz is complemented by typically Blackpoolian entrepreneurial flair: the giant hot dog hanging over the serving hatch facing out on to the promenade would look equally at home in a Pop Art gallery exhibition. Deals and specials are advertised on every surface. For £2.99 you can get a portion of chips in a traditional seaside bucket, and you can 'keep your souvenir bucket!'

Inside, the main restaurant is a utilitarian space with a Formica floor and a mix of blue tiles and fake bare brickwork on the walls. Red, white and blue bunting spells out 'FISH AND CHIPS' above our heads, reminding us why we're here – as if we could forget. The menu is two sides of laminated, stylishly designed A4, and I could spend an entire week exploring it. All the classics are here, with a few tweaks of imagination, such as a 'seafood basket' of butterfly prawns, squid and cockles with chips. The fish and chips are half the price of Harry Ramsden's. There are also burgers, hot dogs, baked potatoes, even a full English breakfast. But unlike Harry Ramsden's, all feel like their part of a chippyish whole rather than the restaurant trying to extend into something it's not.

I decide to order regular fish and chips with curry sauce, a bread bap on the side to make a chip buttie. As an adult, I have both the budget and the appetite for all this. I feel like my childhood dreams have come true. When I was a kid, this would have been 'too dear' for me to have in its entirety. When we loved something as kids, we used to say, 'I'm going to have this all the time, when I grow up.' We couldn't even imagine what it might be like to get fat. Now I know only too well. But weight worries can wait: I owe this meal to my childhood self.

At the counter there's a list of instructions on how to order correctly, which would be intimidating were it not for the line at the bottom reassuring us that 'It's easy peasy!' Around the shop the firm but gentle hand of maternal authority makes its presence felt in a variety of polite notices, such as, 'If you take the lid off our salt pots, please consider the next customer to use them and screw them back on tightly! Thank you for your cooperation.'

Chief among these is the code of conduct for using the Ikea-style drinks refill station:

- Please only use Blackpool Fish Factory cold or hot drink refill cups provided at purchase
- Valid at time of purchase, for one visit only
- One cup per person, per visit
- Once you have left the premises, you forfeit your right to refill
- We reserve the right to charge people for the abuse of this facility

This has me imagining stories of the various incidents that must have led to the formulation and publication of this policy. I resolve to refill my diet cola as many times as I can while staying within the rules. My inner child starts doing backflips.

Our dishes are brought out to the table in minutes. In a big operation like this, there's someone at the fryer continuously – that's their job, and there's no time to stop or do anything else. A big silver range is filled from one side and emptied from the other, golden chips passing through quickly without the chance to sit and go stale. Everything is freshly cooked because even here at the start of November, in the last few days of Blackpool's Illumin-ations, the shop is so busy that it can't be anything else.

My fish crumbles under the knife into flecks of fish and

jigsaw pieces of batter, just slightly overdone. As I work my way through, the separate, shattered parts are all running together with the gravy and curry sauce (yes, I have both – do you have a problem with that? And ketchup). Some people believe fries should be crispy. I prefer them when they're soft and sweaty, like a humid day in India. I'm searching my plate for the best ones, those thick enough to have a generous potato content inside. Some have eyes, and there are a few crispy, emaciated ones but, overall, they're pretty good. The curry sauce is fluorescent yellow with unidentifiable lumps, just as it should be. But it doesn't shine as brightly as the 'butter' on my side order of bread. Despite the name, and despite the promise on the menu, a perfect chip buttie should of course be made with cheap, oily margarine, and this stuff is glowing like the setting sun. The slick melt of the marge makes the chips sing. Cheap, sugary ketchup – not posh Heinz – caps everything off perfectly.

In his essay 'British Cookery' Orwell writes that our 'simple, rather heavy, perhaps slightly barbarous diet, [draws] much of its virtue from the excellence of the local materials, and with its main emphasis on sugar and animal fats. It is the diet of a wet northern country where butter is plentiful and vegetable oils are scarce, where hot drinks are acceptable at most hours of the day . . .' I feel as though he is describing this very meal, right here in this restaurant. Clearly, I won't need to eat again today. But there really is wholesome virtue in fish and chips that sets it apart from modern 'junk food'.

I feel as if time has concertinaed and versions of myself from childhood to dotage are all sitting here together enjoying this meal. The inner child is partying with abandon but at the same time feeling protected and nourished.

Talk to anyone about food, especially about the food that means something to them, and they invariably talk about childhood experiences. Food academic Warren Belasco argues that we all have our own Proustian madeleines and runs classes in which he urges students to write about theirs. The results are always interesting, mostly positive, sometimes negative and often very moving. The foods that do this are almost always meals that were first experienced in early childhood, and this prompts Belasco to modify the common phrasing of Brillat-Savarin's most famous aphorism: more than telling us we are what we eat, we are in fact what we *ate*.

This could be another powerful explanation as to why all those survey lists of favourite foods seem a generation behind what we actually eat today. My cheese-and-pickle sandwich in the Sandwich Shop in Sandwich almost got there, before fading away. But with fish and chips the memories flood out.

In the closing stages of my meal my plate is a vivid palette of browns, golds and reds. Blobs of tomato ketchup, gravy, curry sauce and flecks of fish all gleam under the fluorescent strip-lights. It really is quite beautiful. I could clear my plate completely, but I'm pleasantly full, without feeling stuffed, and I want to keep it that way.

It's perfect, and it fills me with great pride, that fish and chips is Britain's national dish. It's a working-class meal that has won hearts across all social strata. It's not trying to be anything it isn't. In peak season on the prom people aren't here for a premium dining experience. They're here for salt, vinegar and grease on their fingers as they head over to the beach. Here at the seaside, in the bright sunlight (if you're fortunate) and ozone-rich air, it's comfort food for when you don't need comforting, a celebration when there's no special occasion, a democratic, unpretentious indulgence that helped shape us and save us.

4.

Spag Bol

'It was a Brexit Bolognese. We don't need the Italians to tell us how to cook any more. We've taken back control of pasta dishes. #MaryBerry.'

– Lewis Goodall, Sky News Political Correspondent, on Twitter, 7 March 2017

1.

It feels a bit cheeky to just ask someone to make me spag bol, out of the blue, but it has to be done. This is a meal that's more widely available in British restaurants than many of the more traditional meals in this book but, unlike some others, that's not where it belongs in our collective heart. For most of us this is a meal about family. It's a meal each British cook makes their own, to share with the people they care about. This one has to be eaten at someone's house, during the week, ideally during winter, prepared after they've got home from work. It shouldn't be with someone terribly foodie but someone who does take it seriously rather than getting everything out of a packet.

I've known the Gittner family since I was nine years old. Dad George, the local Methodist minister who got a hint of what made Gerald Ramsden's batter so great, was married to Margaret, who started the Cub Scout pack in Mapplewell, where I met people who remain some of my closest friends today. Brothers Al, Chris and Steve are three of them, with Chris, a year younger than me, being in any meaningful sense my second brother. He travelled across Europe with me for my second book, unwittingly inspired my third and gave that book its title, and drove me around the north of England for my sixth. He has the biggest heart of anyone I know, is a passionate cook and relentlessly competitive with his brothers, especially big brother Al. After leaving Barnsley for university and then living elsewhere for a while, the pair now live a few miles apart from each other in more of those little villages surrounding t'Tarn.

'I am sweating my mirepoix,' writes Chris on Facebook a few days before I'm due to go and see him. This is the latest in a line of culinary sort-of-double-entendres that make up a significant proportion of Chris's Facebook posts, which may or may not have started with 'I am pulling my pork' or something similar, before becoming ever more esoteric.

'If you're doing what I think you're doing, you're actually sweating your sofrito,' replies Al.

Later, when I see Chris, I tell him that this is the most Gittnerish exchange I have ever witnessed.

'He was bloody right as well,' says Chris. 'That's the worst bit. I hate it when that happens!'

The sofrito of finely chopped carrots, onion and celery is pretty much the only constant in every single recipe for spag bol that's worth the name. If we were talking French food, we would indeed refer to it as a mirepoix, but sofrito, the very foundation of the dish, is authentically Italian. Chop finely and sweat gently enough and the pile of veg you start with fades away into the sauce, adding sweetness and depth.

Different cuisines are noted for having different 'flavour principles' – the distinctive, characteristic combinations that define a range of typical dishes. For example, put soy sauce, garlic, ginger and sesame oil together and you're probably cooking Chinese, whereas chilli, cumin, garlic and tomato might be Mexican or Indian. In *Acid, Salt, Fat, Heat*, chef Samin Nosrat gives a wonderful graphic that shows the subtle differences between the 'flavour bases' – the mixture of herbs, roots and aromatics – that underpin various cuisines: a French mirepoix and an Italian sofrito are usually identical, but substitute bell pepper for carrot and chuck in a bit more onion and you have a Cajun 'Holy Trinity'. Remove the celery from this and add garlic and tomato and it becomes a sofrito again, but now it's the Spanish version. Leave out the pepper from this one and it's a Filipino ginisà. The Germans have their Suppengrün ('soup greens') and the Poles włoszczyzna (literally, 'Italian stuff'), but there's not really an English equivalent that has the same cultural importance as the basis for a large chunk of our dishes. That's why Chris's Facebook jokes seem funny to us – or to me and a few of his other friends at least – because the concepts aren't familiar to us. It's also one reason why there really isn't much about vegetables in this book. Historically, the British have always considered them something of a nuisance.

Chris and I arrive at Al's house just after 4.30 p.m., just

in time to catch Al chopping the ingredients for his sofrito. Al is cooking what he refers to as his ragù for me, Chris, and Al's wife, Barbara. It would be unthinkable to show favour towards Al over Chris, but I only have one night here, so Chris made his own ragù a few nights ago. He's brought some round in a plastic tub so we can compare it to Al's. I've already told them I'm not going to choose a favourite.

When I emailed Al to ask if he could cook me my spag bol for this book he wrote back that he has three different versions in his repertoire:

1. Whatever mince I can get, usually not the best steak mince as it doesn't have enough fat and therefore can be a bit bland. With tinned tomatoes and tomato purée.

2. As above but if I can organize it I make it with minced skirt. Skirt is an excellent cut for ragù as it has excellent flavour. I only get this 2 or 3 times a year if I can get into Barnsley Market and my favourite butcher has it. Again, this contains lots of tomatoes.

3. Traditional ragù. This is much more specialized and I believe is more authentic to ragù from Bologna. This again uses the best mince I can get hold of, with chicken livers and only minimal tomatoes, it is cooked in milk but is cooked with minimal liquid, it is quite a dry sauce (let down with pasta cooking water on serving) and you add more milk as it's cooking, just before serving it has quite a lot of Parmesan stirred through the sauce

with further Parmesan stirred through the pasta on serving.

I ask him to do whichever feels most typical.

Al is Head of Science at a nearby school. His genuine passion for the subject means he never really stops explaining the science behind the everyday. With its requirement for sautéing and braising as well as sweating, that's one reason he loves this dish so much. He's gone for the minced-skirt option, which is darker and smells richer than the packet mince you usually get from the supermarket.

'The first thing I do is brown the meat,' he says. 'I always brown the meat, even in recipes that don't call for it. I do it in small batches with just a bit of oil. You're looking for the Maillard reaction to get that extra layer of flavour. If you put too much in the pan, you end up boiling it at a hundred degrees, whereas it needs to be 120 to 160 for the Maillard reaction. If you boil it, you end up tightening the collagen in the meat so it can go chewy and lumpy.'

With all the meat gently browned, next he sweats his sofrito of onion, celery, carrot and bacon, 'to make the onions transparent, not to colour them'.

'I start by rendering some streaky bacon,' says Chris, 'and use the fat off it to brown the meat. Then I do the same sofrito as Al.'

With the sofrito glistening and moist, the meat goes back in along with tomatoes, mixed herbs ('or fresh from garden in summer'), some roasted garlic that's been preserved in oil and a little water. 'I'll also add any stock or gravy left-overs,' says Al. 'This has got the gravy from Sunday's roast beef.'

'Sometimes I'll add a de-cased, herby sausage as well,' says Chris. I'll put the garlic in when it's liquid. I use passata rather than tinned tomatoes. A bit of tomato concentrate, some mixed herbs, er . . . some Henderson's Relish, and my secret ingredient – a spoonful of Bovril.'

Where do these recipes come from?

'It has aspects of a classical Bolognese, but it's developed gradually over the years,' says Al.

'Mine started when I was cooking at college,' says Chris. 'I got some advice on the basics from a mate's mum. Then I picked up tips off the telly, some bits from *The Godfather*, some from *Goodfellas* . . . it's never been a written recipe.'

'We've both always enjoyed cooking,' says Al. 'I learned the basics from Delia, from this old copy here which I still have –'

'If everyone used Delia, we would be the greatest cooking nation in the world!' interrupts Chris.

'I usually make this on a Tuesday. Barbara has a gym class so we eat late. That way, it gets the cooking time it needs.'

Both brothers are adamant that, whatever you put in it, the key to a good ragù or Bolognese is a long, slow cooking time. Few Italians would disagree. And if you think of Bovril and the weekend's gravy as stock, neither is using anything here that at least some of the chefs I've consulted would not countenance. Is authenticity important?

Al pauses and thinks. 'I learned to cook because I like to eat. I just want to eat well. When we went to school, no one had spaghetti, but I've now been eating it for forty years. Authenticity is partly important but not as much as it being something that tastes good. And anyway, talk to Italians and it varies across the country. The more important thing for me, with all these health scares going around, is that it's made from scratch.'

Now the ingredients in the pan have to bubble away for a couple of hours. We sit around the kitchen table, talking and drinking cups of tea. There'll be wine later, with the meal, but this is, literally for Al, a school night. There's a delicious anticipation over the cooking time but, before the eating, there's deep satisfaction in preparing this meal too.

'I like chopping things,' says Chris. 'Put the radio on in the kitchen and just zone out while I'm doing it.'

'I'm lucky in that I've got a fifteen-minute commute from work,' says Al. 'I get in, and I just love the therapy of doing it after work. Before the kids grew up, we'd all be in the kitchen together doing it.'

We start catching up on each other's news, picking up where we left off when we last saw each other. Two hours pass quickly and, now, over its generous cooking time, the liquid that was in the pan has been either absorbed or evaporated and the sauce has come together. It's one thing now rather than a collection of separate ingredients. With a nod to our reflections on childhood, Al serves it in the traditional English manner, atop a pile of spaghetti, and we dollop some of Chris's sauce on the side for comparison.

It goes without saying that they are equally delicious, and I would obviously say that even if it were not true. Both are warming and comforting, convivial and gener-ous. Al's is slightly more refined and subtle while Chris's is bigger and heartier, slightly spicier.

All too soon my plate is empty, the last bit being the

final, generous dollop of sauce. Apart from the flavour, the physical experience of eating spag bol – just like the experience of cooking it – is pleasurable too. When I get to the end I'm often ready to start all over again with another plateful.

'I know the feeling,' says Al. 'That's why I usually carton up the leftovers and get them in the freezer before we sit down to eat.'

He's always been this organized. Even when he was my patrol leader in Scouts.

The windows have steamed up from the cooking of the spaghetti. It's the middle of winter and the sky beyond the panes looks like liquid ink. On nights like this, there's no better meal. It's reassuring and wholesome, and I imagine we're having pretty much an identical experience to millions of families across the country. I almost feel sorry for the Italians with their balmier Mediterranean climate. Bolognese simply can't taste this good when the weather's warm and sunny.

We talk of learning to cook at the Scout camps we all attended, of packed lunches and fish and chips. When you've had friends from such a young age and stayed close for this long, your impressions are fixed in childhood. We may all be hovering either side of fifty now, but I can't help thinking of us as three teenagers playing at being grown up. It's bizarre that Al owns this house and has grown-up children, that Chris has his own house a few miles away and drove us here in a car and that I'm writing a real book for an actual publisher. Along the way to this point all of us have, in different ways, used spag bol as one of the markers of our maturity and self-sufficiency: first, learning how to cook for ourselves, and then educating ourselves in how to improve, tailor and adapt the dish to our individual tastes. We've come a long way from the summer camp where we first burned baked beans on to the bottom of a saucepan and I was making a version of this dish at home that would have been barely recognizable as the one we've just enjoyed.

2.

Spag bol was the first meal I ever learned to cook. I must have been around twelve when I announced that I wanted to make 'spaghetti bollocknaise', before being gently corrected by my mum.

When I say 'cooked' – and when I say 'learned', for that matter – I beg to be allowed a little artistic licence in my use of those terms. My first spag bol entailed me buying a jar of 'Ragu' tomato sauce, finding a tin of Prince's cooked minced beef in gravy in the pantry that must have been left over from a Christmas hamper, getting out a tin of sliced mushrooms in water just to be exotic and controversial and mixing them all together in a saucepan until they were boiling. Like I'd seen on the telly, I served it as a sloppy island atop a mound of dried spaghetti, which I had boiled until I was sure it was dead.

Flushed by success, I quickly expanded my home-cooking repertoire to include frozen mini-steaks. These were essentially cheap burger meat shaped to resemble the vaguely triangular steaks you saw in cartoons. You were meant to fry them, but I grilled them instead, already a fan of the char. I developed a morbid fascination with how the meat would swell into blisters which, when forked, shot boiling fat into the blue grill flame and made it flare yellow. I'd serve my mini-steak with a tin of boiled potatoes and a tin of garden peas, a resolutely English dish that matched my exotic bollocknaise in its sophistication. Steaks – mini or otherwise – were rarely seen anywhere near our house. The one time my dad brought real, juicy, fresh steak home – midweek, on a night when neither parent had been to the shops – my brother and I were given sausages instead because the steak was 'too good' for us.

The third dish to enter my repertoire was a frozen bag of Birds Eye Chinese stir-fry that cooked as it defrosted in the microwave. It was the first time water chestnuts, bean sprouts or bamboo shoots had ever been seen by anyone in my family, the rest of whom steered well clear of it. It wasn't pleasant, but it was different. And to me, in 1981, that was almost as good.

But the spag bol was the meal I actually *made* rather than assembled or reheated and, for that reason at least, it was my favourite. I can see now that, as time went on, it became more important than that. There were various reasons it outlasted the mini-steaks and frozen stir-fry, beyond the fact that it was the least disgusting of the three.

Belgian food historian Peter Scholliers opens *Food, Drink and Identity* – an anthology of essays he edited – by recalling how, when he was fifteen years old, he announced to his parents that he was vegetarian. He remembers it as being mainly to do with establishing a position on his own terms within the family and the beginning of creating an identity outside the family in the broader world, in relation to groups of people with whom he wanted to bond with. He didn't have the moral, political or nutritional arguments to back up his position when he made his announcement – these came later, from the people he was keen to be like. But his paternal grandfather had been a butcher, and his father opposed his decision more fiercely than his mother, bringing the two into a conflict which Scholliers later interpreted as being more about masculinity than diet. It's no coincidence that deciding to become vegetarian or vegan happens more often in adolescence than at any other time in our lives. The moral, economic, diet or political issues may be genuine, but it's mainly about taking control of your identity as well as your body, one of the first ways in which we define ourselves as separate and distinct from our parents or siblings, a dramatic later attempt to win the war with your parents that begins in infancy over what and how much you eat.

Of course, I had no idea that I was doing something very similar when I began adding fresh garlic to my spag bol, but I absolutely was. My dad hated garlic because 'the Hungarian pilots stationed over here during the war used to stink of it'. How he knew this, given that he was only seven by the time the war ended and grew up in Barnsley, where there were no airfields nearby because there's no flat land to build one on, what with us being on the edge of the Pennines, I have no idea. This was my first brush with albeit mild racism, and I was as confused by it then as I remain now, because up until that point Dad had brought me up to want to be a Spitfire pilot, and I knew I was going to be one, and now here he was saying that some of them smelled.

When my mum was mad at him, which was most of the time, she pretended to like garlic too.

I made my interpretation of spag bol once a week, every week, from when I was twelve until I left home to go to university. It was my first step towards independence in more ways than one. And in a very specific sense – within the culture of my family – it was a giant leap towards being a man of the house.

When my parents did the weekly shop they bought the same items every Friday and each item had its specific place in the weekly routine. The frozen joint of beef was, obviously, for Sunday. The iceberg lettuce, tomatoes, cucumber and tinned ham were for Saturday teatime salad. These were the only two meals we ever ate together as a family. The pack of Weetabix was for my and my brother's breakfast. The tin of baked beans with little sausages in was for Dad's tea on Tuesdays. The pork chops were for Mum and Dad on Thursdays. The six-pack of crisps, four-pack of Smarties and five-pack of Milky Ways were for me and my brother to squabble over and finish before the weekend was out so Mum and Dad could shout at us for being greedy and threaten not to buy them again next week, while we protested that we were perfectly happy to scoff the lot at the weekend and not have any more sweets until the following Friday.

Everything had its place. So, as I grew more curious about food, if I said on Monday that I quite fancied baked beans and sausages, my mum would shout, 'No! Them's yer dad's for tomorrow!' The idea of buying a second tin, just in case, or even the idea of replacing the one we had with a trip to the corner shop before Tuesday teatime, was inconceivable. A change to the weekly shop was a rare and special event, usually in response to a TV ad for some new item that caught the attention of the majority of the family.

So I imagine it must have been a TV ad for Ragu that sparked the beginning of my culinary independence. And after some initial conflict, my Ragu, tin of minced beef and onions and tin of sliced mushrooms in water became part of the weekly shop and gained the same status in the pantry as the rest of its precious items. When my brother, who had to have anything I had, eventually asked if he could have some of that Ragu in the pantry, my mum shouted, 'No! That's our Pete's for Tuesday!'

I had become a man.

I still cook spag bol fairly regularly, but my expanded culinary repertoire means I no longer make it every Tuesday. And you may be surprised to hear that my recipe has changed somewhat. But reminiscing now, thinking about madeleines, I'm struck by the urge to go back and re-create the first meal I ever cooked, before I go in search of its typical modern equivalent.

It goes wrong almost immediately.

3.

The first thing I do is open a tin of Prince's 'minced beef with onions in a rich gravy'. It looks and smells exactly like dog food. That can't be right. We always had dogs when I was a kid, and we always had dog food in the kitchen. It smelled disgusting, just like this does now. If this same brand of tinned minced beef had smelled of dog food back in the day, I would never have cooked with it. I check the list of ingredients on the side of the can. My tin of minced beef with onions in gravy contains just 36 per cent minced beef and 12 per cent onions – the promised ingredients together accounting for less than half of what is supposedly in the tin. The biggest ingredient of all is water. It also contains, in size order: modified maize starch, wheat flour that has been fortified with calcium carbonate, iron, niacin and thiamin,* concentrated tomato paste, beef stock (made from beef extract, more water, glucose, salt, yeast extract, sugar and 'flavouring'), salt, roasted barley malt extract and a dash of ground white pepper. I try not to let my imagination get on to what part of the cow the 36 per cent minced beef comes from.

The Ragu brand in Britain has long since been seen off by its rival Dolmio, so I'm forced to make the substitution. When I unscrew the lid it smells pretty good, all rich and tomatoey and herby, and there's nothing listed on the ingredients here that I couldn't or wouldn't put in my own scratch-made sauce: tomatoes, tomato paste, lemon juice, cornflour, onion, sugar, salt, basil, garlic, herbs, parsley and spices. Apparently, it's designed for lasagne rather than Bolognese, but it'll do.

I mix the contents of the tin and the jar together – along

* Niacin and thiamin are essential B vitamins that are present in many different foods. However, they are very prone to being destroyed by modern food-processing techniques. The more your food goes through between its natural state and the state it reaches you in, the more likely its vitamins will have been destroyed. So manufacturers who heavily process their food add them back in as supplements.

with the tinned, sliced mushrooms that make this an authentic spaghetti Barnsleyaise – and bring it to a simmer.

Once it's stirred through, it is at least kind of the right colour for a Bolognese sauce. You have to give it that. But it's slimy and soupy and I realize I need to reduce and thicken it if I'm going to eat it from a plate rather than a bowl. The surface of the pan begins to fart and plop like boiling mud. The smell is making me feel slightly nauseous. I take a spoonful to taste. It's beefy and incredibly, overwhelmingly sweet, with a touch of sourness that clashes rather than balances. And that's it. I resist the urge to add seasoning, herbs, red wine – anything that I'd instinctively use to try to improve its flavour.

Even with constant stirring, I can feel the gloop burning on to the bottom of the pan, I guess because it's mainly flour and water. And stirring is becoming increasingly dangerous: it's spitting at me aggressively now, a punk-rock sauce. I swear it never did this when I was a teenager. But then, I never had to try to reduce it when I was a teenager either. The only possible explanation is that it's significantly waterier and flourier now than it was then. I decide to turn the heat off and serve it, partly in the name of authenticity, and partly for my own safety.

After draining the pasta my instinct is to mix the sauce through it because, if nothing else, it might help the still-soupy consistency. But then I remember the authentic eighties serving suggestion and arrange the spaghetti in a shallow doughnut shape on the plate with the sauce poured into the indentation in the middle. This does prove initially useful at containing the sauce, which pours and dribbles with a greasy sheen.

It tastes of not very much at all. Somehow, in contact with the pasta, the sweetness and beefiness I detected earlier have disappeared. Maybe I boiled the flavour away. That doesn't happen with real food, but I'm in unfamiliar territory here. My palate is craving something – anything – to engage it. Even the mushrooms are tasteless. And now, off the heat, the sauce is congealing, turning even starchier and gloopier.

I give in and cover the whole mess with freshly ground black pepper and freshly grated Parmesan. This helps me get about half of it down, but then I start to feel like I'm about to throw up. I pour the rest of the contents of my plate, and what's left in the pan, into the bin, double-bagging it in the vain hope that it won't leak, settle, develop sentience and come for me in the night.

This is the worst thing I've tasted in years, and I used to make it every week and love it. There are two possible reasons for our reunion going so catastrophically wrong: either it's changed, or I have.

My palate is, without doubt, different now from how it was when I was twelve years old. Apart from the evolving tastes that most people experience as they mature, my work as a judge in food and drink competitions means I've studied flavour and trained my palate: or rather, trained my brain to decode and appreciate what my palate is telling it better. I was lucky enough to discuss this issue with Giorgio Locatelli while we were waiting to do our respective bits on *The Food Programme*. He was remarkably polite when I told him what my early version of spag bol consisted of. If he had any desire to inflict grievous bodily harm on me for what I'd done to the dish, he hid it very well. Diplomatically, he put my revulsion down to my more developed palate – it's a common experience, he said, for any chef who attempts to re-create the simple beauty of the childhood dishes that inspired them.

But there's no way my teenage dish was the same awful quality as the thing I just made. It wasn't just the flavour that was different; the texture was bizarre, to the point of being uncookable and inedible. Something had definitely changed.

There's an apocryphal story in the marketing world about a new chief executive starting work at a famous food company: the first version I heard was that he was taking over at Campbell's soups, but I've heard it told about different products since, so I'm sure it's parable rather than fact. Each year, the accountants would try to trim the cost of a product. The challenge was to alter the recipe without creating any discernible change to the flavour. One day, the research-and-development department presented two bowls of soup to the new CEO, one made to the existing recipe, the other to a new recipe that would save the company a few million in costs annually. They challenged the CEO to taste the difference: the deal was that, if he could, the new recipe was a failure and they had to try again. However, he could taste no difference between the two bowls and the R&D guys and the accountants jumped for joy. But then the new CEO said, 'Now make me a bowl to the recipe we used twenty years ago.' Reluctantly, they did so, and everyone tasted the twenty-year-old recipe against the current recipe and the proposed new one, and cried as they were reintroduced to the taste of their childhood, a taste they had previously believed was still there, even if their palates had become dulled to it.*

I decide to explore further. As a child, when I couldn't make my own spag bol, I'd sometimes be lucky enough to have a tin of Heinz ready-made Spaghetti Bolognese. We often had tinned spaghetti on toast as a quick lunch, either in its standard version of neat, two-inch-long strands, as Hoops or, on special occasions such as birthdays, Alphabetti Spaghetti. Each one came in a silky red-orange sauce, and to this day the soft, dissolving texture of tinned pasta is the reason I can never quite bear to cook my own pasta al dente. Tinned spag bol was more luxurious. It had a darker sauce. It was meaty. So, to continue my experiment, just before I finally give in and leap to the present, I buy a tin of Heinz spag bol to have on toast.

It's not nearly as catastrophic. But it's every bit as disappointing.

As far as I can tell, the current version of Heinz spag bol is spaghetti in whatever it is they sell as oxtail soup, rather than their ordinary spaghetti which comes in the same sauce they use for baked beans. I need to put it in a bowl and eat it with a spoon – not a spoon and fork, twirling the pasta around the tines and catching the sauce with the

* When I searched to see if there was any credible reference for this story, I discovered that in 2016 Campbell's *did* re-create the century-old first soup recipe on which the company was founded, using only locally sourced tomatoes and no artificial additives. Employees described it as the best day they'd ever had working for the company, and the president of Campbell's American division said the experiment was part of 'rethinking who we are and how we want to show up in this world'.

spoon – just in a bowl, with a spoon, like soup. It's mostly liquid and, if I were to try to pile it on to toast, like I used to, it would just run over the sides of the plate. It tastes meaty, and tomatoey, and quite comforting, though that might just be the madeleine working its magic in reverse. I'm not convinced the meat is meat – there are just a few tiny flecks really, a fraction of the size of the grounds you get from minced beef. And these don't *feel* like meat either – they have a strange, crumbly consistency that I think I recognize as something else. I check the can. Sure enough, with the ingredients listed in size order, 'textured soya protein' comes just before beef (4%), just ahead of herb extracts, natural flavouring and spice. I learn that the brown colour of the sauce is attributable to 'plain caramel'. It's comforting due to its consistency more than anything else – after the first mouthful, it doesn't really taste of anything. According to the script on the can, written in a font that suggests this is a dish aimed exclusively at children, even though it isn't, this is one of my five a day 'when eaten as part of a balanced diet' and, to be fair, it does claim to be 'meaty' rather than contain actual meat. They recommend eating half a can, which is not enough for a meal for anyone over five years of age and yet still contains 25 per cent of my recommended daily salt intake. The can boasts proudly that one whole tomato is squeezed into every portion. It's made with fresh pasta, which I find hilarious: all pasta was freshly made at some point – how long has it been in the can, which contains 'absolutely no preservatives' but is good for another nine months after the date I buy it?

Across the board, large firms such as Heinz and Unilever

are eternally looking for areas where they can cut costs so they can be competitive in the supermarket. Food-price inflation data over the last few decades shows that the cost of food has in fact been in decline for long periods. We demand cheap, plentiful food, a huge variety of it to choose from, all year round and, because we buy most of it from supermarkets, we put enormous power in the hands of a few chains. These chains demand cheap prices from producers, often stipulating lower prices with each passing year, and the only way producers can meet those prices is to make their food for less. Incremental cuts make significant savings in return for incrementally imperceptible reductions in quality, and it's an addictive process – you can deliver savings every year! This is why we end up with horse meat in 'beef' burgers, why most commercial cider brands consist of less than 40 per cent apple juice, why a supermarket pizza 'made in Ireland' contains ingredients that have passed through sixty different countries and why a product claiming to be minced beef and onions should more accurately be labelled 'water and cornflour'. It's why Michael Pollan, in *The Omnivore's Dilemma*, was forced to ask the question, 'How did we ever get to a point where we need investigative journalists to tell us where our food comes from . . . ?' My early adventures in spag bol may not have produced the best meal in the world – we're not talking fish and chips here – but as aggregate wealth, farming technology, ethical standards in food production and the nation's palate have all improved, the result you get when you mix a tin of Prince's minced beef and onions with a jar of Dolmio has become dramatically worse.

At the time I started making it, it didn't seem unusual to me that my spag bol was constituted from the contents of tins and jars – pretty much everything we ate back then was. Given that we couldn't afford a dishwasher, it would have been unseemly to cook from scratch, messing up loads of pans and utensils in the middle of the week, when everyone was busy.

When I make a spag bol now, it's turned into quite a big production that takes several hours, just like when Chris and Al do it. For me now, as for them, that's part of its appeal. I make it when I have time to relax – often, when I really *need* to relax, the cooking a form of therapy, the kitchen a cocoon. I appreciate that this puts me in a dramatically different situation from the parent arriving home at the end of a knackering day and needing to get something on the table within forty-five minutes before the kids start screaming, and their spag bol may still come out of a tin, or perhaps in the form of a microwaved ready-meal. Or maybe they still make it from scratch, in their own way. Spag bol is the nation's favourite meal when it comes to cooking for ourselves at home, partly because it's so adaptable and variable and can be tailored to anyone's level of culinary skill.

'Cooking from scratch' is itself a variable term. You might argue that you're cooking your spag bol from scratch if you chop an onion, brown some meat and pour on a jar of Dolmio. I'd see you and raise you, though, because when I prepare mine I sauté my onions and garlic with some carrot and celery, then brown the mince, before adding chopped tinned tomatoes, wine, herbs and seasoning. In turn, someone might dismiss my version because I'm using tinned tomatoes instead of skinned and de-seeded fresh, ready-bought mince instead of grinding my own and shop-bought dried pasta rather than home-made. The more 'from scratch' it is, the more wholesome it's likely to be – I don't know about you, but I always forget to add the modified maize starch, yeast extract, potato starch, chicory extract, carrot extract, barley malt extract, unspecified 'flavouring' and ten grams of sugar per serving that comes in every pack of Iceland Spaghetti Bolognese when I'm making my own. But scratch-made is also likely to be increasingly expensive per portion. In that, it represents a trade-off that most British families deal with on a daily basis.

Beyond its simple economy and time and health considerations, cooking spag bol from scratch also potentially exposes you to a cultural minefield.

4.

As a patriotic citizen of the United Kingdom of Great Britain and Northern Ireland, I feel I might be putting my personal safety at risk by admitting this, but I don't care very much for Mary Berry.

Before she found immense fame as the matriarch of *The Great British Bake Off*, Mary was a jobbing food writer who did what we all do: turn out books and articles and grab appearances on TV and radio wherever you can. She'd been doing it for years and, if you knew your food writers in pre-celebrity-chef days, she had done more than enough to establish herself as a legend in the genre. But I *didn't* know my stuff at that time, and I hadn't heard of her before I met her on the set of a cable-TV food show called *Great Food Live*. In the odd way these things work, at that point it seemed she was coasting gently down the curve towards retirement as a veteran of the scene while I was being thrust up into the limelight for the first time as a promising newcomer. The trajectories of our respective TV careers since then show that anything is possible and nothing should be assumed – or even hoped for.

On the show Mary talked about her life and the changes she'd seen in the decades she'd been writing cookbooks. I was there in my capacity as a semi-regular beer-and-cider correspondent. On this episode – it might have been my third or fourth appearance – on top of the segment I'd been asked to do, at the last minute the producers asked me to pair a beer with a treacly pudding another one of the aspiring-to-celebrity chefs had cooked for the programme. They had a cupboard full of samples they'd been sent by hopeful brewers and I chose a wonderfully strong, treacly barley wine that would pair perfectly with the sticky, sweet pudding. As we were getting ready for the shot Mary Berry and I were positioned next to each other behind the kitchen counter. I had the beer in my hand, ready to pour as I talked about it. And just before they called, 'Action!' Mary leaned in, pointed to the beer and said, 'I hope you're not expecting *me* to drink *that*.'

Shaken, I had just enough time to say, 'Well, I expect you to do your job on this programme and eat and drink what you're given on camera,' and then I was on, cheeks burning, feeling like a scolded child. I didn't have chance to look and see whether she even touched her glass or not.

We haven't spoken since. (Why on earth would we?) But years later, I was on the front row at the BBC Radio 4 Food and Farming Awards ceremony because I'd been a judge and had therefore been asked to present one of the awards. Mary Berry was there and, before the ceremony began she spotted someone she wanted to talk to sitting directly behind me. She had to lean over me to chat, and she dug her fingers deeply and painfully into my shoulder, using me to support her entire weight for around five minutes while she chatted away. She may be slight, but those fingers are sharp. By the time she finished I was wincing with pain, but when she finally, mercifully, let me go, she walked off without a comment, apology or even the slightest acknowledgement that I was a sentient, living being rather than a wooden post.

So I have to confess to feelings of glee when, early in 2017, Mary Berry's crown momentarily slipped in the eyes of the British public and she attracted nationwide condemnation. Viewers took to social media to say they were 'shocked and appalled' by her antics on the BBC2 Programme *Hearty and Wholesome*. 'Turned it off. Shudders,' wrote one former fan who was quoted in national newspapers the following day. 'I can't cope,' chimed in another.

Her crime was the wanton adulteration of a British classic. While daring to tell the nation how to cook spaghetti Bolognese, she suggested adding white wine instead of red, as well as a large dollop of double cream at the end. And the damned BBC let her do it.

The dirty bastards.

Briefly, the Twittersphere resembled the outbreak of civil war. Those still loyal to the Great Leader rallied around her and formed a human shield to protect her from the dissidents. She had done nothing wrong, they said. In fact, her recipe was closer to the 'correct' recipe for ragù alla Bolognese than that cooked by most Britons.

But they'd missed the point.

5.

The ingredients of spaghetti Bolognese vary from store to store, from kitchen to kitchen, from budget to budget, even from one cooking occasion to the next. This means there's often debate about what should and shouldn't go into a Bolognese sauce, with Mary Berry's brief wobble being just one example. In fact, one of the first things every aspiring foodie learns is that the British idea of spaghetti Bolognese is not authentic. It's not a real Italian dish. Many Italians go further, arguing that good old British spag bol is a travesty, an 'abuse' of their national cuisine.

'Authenticity' is an important concept to people who care about food. In a world of fake news, spin and the total dominance of brand marketing, many of us seek something 'genuine' even if we can't quite explain what that is. For some of us it simply means an experience that's been unmediated, one that we can experience and evaluate for ourselves. But for others, authenticity really just means a superior form of marketing. In his 2009 book *The Authenticity Hoax*, Canadian journalist Andrew Potter argues that the notion of 'cool' in society has been badly damaged. Style 'tribes' have largely disappeared and any new counter-cultural trend is spread and assimilated instantly by social media and modern marketing. So instead of trying to be cool by knowing about a hip band we've probably never heard, we try to be authentic, and this quest covers much more than music and fashion. Food is just one aspect of our lives that's become much more prominent as a means of self-expression and identity and, therefore, a source of this modified cool. Because this trend is driven, by definition, by a belief that mainstream culture is inauthentic, it is by nature individualistic and status-seeking, creating 'competitive pressures to constantly run away from the masses and their conformist, homogenised lives', resulting in 'a disguised form of status seeking, the principal effect of which is to generate resentment among others'.

Potter argues that symptoms of this malaise include 'the fetishisation of our pre-modern past and its contemporary incarnation in exotic cultures; the search for increasingly obscure and rarefied forms of consumption and experience; a preference for local forms of community and economic organisation; and, most obviously, an almost violent hostility to the perceived shallowness of Western forms of consumption and entertainment.'

If you were being critical, that's a pretty accurate description of modern British foodism. When the late Antonio Carluccio accused Britain of ruining a classic Italian dish at the Cheltenham Literary Festival in 2016, newspapers ate it up and asked for more. 'Spaghetti Bolognese . . . does not exist in Italy,' he said. 'In Italy it is tagliatelle Bolognese, with freshly made tagliatelle and Bolognese without any herbs whatsoever. When you think Italy, you start to put oregano, basil, parsley, garlic, which is not at all right.' A slew of articles and recipes explaining the 'proper' or 'correct' way to prepare a meaty Italian sauce – or ragù – with pasta followed. 'Spaghetti' and 'Bolognese' may be two Italian words, but put them together, the argument goes, and you do not have an Italian dish.

There are two issues with the British version of spaghetti Bolognese that anger purists. The first is that the shape of pasta is not simply aesthetic: different shapes work with different sauces or accompaniments. A meaty Bolognese ragù does not mix well with long, thin spaghetti – flat noodles, such as tagliatelle, hold the sauce much better. So instead of spag bol, if you want to go authentic, you should be cooking 'tag rag' instead. I can't believe no one calls it this.

The second issue is the sauce itself. Carluccio's beef – so to speak – with herbs is just one issue of contention around what should really go into a ragù alla Bolognese. In 1982, the chamber of commerce for Emilia-Romagna, the northern Italian region of which Bologna is the capital, asked the Accademia Italiana della Cucina, an organization dedicated to preserving Italy's culinary heritage, to record a definitive recipe for their ragù. This 'official' version contains beef, pancetta, onions, carrot, celery, a bit of passata, meat broth, dry white wine, milk, salt and pepper. That's it: no chopped tomatoes, no herbs, no red wine, and no cornflour, barley malt extract or chicory extract. With her white wine and cream, Mary Berry was closer to the 'correct' version of Bolognese sauce than most of us. Of course she was.

Food historians believe that when the dish went abroad it became confused and mixed up with ragù alla Napoletana from the south of the country, which is rich in tomatoes and basil, uses red wine and features bigger chunks of meat rather than mince.

The difference between these traditional sauces from Bologna and Naples illustrates an important point about Italian cuisine: it varies depending on where you go. Many who write about it would argue that there is in fact no such thing as Italian cuisine but rather an array of different regional cuisines that have been artificially jammed together and labelled after a country that completed its unification only in 1871. These cuisines vary with the climate and, most importantly, with what's readily available. Is there any such thing as an 'authentic' *Italian* recipe as opposed to a recipe from one of Italy's many regional traditions?

In the wake of Mary Berry's Ragùgate, Giorgio Locatelli told the *Daily Telegraph*, 'In Italy, it is different from house to house, not even village to village. We didn't have tomatoes until the 1600s in Italy and ragù was cooked well before that, so if you go to places in northern Italy there is no tomato . . . in some places in Italy they put white wine because that's what they have. Some people use pork, some use beef, some use veal, pork and beef. Some put herbs, some don't put any herbs at all.'

So, the authenticity of your sauce depends on where you reckon it comes from. Should we just start calling our dish 'spag nap' instead? You might assume that would make everyone happy. But no, I'm not letting the Italians off the hook that easily. I'd have a lot more time for the guardians of culinary tradition if they practised what they preach.

Compared to the official, correct recipe for ragù à la Bolognese laid down by the Accademia Italiana della

Cucina in 1982, Carluccio's own 'authentic' version is quite different. He ditches the milk, switches white wine for red and uses pork and sometimes veal instead of just beef. Massimo Bottura, a Bolognese 'virtuoso' who runs a restaurant in Modena and refers to spaghetti Bolognese as 'the most abused Italian dish', has published a recipe that includes veal, bone marrow, sausage meat, bay, rosemary and red wine 'such as Sangiovese' instead of white, and no milk. Even the official 1982 recipe itself differs from the earliest known recipe, discovered by Pellegrino Artusi in Bologna. It is believed to date from the late eighteenth century and he put it in a cookbook in 1891, called it Maccheroni alla Bolognese ('maccheroni' then being a generic term for pasta, both dried and fresh) and suggested it be made using lean veal fillet rather than beef, with dried mushroom, truffle or chicken liver added for extra flavour, and with cream stirred in at the end. He also suggested it be served with 'horse teeth' pasta, better known as rigatoni, the ridged pasta tubes that are more often served with ragù alla Napoletana, rather than tagliatelle. The message seems to be that, if you're Italian, you can make it up as you go along, changing whatever aspects you feel like changing, and that's OK. But if someone from another country does exactly the same thing, that's a travesty, an abuse of national tradition.

This is of course understandable, at least to a point. But the other annoying aspect of this whole debate is the regularly repeated idea that we, the British, are responsible for the abominations visited on poor old tag rag.

Along with lasagne, spaghetti Bolognese is now one of the world's most popular pasta dishes. It's unclear how, or when, ragù alla Bolognese left home, went travelling and turned into spaghetti Bolognese. Some writers claim it to be an American invention, created after American troops enjoyed tagliatelle alla ragù while fighting in Italy in the Second World War and made it using spaghetti when they came home because it was the kind of pasta that was most easily available, and meatballs because they felt like it. As soon as it began travelling, pasta was always going to be an international hit: it's very cheap, light and easy to transport, and very versatile, with a long shelf life. Kids love it. And for a long time spaghetti was the only shape you really saw around. Recent research shows that spaghetti Bolognese is now also the third most eaten meal in Germany. In Belgium, it's arguably the national dish, available on the menu in almost any restaurant you visit, slightly orange hued, with very fine mince and a bland but compulsively sweet nature. Pasta recently overtook rice as the most consumed staple around the world and in most places it's eaten it's accompanied by a meaty, tomatoey sauce.

Yet Carluccio wasn't the first person specifically to accuse the British of aggravated assault on the dish he himself kept messing about with, and he won't be the last. We love beating ourselves up over this kind of thing. 'The secret of perfect spag bol? Don't let a Brit cook it', ran a *Daily Mail* headline over a piece by – oh, Antonio Carluccio – in 2010, in which he specifically refers to spag bol as a 'purely British invention'. His 2016 attack was reported almost gleefully, headline news in every newspaper from the *Mirror* to the *Telegraph*. It's not enough that our own cuisine is awful, we insist on debasing others' too, bringing them down to our level. If the Brits are to blame for the horror that is spag bol, somehow it must be our fault that it's enjoyed in Texas, Guatemala, Brussels, Berlin, Sydney, Moscow and São Paolo too.

The UK has a long tradition of welcoming immigrants who open food businesses, from Chinese takeaways to Italian ice-cream parlours. After the Second World War, many former Italian prisoners of war opted to stay in Britain, and more of their countrymen joined them. By the 1960s, they were serving spaghetti Bolognese to the natives. It was Italian immigrants, not British diners, who created the dish, and they did so not out of some sense of cultural vandalism but because, just like the guardians of the various different ragùs back home, they had to work with what was available locally.

In Britain today we're following this rule just as any Italian chef or mother would. Talking about a 'correct' version may be a well-meaning attempt to preserve a culinary legacy, but recipes adapt constantly – even the differences between the current 'official' recipe for ragù alla Bolognese and the earliest recorded version demonstrate that. To try to deny this is to tie a popular recipe to a set of circumstances and contexts that no longer exist and, for most people who cook it, never have.

It's not that I don't have sympathy with the Italians. If I try to imagine the sense of outrage and disgust an Italian restaurateur experiences when asked for spag bol in Bologna, I only have to imagine how I would feel if there was a widespread belief among foreign tourists that roast beef and Yorkshire pudding are best accompanied by French fries and mayonnaise rather than roast potatoes and gravy. But the British self-flagellation over authenticity, the obsession in some quarters with creating a 'correct' version, misses one important point: what if our version is *nicer*?

If tomatoes had been plentiful in northern Italy, they would likely have gone into the Bolognese version, just as they did in the Neapolitan one. Because when you do put tomatoes and herbs in, it tastes nicer than if you don't. When Felicity Cloake went in search of the perfect Bolognese as part of her excellent recipe series for the *Guardian*, she found the chicken liver in Elizabeth David's 'authentic' version to be too overpowering, the big chunks of meat in Marcella Hazan's – often considered to be a definitive modern version – to be too chewy, and Ursula Ferrigno's (and latterly, Mary Berry's) use of cream to be 'overpoweringly rich'. Giorgio Locatelli's was very tomatoey, inauthentic, but quite delicious, and after a bit of experimentation myself, it's closest to the version I now make.

And so what if it's the 'wrong' pasta? I enjoy the separation of pasta and sauce, and the eternal struggle to bring them together on the fork. You can concentrate on twirling the spaghetti, which does get enough sauce on it to be tasty. And the more you eat, the more you start to end up with little mounds of the sauce on its own and spoon these up greedily as both a reward for and intermission from your neat fork work.

Recipes evolve, like language does. They become part of us and we impose ourselves on them.

Spaghetti Bolognese is not Italian. It's international, a global standard. And if everyone else in the world is making it wrong by splashing in the tomatoes, herbs and red wine and a few chefs who insist on making a traditional sauce which doesn't taste as good are right, then I'm happy to be wrong. Here in Britain, we've adapted it to suit our tastes, just like everyone else has. And that's why spag bol is, in fact, 100 per cent British, independent of its confused origins. Mary Berry got into trouble because, while she may have been making an authentic ragù alla Bolognese on her TV show, she was screwing up an authentic British dish.

6.

Of course, any meal that's this popular, this accessible, this much fun, will inevitably attract a degree of criticism from food snobs, quite apart from any arguments about authenticity. Giles Coren described spag bol as 'overrated gloppy stuff' that appeals only to children. 'Ask a footballer what they can cook and they always say spaghetti. It is what you reach for when there is nothing else left in the larder. It's poor people's food and it's unsophisticated,' he said.

At the time of writing Coren is an 'ambassador' for an upmarket fresh-pasta company whose products – 'artisanal' pasta and sauces that are, of course, 'authentic' – are so expensive that there's no danger of them cropping up in any poor person's 'larder' any time soon.

Giles Coren is a perfect example of what Potter calls 'conspicuous authenticity', where a desire for an authentic experience turns into snobbery. I fantasize for a while about kidnapping Coren, starving him and then feeding him my recent re-creation of the first meal I ever cooked. I remember how it felt to be bullied at school for being poor, for not having the right trainers or the correct brand of sports bag. Coren is no better than the twelve-year-old kids who did that. When he sneers, or even when someone far more well-meaning suggests you make a big batch of sauce and store it in your freezer, they're missing the point that many people don't have the money or the space for a big freezer, and that Iceland's 500-gramme Spaghetti Bolognese meal for one costs a quid, whereas 500 grams of steak mince in Tesco is £2.50. The ruthless economics of food in Britain have made cooking from scratch – the safest, most nutritious and rewarding way of preparing a meal – into something of a luxury.

On the day I'm writing this, Michelin-starred chef Angela Hartnett appears on *Desert Island Discs*, where she argues that Britain is not 'a foodie nation' and that those on lower incomes are denied decent food: 'We've lost home economics in a lot of schools. People aren't taught to shop,' she says. 'Our food culture is about money. People who have money can afford good food in this country. When you haven't got any money [and] you're living on a low income, to patronize and sit there and say, "You've got to have an organic chicken" is wrong. People don't have the time to shop and the time to cook. Everyone says we're a more unhealthy nation than ever and yet we're not doing anything about it.'

Over time, the divide has become institutionalized and working-class people have become complicit in it. There's a defeated underbelly of Janice and Ray's judgemental dismissal of the Other, a knowing of place, that's summed up in Yorkshire by the phrase 'It's too good for the likes of us'. Under this self-policing yoke, food that is objectively awful is accepted as 'good enough for the likes of us' and can even be worn as a badge of honour. Anyone who disagrees is treated with suspicion: by declaring that a cheap ready-meal full of crap isn't good enough for us at all, you're implying that you think you're better than everyone else. This tall-poppy thinking is one of the reasons I had to leave Barnsley. But if Chris and Al Gittner ever thought they were better than everyone else when they buy their skirt steak or sweat their sofrito, they would never have moved back there. As the continued survival of Barnsley Market demonstrates, making a decent meal from scratch – British or foreign, traditional or new-fangled – could and should be an option for anyone.

More important than whether or not it's what some Italian artisan was eating 200 years ago is that, wherever it comes from, food should be honest, deriving its authenticity from being what it claims to be. If you buy a tin that reads, 'Minced beef and onions', you'd expect those ingredients to account for more than half of what's inside.

Or maybe we should all just have the version we prefer, whether that's spag bol, spaghetti Bolognese, ragù alla Bolognese or something in between. Like the cheese sandwich, part of its appeal is its flexibility. Andrew Potter quotes *Sincerity and Authenticity*, published in 1972, in which literary critic Lionel Trilling discusses the line from *Hamlet* 'To thine own self be true.' He argues that true authenticity is loyalty to one's own self, knowing who you are and what you want, sticking to that and not dissembling. If you're skilled enough to make your spag bol just how you like it and don't apologize for that, by this logic you're being far more authentic than someone who delights in telling you you're not making the 'correct' version of the dish.

When William Drew, group editor of *The World's 50*

Best Restaurants and *The World's 50 Best Bars*, was asked if Italian food was losing its authenticity back in 2012, he said that, more than ingredients and method, for true authenticity you can't beat the right ambience. 'What really makes an Italian restaurant "authentic" is conviviality. Eating together being a communal, family process, so you want a welcoming maître d' or chef patron – it's that combination of eating and experience.'

By that measure, the Gittners' spag bols are the most authentic I've ever eaten.

5.

Devonshire Cream Tea

'Sorry! I don't want any adventures, thank you.
Not today. Good morning! But please come to tea – any
time you like! Why not tomorrow? Come tomorrow!
Good bye!'

– Bilbo Baggins in *The Hobbit*, by J. R. R. Tolkien

1.

If you read a lot of books about food, you probably weren't expecting to be spending so much time in places like Blackpool and Barnsley in this one. We're halfway through, so let's go for a treat.

Looking for a symbol of old-school, keep-calm-and-carry-on Britain, where upper lips are still stiff and everyone knows their place, you could do a lot worse than head to the Ritz. With rooms starting at £500 a night and people wearing trainers or sportswear banned from any of its restaurants or bars, the Ritz London makes a terrible venue for stag and hen parties or regional sales conferences. But for ladies of a certain age, tourists from around the globe and recipients of vouchers from friends or relatives who can't think of a better birthday present, afternoon tea at the Ritz is an experience akin to marrying into the royal family.

The Ritz Hotel's website boasts of eighteen different types of loose-leaf tea, including the Ritz Royal Blend, exclusive to the hotel, all overseen by the only certified tea sommelier working in any British hotel. The tea (or a glass of Champagne if you prefer) accompanies 'a selection of finely cut sandwiches, freshly baked scones with Cornish clotted cream and strawberry preserve, and a mouth-watering range of exquisitely presented pastries and teacakes', enjoyed in the splendour of 'the spectacular Palm Court, with glittering chandeliers and elegant mirrors, which add a light and stylish flourish to the room'. Prices start at £57 per head for adults and £30 for children.

In December 2017, Janet Wilson won a small-claims case in Canterbury County Court against the Ritz, which was ordered to pay her £108 plus £35 costs. The £108 was a 50 per cent refund on the £216 afternoon tea Mrs Wilson had bought for her husband and two daughters. She claimed that the scones were hard – 'I've made better scones than that. There's no way they were fresh' – and 'the sandwiches tasted like they had just been brought out of the fridge. The tea was not served properly. It was served over us, not to the side of us.' Their teapot was not refilled until they asked and the staff serving them 'didn't look very happy' about their request for more. 'They put the bill on the table before we had even finished and when we put the card down they removed the food before we were finished. It was very much get in, sit down, food put in front of you, and then out for the next people,' she told newspapers.*

Mrs Wilson complained and asked for a refund. The Ritz refused, offering a gift voucher instead, and Mrs Wilson successfully sued the hotel. 'I complained, and they didn't want to know. I didn't think it would get as far as court, but I'm pleased with the outcome. I just didn't think they should get away with it. I wasn't greedy – we weren't happy with the food but we stayed to eat, so feel 50 per cent was adequate,' she said.

The case was reported in several national newspapers, with below-the-line comments split fairly evenly between those condemning the hotel for declining standards that were typical of rip-off Britain (the cheapening of heavily marketed food is not just confined to mass-market groceries, it seems) and those accusing the family of freeloading. It was newsworthy because, either way, it demonstrates the changing nature of British life. We're losing faith in the great institutions that define us, be that one of the poshest hotels in the world or the British habit of insisting that everything is absolutely fine with your meal even when you can barely force it down because you don't want to make a scene. (Mrs Wilson didn't complain at the time but waited until the day after because she didn't want to spoil the occasion.)

This story stirred up old prejudices within me. I may know what a sofrito is and say the word with a straight face

* I don't know why she was so shocked: a Google image search reveals that the sandwiches aren't even cut diagonally.

but I can't help but think of the Ritz as a place that's 'too good for the likes of us'. I may have been on the receiving end of this attitude when I passed exams and, later, moved to London, with older relatives saying things like, 'Ooh, you'll not want to know us soon,' but when I think of the Ritz I'm no longer a member of the hated metropolitan middle-class media elite but a poor kid from Barnsley who has no right to be there. I have no idea how well-off the Wilson family are, but I cheered that they'd stuck it to the snobby Ritz on my behalf.

This is of course pure fantasy and projection on my part, as surely as the idea of my older relatives and family thinking I won't want to know them now I live darn south in That London was.* But these attitudes and biases stubbornly resist reality and common sense. They go deep because they were formed early.

So of all the meals I'm exploring in this book the cream tea is the only one I come to reluctantly. Of course, cream tea is not quite the same as afternoon or high tea. You get sandwiches with afternoon tea and, even if they're pointlessly filled with cucumber and airily shorn of their crusts, there's very little about a sandwich that's not to love. But the core of the afternoon tea is the cream tea, and that's the bit that gives me problems. It's the exception among all these meals in the way it makes me feel. I have no personal history of it, no leaping of the heart when it's mentioned.

And it's so intensely codified and ritualized, and these things are often designed specifically to be exclusive. I went to university in St Andrews and genuinely couldn't

* There are some of them I really don't want to know, but not for that reason.

understand why, during Freshers' Week, when you met a fellow new student, they would ask your name, what you were studying and then where you went to school. None of them had heard of Darton High School. I hadn't expected them to, but they would seem confused by this. When they then told me they'd been to Ampleforth or Fettes (without my having asked the question back) I'd say I hadn't heard of their schools either and wonder why everyone was asking such an obscure question. When I finally realized why the name of your school was important to them, I felt as though I'd been relegated to a lower tier and that feeling continued throughout my university career. Whenever there was a formal dinner or ball there were so many customs and codes that I wasn't aware of, and that these people seemed to know innately, that I felt dumb and brutish as a result.

Table manners have steadily increased in complexity over time and they're invariably instigated by the rich before trickling down. As one 1879 rulebook put it, etiquette 'is the barrier which society draws around itself, a shield against the impertinent, the improper, and the vulgar' – all words which I'm sure a society hostess would regularly apply to people too poor to have been coached in gentle manners. So, when I see people arguing about whether you should put jam or cream on your scone first and whether or not it's correct to extend your pinkie while drinking, those old feelings of inferiority and inadequacy flare up.

Even stripped of its cultural baggage, the physical reality of the cream tea simply doesn't fit my notion of what's good to eat. When you look at what it consists of I can't understand why anyone would regard it as a treat in any way.

I've never liked any of the constituent parts of the cream tea, so I'm genuinely aghast at the idea of bringing them together.

Scones suck so much moisture from your mouth that your tongue turns to dust and is scattered by the wind like a mummy whose curse has been lifted. Their punishing aridity is supposedly tempered by lashings of clotted cream. Many otherwise sane people I know genuinely seem to believe that cream is some kind of special treat. But it has the same consistency and appeal as axle grease and the thought of eating any kind of cream makes me gag. As for clotted cream? Can you think of one other substance that the word 'clotting' brings to mind? That's right, blood. Blood clots inside the body are horrible, traumatic and often fatal and I see no reason to believe that clotted cream would be any different.

And jam is wrong. Fruit is nice. I like fruit, especially the kind that gets made into jam, like strawberries and raspberries. I suppose the clue is in the term 'preserves', because fruit in its raw state goes off quickly whereas jam lasts for ever (especially in my house, because I don't eat it). But we have a choice now. We have refrigeration and deep freezes and controlled-atmosphere storage facilities and sea and air freight across two hemispheres. Our 'fresh' fruit may well have been kept in oxygen-starved warehouses for a year and we may be killing the planet by flying it here from Australia or China, but that's still better than jam.

Sweet things do not belong on bread. And of all sweet things jam is far too sweet. Fruit is already sweet and you make jam by adding loads more sugar to it. How can that be right to anyone with taste buds?

Scones. Clotted cream. And jam. I suppose the greatest question that troubles me is why the hell would Janet Wilson – or anyone else – pay over fifty quid a head for this rubbish in the first place?

2.

I'm not alone in my disdain for the cream tea. Of all the meals in this book it's had the least written about it by food historians. But oh my, I love tea, the drink. If I ever had to give up alcohol, I would instantly become a tea geek. I genuinely think there's something wrong with people who claim they don't like it – either their palates or their sense of themselves have been wired up wrong. And as the name suggests, this meal is built around tea, the drink: it was the rituals around the pouring and sharing of tea that laid the foundations for the etiquette that surrounds the cream tea today.

Tea first arrived in Britain in the mid-seventeenth century, in the hands of the British East India Company, who had fought to control its trade from China and introduce it to India. An advertisement in *Mercurius Politicus* in September 1658 confirms that it was then on sale at a London coffee house: 'That Excellent, and by all Physicians approved, *China* drink, called by the *Chinese*, *Tcha*, by other nations *Tay alias Tee*, . . . sold at the Sultaness-head, ye *Cophee-house* in Sweetings-Rents, by the Royal Exchange, *London.*'

In the early days people weren't sure how to prepare or drink it. In the coffee houses the leaves were boiled up in a large cauldron and then siphoned off to a beer barrel, where a strong, stewing brew would sit cooling until someone ordered it, at which point it was drawn from the barrel into a cup and had boiling water added to it. It would have been incredibly bitter, as milk wasn't yet added and, at this point, sugar was still a rare luxury.

Coffee houses, like taverns, were exclusively for men and would go on to give birth to both gentlemen's clubs and the stock exchange. The fortunes of tea were made when, following a presentation of two pounds of tea to Charles II by the East India Company, his new Portuguese bride, Catherine of Braganza, proclaimed it her non-alcoholic drink of choice, giving it an instant fashionable cachet among the aristocracy.

Thomas Twining began selling tea when he bought Tom's Coffee House on the Strand in 1706. His genius was that he expanded and opened a shop selling dry-leaf tea. Women who could never have entered a coffee house could now buy tea and make it in their own homes, to their own tastes.

In the typical upper- or middle-class household of the eighteenth century the steady encroachment of industrialized work, coupled with the growth of practical artificial lighting, began to move breakfast earlier and dinner later, leaving a chasm in the afternoon for the sociable lady. She would fill this by inviting friends around for tea. A servant would bring the tea set into the drawing room around three in the afternoon, followed by a kettle that had just boiled. The hostess would then unlock the caddy or cabinet where her tea supply was safely kept, infuse the tea and pass it around.

To an outside observer this sounds as ritualized as communal drug-taking, which in a way it was. Tea has always had the reputation for being a stimulant and everywhere it is taken there is some element of ritual around it. But the occasion of tea drinking quickly became much bigger than the ingestion of the substance itself. Men had always had the alehouse or tavern, and more recently the coffee house and club – not to mention parliament – in which to scheme, plot and put the world to rights. Women were entirely excluded from this world. Now, for the first time in the history of polite society, they had a forum of their own.

They quickly filled it with elaborate codes of etiquette around the correct way to pour and drink, to ask for more or to indicate you didn't want any more (and to know which of these was correct). That extended pinkie finger of the hand holding the cup handle is possibly the last remaining element of a system that was far more complex. And beyond the drink itself there were codes of behaviour that governed the occasion. Afternoon tea soon gained a reputation for the exchange of gossip and opinion. One French (male) visitor to an English drawing room in 1796 remarked, 'Many English women of high standing . . . take a particularly exquisite delight in speaking ill of their neighbours.'

This was two years after the invention of gas lighting, which made the gap between breakfast and dinner – then still the only two main meals of the day – even longer. By the early nineteenth century, tea was being accompanied by cake, bread and butter and, later, sandwiches. The newly founded potteries in Stoke-on-Trent (Josiah Wedgwood established his business in 1759) were turning out exquisite, delicate cups, saucers and cake stands that catered perfectly to the needs of these refined occasions. The afternoon tea was born.

In 1784 and 1785, the price of tea crashed. Tea drinking had been creeping down the social scale for a century, from the nobility to the middle classes who aped their manners, and had already entered the working-class diet. Now, it was easily affordable to everyone. One Scottish legal luminary wrote in 1743, 'Tea has now become so common, that the meanest familys, even of labouring people, particularly in the Burroughs, make their morning's Meal of it.'

For the working classes tea was a stimulant. Tea breaks were a pause from grinding work, a chance to refresh and bond with fellow workers. Such was its appeal it began to take the place of beer in the working-class diet. Tea was an excellent source of safe hydration because, like beer, it was boiled in its preparation. But beer has nutritional value – around 220 calories a pint, plus lots of B-vitamins. Tea has none. Soon, commentators began to realize that widespread tea consumption was actually harming the nutrition of the poor.

What this meant to the upper classes was that their tea drinking had to be kept quite distinct from that of the poor. The ritual and etiquette around tea – and afternoon tea in particular – became ever more complex and refined, as different from the way the poor consumed it as possible. At one point it was fashionable to drink from the saucer rather than the cup. If you were seated at a table, you should never touch your saucer, only raise the cup and lower it again. If you were standing, you should hold your cup and saucer no higher than waist height. And apparently, if you were really in the know, that pinkie finger should be curled inwards, like all the rest.

The variant of afternoon tea that came to be known specifically as cream tea has murky origins. In the few historical analyses that exist there's furious debate as to when the first cream tea was served and who served it – mainly between the counties of Devon and Cornwall, who both claim cream-tea supremacy. Really, all that's happening amid the claims and counter-claims is that the cream tea evolved gradually into its current form, like any other meal. There's a record of the monks of Tavistock Abbey in Devon feeding builders with bread, clotted cream and preserves in the eleventh century, but clearly tea – builders' or otherwise – wasn't served because it wouldn't arrive in Britain for another 600 years. In 1542, Andrew Boorde declared that 'Rawe crayme undecocted, eaten with strawberries or hurtes [whortleberries] is a rural man's banquet,' but that's strawberries and cream, not cream tea. It's clear that these are flavours and ingredients that have long been known to go together, and Devon and Cornwall, with the long-standing tradition of fine dairy cattle that also gave us Cheddar cheese in neighbouring Somerset, have always enjoyed an unsurpassed reputation for their cream.

It's possible that clotted cream – an essential distinction for the cream tea – was originally created in Syria, with the method being introduced to south-west England by Phoenician traders. But recent archaeological evidence suggests it may have developed independently, albeit later, in England. Fruits cooked in sugar to preserve them were also brought back to Britain by crusaders in the late thirteenth century. So it's tempting to speculate that the great British cream tea may owe more to the Middle East than anywhere else.

In the early nineteenth century, the Napoleonic Wars and their blockade of continental Europe put paid to the idea of the Grand Tour, which had been popular among the aristocracy in the eighteenth. The Prince Regent's fondness for bathing made coastal towns fashionable and, in 1848, Brunel's Great Western Railway admitted towns along 'the English Riviera' to the club. When butter production was industrialized in the 1870s it became less profitable for dairy farmers to sell their raw milk to big dairies and West Country farmers focused on cream, cheese and ice cream. Around the same time self-raising flour and baking powder meant scones could be made much lighter than the dense, Scottish original. With cheap sugar from the Caribbean, jam was now also available to anyone. By the end of the nineteenth century, all the ingredients for the modern cream tea were assembled in Devon and Cornwall.

No one knows exactly where or when they came together to be called a cream tea. The term is not mentioned by Mrs Beeton, nor even in *Entertaining Made Easy*, an exhaustive analysis of teas, luncheons and small meals written in 1919 by Emily Rose Burt. The earliest known reference to a 'cream tea' comes in a letter of complaint to the *Cornishman* newspaper, where a disgruntled reader writes:

> There is too much blatant profiteering going on! Visitors are being frightened away. For an alleged 'Cornish Cream Tea' consisting of three slices of

bread and butter, a splashing of cream and jam and two cakes, I was charged 1 shilling and sixpence.

Another, similar mention occurs in September 1942, when a Food Enforcement Inspector basically entraps a Mrs Lily Crocker of Willis Farm, Bickleigh, South Devon. Under the headline 'Inspector has a Cream Tea' the *Western Morning News* tells how Mr Sidney Snell visited the farm and asked for tea for one and was given 'a pot of tea, milk, sugar, bread and butter, plain bread, as well as jam, and a glass of cream about three or four ounces'. Because milk was rationed, she was fined £5 for making cream and £5 for selling it.

You'll have spotted straightaway that the bread and butter in these stories means whatever the *Cornishman's* correspondent and *Western Morning News'* sub-editor thought of as a cream tea doesn't meet our modern definition. That's why the *Oxford English Dictionary* cites the earliest reference as being a 1964 novel, *Picture of Millie* by Philip Maitland Hubbard, a murder mystery set in the West Country, which contains the line, 'We just bathe and moon about and eat cream teas,' but even that doesn't specify what these cream teas consist of. *Aargh!*

The notion of a 'cream tea' may go back a long way, but the term itself is, at most, only a century old. And the very strict stipulation that a cream tea contains only clotted cream, jam and scones is much more recent than that. It's striking that what has become such ornate ceremony and etiquette around the cream tea is such a recent invention and emerged at a time when rules and etiquette in food and drink generally were in retreat. We need our rituals, and over the past few decades we've chosen the cream tea as the meal around which they coalesce over any other.

One e-book I found – *The Great British Cream Tea*, published in 2017 by Rupert Matthews – is perfectly representative of every other guide I've found on how to eat a cream tea. From the outset I should say that, to me, it seems pretty obvious: pour the tea, spread the jam and cream on the scone, eat the scone and drink the tea. But no, it's far more complicated than that. 'Etiquette demands' – *demands*, not suggests – that it be served at 4 p.m. The jam and clotted cream 'need' to be decanted into small serving dishes. You 'should' have a bone-china tea service, and of course you 'should' use a lighter tea such as Earl Grey or Darjeeling rather than 'builder's tea'. Then there's the vexed question of tea or milk first into the cup. Matthews informs us that Orwell's preference for tea first was shared by the upper classes, because expensive porcelain could withstand the heat while cheaper china might crack. Pour hot tea straight in without the cooling milk and you were subtly bragging about the quality of your tea service.

Another online guide tells us that it is 'unacceptable' to reheat scones rather than have them freshly baked, that they should be two and a half inches in diameter and as wide as they are round. The jam 'should' be fairly sweet and smooth. It is 'essential' that the cream be clotted. And according to this expert, you can have either tea or coffee but it is 'important' that they are taken black.

The 'jam or cream first?' debate is only the most notable example of disagreements over the correct etiquette. What matters above all is that the etiquette is there, that the occasion is dripping in it.

Why this particular meal and not another? Partly it's because this is what tea demands. Chinese and Japanese tea ceremonies, the Moroccan mint-tea tradition and India's chai culture suggest that wherever tea is important there's a significant degree of ritual and codification surrounding it. But the particular nature of British tea tradition – its gentility, subtlety and politeness – surely has its roots in a tradition evolved by and for women rather than men. In that, the cream tea tells us something about food and Britishness that's reflected in baking more generally. The nice cup of tea is a reflection of our temperament and attitude. Put it with cake and it's a bastion of heritage.

The Great British Bake Off is more than a programme; in eight years it's become a national institution. It was the most watched television programme of 2015 and 2016, is credited with reinvigorating Britain's love of baking and sparking a sharp rise in national sales of baking ingredients, and has even been credited with reviving the fortunes of the Women's Institute, which has reached its highest level of membership since the 1970s.

Peri Bradley, a lecturer in media theory and editor of *Food, Media and Contemporary Culture*, argues that *Bake Off* 'presents an idyllic view of rural, upper-class Britain that links to heritage TV texts such as *Upstairs Downstairs* and *Downton Abbey* and a national identity that upholds traditional values and a stable national economy'. I'm not sure I buy the conspiracy-theory-sounding implication that this is part of an establishment plot to keep people pliant with an illusion of the good old days, but the programme definitely belongs to an auntyish BBC tradition of 'keep calm and carry on', of Women's Institutes and church fetes, even as it casts a warmly cheeky eye at such institutions. Anna Beattie, the producer who came up with the idea, said, 'I loved that idea of village fetes and an old-fashioned baking competition with people who only wanted to bake a good cake.' Even when it transferred to Channel 4, the producers hired two very different but quintessentially BBC personalities – Sandi Toksvig and Noel Fielding – to replace the presenters who left. It does, as Bradley argues, present 'British identity as reasonable, liberal, calm and sensible', and the large marquee in the grounds of a posh house does give it 'a sense of luxury and occasion'.

Bradley has trouble reconciling the idea of 'heritage' Britain with the diverse, multicultural nation *Bake Off* portrays, and her assertion that there is no working-class presence on the programme is false. But not everyone in Britain is happy about this supposedly 'politically correct' aspect of the programme. Just before the final of series six, *Daily Mail* columnist Amanda Platell wrote:

> When this series of *The Great British Bake Off* began, the BBC was proud it was the most inclusive, multicultural line-up ever. Now we're down to the final three, it's certainly a PC triumph. We are left with Muslim mum Nadiya Hussain, gay doctor Tamal Ray, and New Man Ian Cumming. Poor Flora Shedden never stood a chance. She was far too middle class—and was booted off this week after her chocolate carousel was deemed sub-standard. Perhaps if she'd made a chocolate mosque, she'd have stood a better chance.

As Nadiya Hussain was the only Muslim in the final, this was an obvious jibe at her faith, which was worse somehow than the 'political correctness' of a gay doctor and a new man (whatever that might be in the second decade of the twenty-first century). How cheering it was, then, when Nadiya won and was instantly proclaimed a British national treasure. She now has several books and TV series under her belt, not because of political correctness but because people across all social classes and backgrounds instantly warm to her and because she's incredibly talented. After provoking a media outcry with her earlier comments, Amanda Platell realized she'd misread the popular mood and later delighted in telling her readers how 'We were all moved watching . . . the goddess of *The Great British Bake Off*, as sweet and delectable as her irresistible lemon drizzle wedding cake.'

Bake Off does undeniably present a middle-class, BBC worldview. My family's household was one that only ever watched ITV, because the Beeb was too 'stuck up', but *Bake Off* wouldn't be the phenomenon it is, and Nadiya wouldn't have gone on to be such a big star, if none of this appealed to working-class, ITV- and Channel 5-watching people. The world of village fetes, marquees, the WI, china tea cups and cake stands is one that has as much appeal as fish and chips or a Sunday roast. And that's why the cream tea consistently appears in our favourite foods list alongside them.

3.

'There's a new Wetherspoon's down by the harbour,' says the landlady of our immaculate B&B.

You can sometimes tell the tenor of a town by the way people say a sentence like this. I've been to some coastal towns that are so on their uppers the local Wetherspoon's is the best pub you'll find. Having just arrived, I really don't think Ilfracombe is one of these. But the enthusiastic tone of the landlady does make it sound like the kind of place where the arrival of a Wetherspoon's is a welcome boost rather than a blight.

Of course, she could just have sized us up and decided that we're the kind of people who would be excited by the thought of a Wetherspoon's so far from home.

Like many famous English seaside resorts, Ilfracombe is a town of faded grandeur. My family never came to the West Country for our holidays. Our seaside jaunts were confined strictly to the north of England – I don't think we'd have been able to bear staying in the car with each other long enough to make it anywhere else. As far as I know, I remain the only one of us who's ever made it past Bristol. But slightly posher schoolfriends of mine – still working class, but *comfortable* – would go to Torquay, Paignton, Ilfracombe and Woolacombe. I had no idea what these places looked like, didn't even really know where they were. But onomatopoeically, they were posh. Until we got here, I'd imagined a lofty, superior place with rows of regal-looking tea rooms full of people with their noses in the air, capable of transforming me, with one withering look, back into a snotty-nosed, greasy-haired kid wearing charity-shop clothes. And that's why I simply had to come here for my cream tea, with every intention of sneering back at them.

The buildings are certainly grand and elegant, many of

them displaying a localized fad for Wild West saloon-style verandas. But they're a little shabbier than I expected, most still just about pulling it off, but not all, and some are clearly not just closed after the season but closed for good. Even among those that look like they're still going concerns, many are shuttered up for the winter – a surprise given that we're only at the end of the second week in September. Even taking into account the terrifying rain that assailed us on the way here over Exmoor, Ilfracombe has the feel of a place where the party has ended prematurely.

On that journey over, we passed sign after sign for cream teas, which seemed to be on sale around every bend and down every lane. Now we're here there are an awful lot of tea rooms lining the streets – more than fish-and-chip shops, and there are an awful lot of fish-and-chips shops. From their exteriors, I surprise myself by taking an instant liking to them all. They feel lost in time and remind me for some reason of my early childhood in the 1970s, even though I never recall going to one, and even though most of them look like they'd be far more comfortable in the 1920s. On the street heading down to the harbour sits a microclimate of tea rooms that have evolved together. The buildings are all set quite far back from the street, leaving space for long gardens or sheltered outdoor-seating areas. Each announces itself with a carefully hand-painted sign rising from a rockery or hanging overhead like a teapot-shaped pub sign, displaying names like St James's, Fuchsia or Acorn. I imagine every single one is run by a twinset-and-pearl-clad lady named Miss Blennerhasset.

I like how Ilfracombe huddles beneath the hills on the edge of Exmoor like a child sheltering in the crook of a parent's arm. The harbour sits around the corner from the wild sea, protected by steep cliffs. The landscape and the narrow, winding streets within it evoke the smuggler's coves of Enid Blyton that, as a kid, I used to find impossibly romantic, without ever stopping to consider what dangerous bastards smugglers were capable of being. It's a perfect seaside town that, if we had come here as kids, I could easily have loved – even if the sand on the beaches is Mordor-grey.

The first word that springs to mind when trying to describe Nelly May's Parlour is 'prim'. It's not a word I think I've ever used before, and it must be twenty years since I've heard it or seen it in print, which makes it all the more appropriate now.

In a terrace on Ilfracombe's main shopping street Nelly May's sits between a gift shop and a large fish-and-chip shop and raises the tone with bounteous hanging baskets and window boxes so lush they almost form a complete garland across the front of the building. The walls are salmon pink, the windows trimmed with lace. If you couldn't see the signs, the ancient dolls and stuffed toys in the window displays might trick you into thinking it's an antique shop or a toy museum.

Inside, china plates cover the walls. Roof beams sag low. Old, mismatched chairs and tables covered with bright cloths overlaid with lace sit on the parquet floor. A sinister blond doll, wearing what looks like a prisoner's uniform from the early twentieth century, leers from a shelf in the corner. This place has been here for ever and hasn't changed a jot in all that time.

The polite formality is tinged with the faintest whiff of

passive aggression. The front of the menu tells us that 'At Nelly May's all of our food is prepared and cooked to order. We thank you in advance for your patience.'

Suzanne, our waitress, wears an embroidered name badge with flowers surrounding the letters of her name and a frilly lace border encompassing those in turn. The badge is pinned to an immaculately clean, starchy apron given some levity by a cheery red trim. Her neat and formal manner suggests she's not just the waitress here. She claims to be a little flustered as she serves us, although she seems anything but. We'd probably never have known, but then she explains that the reason she's so flustered is that the environmental-health inspector was here this morning and, amid all the chaos of trying to serve breakfast in a busy shop while setting up for a birthday lunch, they managed to do enough to get the full five stars assessment. I've just been served a masterclass in what was once referred to as the English art of understatement and is better known to the internet generation as the humblebrag.

After lingering over the leather-bound vellum menu for as long as seems appropriate and not a second longer, I decide to order the mini-cream tea for one. I regard this as a perfectly acceptable compromise between my complete antipathy for this meal and the fact that I have to eat it without making a scene. On paper it looks perfectly simple: 'Nelly May's mini Devonshire cream tea – 1 home-made scone, home-made jam, local clotted cream served with tea or a cafetière of coffee for 1', all for the delightfully eccentric price of £4.05. But when Suzanne comes to take my order I start to get a little flustered myself. Would I like plain or sultana scones? Well, plain, obviously. But this proves to be a mere rehearsal for the choice of jam: would I like strawberry, strawberry and lavender, plum, plum and brandy, gooseberry, blackcurrant, or about thirty more I forget in my panic?

'Strawberry and lavender sounds nice.' (It doesn't.)

When our order is finally complete, Suzanne removes the earthenware cups that were sitting empty on the table when we arrived and replaces them with fine china. I feel like I've passed a test – maybe we'd have been left with the cheap, shitty cups if I'd picked the wrong jam. As I always do in moments like this, I picture the ancient grail knight from the climactic scene of *Indiana Jones and the Last Crusade*, his thin, shaky voice saying, 'You have chosen . . . *wisely*.'

As if to confirm this, a few minutes later the tea for my upgraded cup arrives in a traditional cream-coloured tea-pot whose dimensions bring to mind Hattie Jacques playing a *Carry On* matron and which sports a magnificent fluffy, crocheted white tea cosy. Two crocheted red balls – which I think are meant to represent strawberries – and a pair of crocheted green leaves sit gaily on top. A bowl of sugar, complete with a neat little pair of silver tongs, arrives with its modesty preserved by a doily. At some point during the ordering process my sneering, defensive cynicism started to wane. Those tongs grab it daintily and throw it out through the window like a bum from a Wild West saloon brawl, only politely.

And then Suzanne approaches with our cream teas on a three-tier cake stand. And in that moment my resistance crumbles.

OK, I get it now.

As soon as I see the stand – three prettily patterned

plates screwed together and kept apart by slender, delicate steel columns – I'm flooded by the feeling that this is a special occasion. Suzanne could have served our order on a bunch of separate plates, but where would the fun be in that? And besides, with so many different components, the tidy order of our relatively small table would have been ruined. It would have become . . . *unseemly*. The cake stand is a practical solution, giving you enough space to negotiate everything conveniently and at your leisure without having to ask for things to be passed across the table.

But it's also so much more than that.

Practicality is not the point here. This is the kind of apparatus that, if you had one at home, was always kept for best. (I have a vague memory of seeing Bourbon biscuits sitting on something like this when I was small. I can't remember who was visiting who merited the stand being taken out and wiped clean of dust, or the Bourbon biscuits being bought.) The cake stand elevates whatever is placed upon it. It says, Whatever this is, the eating of it is a celebratory ritual.

The basic idea is scalable, depending on the size of your order. As Liz and I have each ordered a mini Devonshire cream tea, they come out together, sharing one three-tier stand. Liz's scone, glass dish of cream and dish of jam are on the bottom tier, mine are on the second tier and a couple of spoons sit on the top tier, so this littlest plate doesn't feel left out. I immediately wish we'd ordered full cream teas rather than minis, just to see what this baby can really do.

Weakened and left vulnerable by the cake stand, I'm then taken out at the knees by the scone and forced to eat my words on every aspect of the cream tea along with it.

The scone is moist. It's warm and fluffy. It's edible. No, it's more than that: it's actually quite nice.

My little glass dish of jam shines under the lights, the colour of claret. The clotted cream stands proudly in peaks. I take my knife in my hand and point it at them.

Come on, you two. Let's dance.

Because we're in Devon, for appearance's sake, and not from any declaration of allegiance, I put some cream on my scone first and top it with a blob of jam. There's something naughty about the way the scone crumbles and surrenders as I bite. The cream is smooth, the jam is fruity and wonderfully elevated by the dab of lavender. The whole thing comes together in a luxurious rush and oh my god this is *fucking gorgeous*. The tannic dryness of the tea provides the perfect foil. But whatever. I want more of this jam-cream-scone action. Or cream-jam-scone action. I don't care.

With the other half of my scone I spread the jam first and dab the cream on top, like some filthy pervert. It makes absolutely no difference whatsoever to the taste or mouthfeel of the assembled components.

By the time I finish this union of three food items I thought I hated, scraping every last bit of jam and cream from their respective bowls and briefly considering wailing that there's no more before checking Suzanne's stern yet friendly mien, I finally understand the point of the cream tea. It's not snobbish or judgemental at all. Or at least, it really doesn't have to be.

There is a sound rationale to etiquette, at least to a point. Legendary food historian Margaret Visser argued in 2003 that 'without [rules] food would be hogged by the physically powerful, civility in general would decline, and eventually society would break down altogether. Furthermore, the specific fashion in which a culture manages eating helps to express, identify, and dramatise that society's ideals and aesthetic style.'

Or as Al Murray's Pub Landlord character put it, 'You've got to have rules. If we didn't have rules, where would we be? France.'

These rules change depending on the social importance of the eating event. The dinner you go for on a first date has different rules from the Sunday lunch with friends. Having the boss around for dinner was a staple of sitcoms like *Terry and June* and was fraught with an anxiety that wouldn't exist if the neighbours came round. The cup of tea in the afternoon with a friend is different in every way from the drink you have with your boss to have a first, informal chat about your next promotion. And they're different for afternoon cream tea than they are for any other meal because that's what people like about afternoon tea. As an occasion, it may have begun in upper-class drawing rooms as a bitchfest but, among the lower classes, it's always been more about communion. So why not make it special and ritualize it? As Linda Hewitt, quoted by Peri Bradley, argues in a celebration of tea:

> One of the most endearing things about the [British] national identity is the ability to take food and drink and turn them not into some grand gustatory adventure but rather into a time of warmth and hospitality, of sociable and delectable sensations. With the tea that is poured from the pot . . . comes a spell

of as much understanding and sympathy, comfort and conviviality, as we mortals are likely to know.

Debating the merits of jam or cream first is hardly alienating to anyone and is clearly done with tongues in cheeks, just like *Bake Off*. The ritual, the ceremony, takes flour, water, cream, fruit and sugar – ingredients that are accessible to anyone and aren't at all special individually – puts them on a fancy tiered plate with some flowers painted on it and makes you feel like a duchess. But not just any duchess – how many duchesses get to pour tea from a pot snuggled in a crocheted cosy gaily decorated with woollen strawberries?

It only really works if your standards are impeccably high, like Suzanne's; if you get out the best stuff you've got, whether that's bone china or a knitted tea cosy, you can declare any afternoon of the week to be a special occasion. The pride in the cream tea – the rigour, the high standards – is exactly what's missing from some examples of our other great British meals. I find myself delighted that it presents itself so strongly in this one.

Perhaps another reason the cream tea has become so much more ritualized is that, today, the influence of etiquette seems to flow from the bottom up rather than the top down. Take forks. They're actually a relatively recent arrival on the dinner table – Louis XIV thought them 'unmanly' – but pretty soon we had complex table settings where knowing the correct fork or spoon to use was a measure of social value. It was terribly important to the Victorians and has still been used as status thing in my lifetime, too, at dinners in places like St Andrews. Now, though, eating with your hands has been destigmatized – to the point where some children are unable to eat with knives and forks, or are at least unable to hold them in a way that doesn't look ridiculous. So has drinking straight from the bottle – go to even an upscale sandwich chain and you will not be offered a glass for your drink or a plate for your food, just a bunch of napkins to wipe your fingers clean, which assumes you're going to make a bit of a mess. Authenticity is replacing superiority. In the main, this is democratic and liberating. But surely, there should still be standards. Deep down, we yearn for them.

As we leave Nelly May's Parlour I check the window for anything I might have missed and spot a printed-out review from an online round-up of the best tea rooms and hotels in Devon. It says that Nelly May's is 'a new tea room opened on July 15'. I wait for the crushing disappointment at the realization this place hasn't been here for ever, and that the picture of 'Nelly May' on the windows and the menus is likely just some contrivance. But the disappointment doesn't come. It doesn't matter. Nelly May's Parlour is already gaining a reputation as one of the best of the many tea rooms that crowd north Devon.

And for £4.05 rather than £57 it offers a far better, more authentic and satisfying occasion than afternoon tea at the Ritz could ever be.

6.

Going for a Curry

'The British Empire was created as a by-product of
generations of desperate Englishmen roaming the
world in search of a decent meal.'

– Bill Marsano, American food writer

1.

In 1986, I left Barnsley for the University of St Andrews –
as far away from home as I could get, in more ways than
one. The first member of my family ever to go to university, I had no idea what to expect and no clue about how
much the experience would change me.

I didn't notice the shift in my food habits at first. For a
couple of years I lived in St Regulus Hall, or 'Regs' – a
Victorian-built hotel that was acquired by the university in
the 1950s and by 1986 housed 140 students a year. Regs
served three meals a day, most of them the same kind
of tasteless, industrialized meat-and-two-veg* familiar to
anyone who has eaten school or hospital meals or has a

---

* My mate Steve was a vegetarian. He had to pay extra for his meals because of
the inconvenience he caused. More than once he was handed the same meal as

canteen at work; generic grey food produced at some awful central depot before being blast-frozen and distributed, then boiled or microwaved until its spirit was broken. Late at night, unsatisfied, we'd go for what's known in Scotland as a 'fish supper', familiar and reassuring save for the 'salt and sauce' it was served with, 'sauce' being a cheap brand of brown sauce heavily watered down with vinegar that should have been as awful as it sounded but was actually quite addictive. If we were out even later, we'd go to the all-night bakery for hot, fresh bread and less hot, less fresh Scotch pies or Forfar bridies that were molten at the edges and sometimes still frozen in the middle.

We tolerated most meals in Regs without really paying attention to them – it was better that way. While I vividly remember the taste of the fish suppers, bridies and pizzas I ate in St Andrews, I can only recall two specific meals from the hall-of-residence dining room: the best and the worst.

Once a week, without fail, we were served beef olives. Now, I've just looked up the recipe for beef olives for the first time ever – it's taken this long to reach closure – and I was shocked by what I read. Apparently, they consist of a stuffing made of bacon and freshly minced pork with sage and onion, garlic, pepper and nutmeg, wrapped up in steak to make hearty parcels of meaty gorgeousness. The beef olives we were served in Regs did not match this description at all. They looked like long, grey turds. They contained something that probably came from an animal,

---

the rest of us and, when he reminded the catering staff that he was vegetarian, they simply scraped the meat off his plate and handed it back to him.

but we didn't like to speculate as to what part of which animal it was. They tasted of February nights and failure. Our disdain – no, our *fear* – of Regs's beef olives reached the point where, as soon as they were served, 140 students would stand up as one, leave the dining room and go and queue outside the pizza place at the top of the road instead.

At the other end of the scale was chicken curry.

Regs's chicken curry bore about as much resemblance to any other chicken curry you've ever seen as their beef olives did to food. But somehow, it worked. Luminous yellow and yet somehow grey at the same time, it had currants in it instead of spices or heat. You couldn't pinpoint the source of its appeal, but when it was on the menu we'd sing, 'Chicken curry, chicken curry, chicken curry,' to the tune of John Philip Sousa's 'The Stars and Stripes Forever', otherwise known to football fans as 'Here We Go', and go back for more until the kitchen was empty. The kitchen served it once for every three times we walked out on the beef olives – proof they were punishing us, basically. It may well have been a travesty of anything we might now consider to be 'proper' curry, but it was the most exciting, flavourful meal that dining room had ever seen.

The standard degree at St Andrews is a four-year Masters compared to the three-year Bachelors in English universities. When there were still vestigial student grants and no tuition fees, this was seen as an advantage, and people who were less rich than Prince William could still afford to go there. Every day I spent in St Andrews felt like a holiday. Even four years didn't feel like enough. I wanted more.

At the end of my third year I was elected Deputy

President of the Students' Association. This was a sabbatical post, which meant I had to take a year off from my degree and work the role as a full-time job. That year, I also moved out of Regs and into a flat with friends and learned how to cook meals that involved chopping fresh garlic and onions, peeling vegetables (for the first six months I used to peel mushrooms – it's quite therapeutic, but very time-consuming), sprinkling in dried herbs and spices and bringing everything to a simmer in a permanent saucepan that slowly evolved, like the colours of a lava lamp, from stew, to chilli, to curry, to soup, and back again.

But I was only at the flat about half the nights of any given week. The others were spent in the Union building, where I organized and helped run discos, gigs and bars, usually working until well after midnight while my flatmates ate my share of the food. One night, Bruce Turner, the former student who never left and instead became the fearsome and universally respected General Manager of the union – basically the grown-up who was there to prevent us students from completely screwing the place up – was enjoying something from a silver foil tray while I was finishing cashing up. When he'd had enough, in a fit of uncharacteristic good-naturedness never exhibited before or after, he leaned over and said, 'Here, Whippet [because I'm from Yorkshire, you see] finish this.'

'What is it?' I asked, already reaching for the foil tray.

'Chicken pathia, from the New Balaka.'

When I'd left Barnsley there still wasn't a single Indian restaurant in town. There were two in St Andrews, but it had never occurred to me to try either of them. I'd never been tempted to find out what had happened to the old Balaka, or even look at the menu of the new one just across the road from the Union building. We had chicken curry in Regs – why did I need to pay a fortune for the same thing in a restaurant?

I looked at the remains of Bruce's meal. It wasn't like any curry I'd ever seen: for one thing, you could recognize most of its ingredients. There were pieces of moist, glistening, cooked tomato, silky slices of red onion and plump chunks of chicken, with some odd leaves that were fresh and vivid green and *alive* scattered on top. The smell was thrilling and outrageously seductive. The rice had flecks of red and gold, and even had an aroma of its own. And then there was the soft, buttery naan, something I'd never seen or even heard of before, until I watched Bruce scooping up chunks of chicken with it and popping the whole lot into his mouth.

The first taste changed my palate for ever, awakening new synapses that perceived and tried to make sense of it. I felt like I was suddenly tasting in colour, a realization that everything my nose and mouth had experienced up to that point had been in black and white. I'll never forget the clarity of the enlivening heat, the soothing, sesame comfort of the naan, the different dimensions and layers of flavour I'd previously had absolutely no idea existed. This wasn't just better than Regs's chicken curry: it was better than anything I'd ever eaten before. There could be no going back.

Chicken pathia isn't all that common on the standard roll-call of 'traditional favourites' on curry-house menus. Where it does crop up alongside the chicken, lamb or prawn kormas, Dhansaks, jalfrezis, madrases and vindaloos, it's usually billed as a fairly hot, sweet-and-sour dish made with a lot of onion and fresh tomato, and is Parsi in origin. The one that took my curry virginity fitted this description; challengingly hot, but not painfully so. But I've also seen pathia described as a mild curry. I used to seek it out when I started visiting Indian restaurants regularly. I'd order it whenever I saw it and was always disappointed. It was too sweet, or not hot enough, or didn't have enough tomato or onion. For a few years I believed the New Balaka must simply have made the best curry in the world. But I eventually realized that even if I could taste that same dish again, it wouldn't be as good. You can never have your palate and mind blown simultaneously like that a second time, never re-experience that same awakening.

I had left Barnsley. I was embracing food that was undeniably foreign, distinctly 'other', unlike anything else I'd ever experienced. Little did I know then that this was a love affair that would grow into an obsession, like it had done for thousands of British people before me.

2.

In 2007, for reasons best known to my therapist, I decided to take a barrel of beer to India, by sea. India Pale Ale (IPA) originated as an export beer that was sent by brewers such as Bass from Burton-on-Trent via London or Liverpool, the Canary Islands, the coast of Brazil, the south Atlantic, the Cape of Good Hope and the Indian Ocean, to slake the thirsts of British troops and civilians in the subcontinent. The legend was that the journey conditioned the beer in some way, just like it did with the Madeira wine carried on the same ships, so that when it reached India it still tasted like very, very good beer but also had a quality that was often compared to champagne. When the modern craft-beer industry revived IPA, it celebrated this journey as an essential part of the beer's character, and yet no twenty-first-century craft brewer was doing anything to even emulate it. So I decided to re-create the journey myself, lugging a heavy metal keg full of beer for three months over 18,000 miles of sea voyage.

On the way, I had a lot of time to explore the legend of IPA. Why couldn't they just brew beer in India? How on earth did this journey make economic sense? How did the British drink it when it got there? What were the British doing in India in the first place?

And so I learned about the history of the 'Honourable' East India Company and, following its demise, the Raj. By the time I got off the boat in Mumbai with a heavy rucksack on my back, a suitcase in one hand and a holdall with a keg of beer inside it in the other, $300 poorer after bribing my way out of the port and with very little idea of a plan of what I was going to do now I was here, I was ready to apologize to every Indian I met on behalf of my ancestors.

Fortunately, a beer marketing executive based in Mumbai had been following my adventures on my blog. Ashish Jasuja insisted on looking after me and showing me around Mumbai (he corrected this to 'Bombay' whenever I used the new name), maintained that the unnecessary deaths of 10 million of his countrymen were not my fault because it all happened a long time ago, and introduced me to the kind of Indian food that people eat in India.

In stylish restaurants catering to Mumbai's burgeoning, affluent middle class, and a week later in street cafés in Old Delhi, I tasted recipes that had been handed down through generations. I learned the difference between spiciness and heat, that it's possible to have one without the other, that a dish could be rich, complex and layered with or without the punch of chilli, and I learned the difference between chilli heat and pepper heat.

That first day in Mumbai I was given a fish tikka dish that again reset the bar as the best thing I had ever eaten. Ash called over the waiter.

'What's in this? I have to know, I have to try and re-create it when I get back home.'

'It's our special red masala,' said the waiter.

'It's amazing,' I replied, reaching for my notebook. 'What's in it?'

'Red masala,' said the waiter, smiling broadly, doing the inscrutable head wobble that can be made to mean anything you want it to and can mean different things at the same time to the person doing it and the person they're doing it to. What the head wobble now meant to me, I realized, was that this man was going to tell me absolutely nothing whatsoever about the secret recipe which was his family's livelihood, in the politest way possible.

India made a hypocrite of me. After arguing that it was absolutely fine to muck around with spag bol, I arrived back home yearning for the authentic Indian experience, boring people with pronouncements like, 'Of course, you do realize that vindaloo was originally a Portuguese dish?'

201

and 'It's not just about the degree of heat; vindaloo and madras originate from opposite sides of the subcontinent and have an entirely different base of spices from each other. You can't just turn one into the other by adding more or less chilli.' I told myself that I just wanted the subtlety and complexity I'd tasted in India, but I fear I had become a curry snob.

If I wanted to champion some Platonic ideal of authentic Indian food, it turns out I was kidding myself. The core flavours and styles of what we now consider to be 'Indian' food are an agglomeration of various cuisines in the region, seasoned with significant influences from Europe and South America. Take biryani, for example. This Indian restaurant staple has its roots in the court of the Mughal emperors, who came from Afghanistan and Persia to conquer much of India in the sixteenth century. Feasting was central to their culture, and they gathered cooks from all over the Muslim world, including Turkey, Arabia and Egypt, to bring their influences and dishes to the royal kitchens. Pilau was a delicately flavoured Persian dish that eventually mated with the pungent, spicy rice dishes of Hindustan to create the biryani, just one result of a cultural mash-up of Hindustani, Persian and central Asian cuisines which were quite discrete until the food-loving Mughals brought them together.

In May 1498, six years after Columbus first crossed the Atlantic, three Portuguese ships anchored off the Malabar coast in India after successfully navigating the Cape of Good Hope. Ships following this route would often end up off the coast of Brazil, partly because of the direction of currents in the Atlantic, and partly because, once you get around the bulge of north-west Africa, the Brazilian coast is only a few degrees west of due south rather than being across the wide ocean displayed on many maps. The capsicums and the tomatoes – also native to South America – that they picked up on the way entered into Indian cuisine astonishingly rapidly.

When the British arrived in India a century later, the cuisine they found wouldn't have been as alien to them as you might think. Like Mughlai cuisine, medieval European cookery was also influenced by Arabian cuisine, and both featured ground almonds, lots of spices and sugar, with sweet and savoury flavours mashed together. It's an often-repeated myth that spices in the medieval court were used to disguise the flavour of rancid meat. This is almost certainly inaccurate: the royal court would have had the best, freshest meat and used spices to enhance the flavour of dishes, making them tastier and more interesting rather than to hide the rot. Conversely, those who had to make do with rotting, mouldy food would not have been able to afford spices to mask those flavours. Until the fifteenth century, the Arabs had a monopoly on the spice trade into Europe, which all came through Venice. The daring sea voyages of the Portuguese and, later, Dutch and English fleets, were driven specifically by a desire to break this monopoly. Imagine planning a manned trip to Mars because chilli powder was cheaper there and you have some idea of how important spices were to our diet in the fifteenth and sixteenth centuries.

The British arrived in India seeking consolation after being routed from the Indonesian spice islands by the Dutch. At first, they came as traders but, gradually, the permanent 'factories' they established through which to trade fabrics became cities. The East India Company had its own navy to protect its cargoes from pirates and its own army to protect its settlements. Inevitably, protection turned into territorial expansion, until a private company whose sole legal obligation was to maximize returns for its shareholders somehow ended up ruling almost the entire subcontinent.

The British adventure in India is full of wonder, shameful atrocity and endless contradiction. Some Britons ventured there with the sole intention of asset-stripping what was once a far wealthier country than we were, and succeeded in that. Some were brutal in their oppression of the native population and pretty much invented institutional racism to help them achieve their goals. Others arrived there and fell in love with a culture that was far older than our own and began to mix and match various elements of European and Indian life, bequeathing gingham, bungalows, pyjamas and especially curry to the nation back home.

As the East India Company gradually gained control of the subcontinent, it imposed its will on what had previously been a diverse collection of religious and cultural factions. The British ruled over a greater area than even the Mughals had and, if the East India Company had any principle at its cynical, amoral heart, it was the principle of bureaucracy. It sucked up the different quirks of each region and synthesized them into a new Anglo-Indian sensibility. What had been a diverse range of different cuisines, some vegetarian, some meat-based, some favouring bread and others rice, some spicy, others mild, all went into the cultural blender and came out as something else. Where Indians talked of rogan josh, dopiaza or quarama (which later became korma), the British lumped the whole lot together as 'curry', a word that has several possible antecedents in the subcontinent but is an entirely European invention. The British in India had traditional British dishes served in the centre of the table, with 'curries' served as side dishes to make them more interesting.

If the servants of the East India Company didn't die of malaria or alcoholism, they could make their fortunes in three years. Many of them returned to England, bringing their preferences for Indian food and India Pale Ale back with them, as well as the money to splash out on the best local versions available. The Hindostanee Coffee House – the oldest recorded Indian restaurant in the UK – opened in London in 1809, offering 'Indian dishes, in the highest perfection . . . unequalled to any curries ever made in England' – a claim that implicitly reveals that curries were already widespread in England by that time. By 1852, curry was so popular that one cookbook claimed, '[F]ew dinners are thought complete unless one is on the table'.

With foods like mulligatawny, kedgeree, chutney and coronation chicken, through the Victorian era curry was as British as – well – potatoes, which achieved widespread acceptance on the tables of polite society only at the same time as 'curry' was being cited as an essential dish for a successful dinner party.

Curry, then, is best thought of not as Indian food but as an Anglo-Indian creation. Some see this as a form of cultural appropriation but, catalogued among British crimes against the Indian people, this would have to rank pretty far down a very long list. Like all cuisines, Indian food was continuously evolving long before European ships arrived and has continued to evolve ever since – both for Indians themselves, and for the people who fell in love with their cooking.

3.

After 1945, immigration into Britain expanded dramatically, both in scale and scope. There had long been communities of Germans and European Jews in London's ghettoes but now Britain welcomed people from around the world, particularly from the Commonwealth. Ever since the tall ships of the East India Company began hiring sailors for six-month, one-way journeys and paying them off on London's docks, there had been a South Asian community in London. While there were a few thousand South Asians in Britain in 1945, by 2001 there were more than 2 million.

When the first sizeable influx from the recently partitioned and troubled subcontinent arrived in Britain, rationing was still in force. Sikhs and Hindus were committed to a vegetarian diet, while Muslims required their meat to be halal. The meagre range of groceries available in Britain forced some of these early immigrants to adapt to their new environment: some vegetarians succumbed to eating meat, while some halal-meat eaters turned vegetarian.

By the 1970s, when war in Bangladesh stepped up immigration another gear, there was a big enough population in Britain to support a supply chain that brought in a broader array of vegetables, herbs and spices. Some British Asians opened shops to cater for their growing communities, while others set up importers and wholesalers to supply them. But by this time, a generation of British-Asians had grown up eating quite different food from that which their grandparents had enjoyed. In 2003, Vicky Bhogal, a British Asian, wrote in *Cooking Like Mummyji: Real British Asian Cooking*:

> As this book is specifically about the food we British Asians have grown up eating – and not food from the Indian subcontinent – I found it impossible not to include the variants on English foods our parents invented to make use of the ingredients readily available at the local supermarket.

She goes on to give recipes for everyday Anglo-Indian dishes such as baked beans with spring onion sabji and masala burgers. The first Indian cookbook I ever bought, a 1988 paperback called *An Indian Housewife's Cookbook* by Laxmi Khurana, cheerfully uses ingredients such as bags of frozen peas and tins of tomatoes, because why wouldn't you? Anjum Anand's books include recipes for Gujarati-style chips, Indian shepherd's pie and spicy cheese on toast.

When Vicky Bhogal writes, 'The food eaten in the vast majority of Indian restaurants bears very little resemblance to the food British Asians eat in their homes,' it's easy for the white English foodie reader to conclude that the food in homes like Bhogal's is 'authentic' while the restaurant food the rest of us eat is not. But what she actually means is that Indian food has evolved to fit its new surroundings in restaurants quite differently from how it has in the British-Asian household.

In 1957, the *Guardian* reported on 'the rising popularity of Indian restaurants in Britain'. It said there were 'about a dozen in the Manchester district, at least a hundred in London, and they are spreading over the rest of the country fast'. In part, the paper attributed this rise to the tendency of Indian restaurants to stay open far later than anywhere else. But it wasn't just a matter of convenience: even then, the British yearned for 'astonishing' flavour. Rationing had only recently ended and Indian food opened up new, previously unimagined vistas: 'Subtract the steak and the eggs from the corner café and you are left with chips: Indian restaurants created curries out of everything,' enthused the *Guardian*. The first restaurants were opened by Pakistani seamen, particularly those from the famine-prone region of Sylhet, and they were a welcome boon to their countrymen. But writing ten years after Indian independence, the paper noted that many British people had returned from the subcontinent having become familiar with the food. The author suggested that three quarters of the business of Indian restaurants was already with the English.

The post-colonial aspect of their trade did occasionally flare up into trouble. Allegedly, one old major became upset when the waiter serving him refused to clean his shoes. 'Why am I freer in your country than in my own?' he yelled, perhaps misunderstanding the nature of freedom entirely, as the manager took the waiter into the kitchen to calm him down and the major left with dirty shoes.

In the 1970s, as Bangladesh was ravaged by war, the influx of Sylhetis increased. Britain was still suffering a labour shortage and the government issued work permits which allowed restaurants to bring in curry cooks because, according to the *Caterer* magazine in 1975, it was 'usually hopeless trying to teach British workers how to prepare and cook Asian food'. The number of restaurants which, to gloss over distinctions of post-Partition origin, we might refer to as 'curry houses' rocketed during the 1970s and 1980s, becoming a defining feature of post-pub British life, before levelling off in the 1990s. In 1995, it was estimated that Bangladeshis owned 7,000 of Britain's 8,000 'Indian' restaurants.

The food these places served had its roots not in the Asian immigrant kitchen but in memories of the Raj. From the start, enterprising curry-house owners, who began by setting up in bomb-damaged cafés and serving curry alongside fish and chips, knew what kind of thing had worked in India because their families had spent generations serving these dishes to the occupying British. Their astonishing success showed that it wasn't just in India that the British wanted something spicy. Perhaps influenced by its post-pub popularity, curry for the British was blunter, less subtle, than the cuisine that spawned it. Shorn of the religious or regional detail that had previously kept cuisines separate, and with an ever-growing list of available ingredients, South Asian entrepreneurs looked closely at what worked and tweaked their dishes to appeal to the British palate. In *Spicing Up Britain: The Multicultural History of British Food*, Panikos Panayi wrote:

> Originating in the British colonization of India, the spread of curry in post-war Britain represents an example of the Empire striking back. It has become a type of cult food, taking on a life of its own, quite

distinct from the products eaten by South Asian immigrants in Britain.

While British Asians eat a fusion of what's available here with tastes from home, the rest of us are eating a fusion of what the Raj remembered as tastes from home and what was available in India, brought back here and reinterpreted once more. In a way, curry is British food that has gone abroad, taken on some exotic notes and returned home more than it is the food of India.

The process of evolution has been continuous and shows little sign of stopping. And that's why we have balti.

'I do not know how the Bermuda Triangle got its spooky reputation, I find the Balti Triangle is far more taxing,' wrote restaurant critic and food writer Charles Campion on his first visit to South Birmingham's fabled curry paradise. A few years later, when he decided to initiate me into the twin mysteries of Batham's beer and Brummie balti – each, as far as Charles is concerned, the pinnacle of their art – it seemed that greater familiarity with the route had changed nothing. His satnav would point him in one direction and he'd say, 'Oh no, I really don't think that's right,' and we'd go the other way instead. I swear the recorded female voice saying, 'Recalculating . . .' grew testier and more exasperated each time he did it, and the tension between the two of them began to grow uncomfortable. But we got there eventually, and it was worth the trip.

Now, when it comes to choosing where to go for the typical British curry, I feel almost as if I need to ask Charles's permission. The balti and the chicken tikka masala are two curries that are famous for being relatively recent

Anglo-Indian (or Indo-British?) creations so, for the first one, I suggest to Charles that he might want to accompany me on a trip to Adil's, the restaurant where the first balti was allegedly served in 1977, which is still open in Stoney Lane in the Birmingham suburb of Sparkbrook, the heart of what is now known as the Balti Triangle. Charles loves the idea but, by the time we're in the car to Sparkbrook again, the 'original' has been subtly replaced by 'the best'.

Al Frash translates as 'the butterfly' and is, according to Charles, 'supposed to make us think of delicate flavours'. It sits on Ladypool Road, which runs right through the heart of the Balti Triangle, roughly parallel to Stoney Lane. The road feels instantly cheering. The grey sky, red-brick buildings and grey slate roofs couldn't feel more English, but they've been covered in bright, colourful signs and made to look more exciting and vibrant than those who built these streets could ever have imagined them. In that respect it vaguely reminds me of Brick Lane in London, but really it's quite different. It's impossible to walk down Brick Lane without hawkers trying to drag you into their restaurants. The hardest thing to find there is a restaurant that doesn't claim to have won every curry award going for the last several years, including awards that I can find no mention of anywhere else apart from on the banners hanging in their windows. Gullible visitors can quickly become convinced that every member of the cast of *Goodness Gracious Me* eats in every single one of these restaurants every night of the week. I often hear people say that, if you're in the know, the curries of Brick Lane are actually pretty poor. I don't think they are – the ones I've had are fine – but the experience of eating there is neither the best I've ever had, nor the cheapest, the most enjoyable, the most authentic, nor the most typical of the British experience of eating Indian food. Birmingham's Balti Triangle feels like it might be a better bet.

Al Frash is a modern, stylish space with abstract art on the walls and blue-tinted lights tucked into the ceiling creating a mellow, ambient mood, but the music is familiar and reassuring – the same sweeping strings and washes, the same siren vocal style of Indian restaurant music across the country.

People who are upset by the idea of cuisines adapting to new homes and people who don't like or understand Anglo-Indian food at all can often be heard to say, 'And you know what the word "balti" means? It means bucket! You're eating food out of a bucket!' as if this is in itself some kind of argument against the quality of the food or a demonstration of how far we have defiled authentic Indian cuisine, as if we're no better than livestock feeding from buckets of swill. Such blind prejudice shows a complete ignorance of what a balti is. The pan in which it's served resembles a small, heavy wok. If Hindus do refer to it as a bucket, they clearly have a different idea of how that word is used than we do. It bears no resemblance at all to a garbage receptacle but looks much more similar to cooking pots used in Asia than most serving dishes in a typical Indian restaurant.

I hadn't realized how significant breads were to the balti. When Liz and I visit a typical high-street Indian restaurant, our default is to order plain naan and rice to share, but in different parts of India you tend to find one or the other. The balti restaurant favours bread. While the Al Frash menu caters more than adequately for rice lovers, the breads get much more prominent billing and are traditionally used to scoop up your food.

Our starters arrive with puffy, light mini-chapattis. The mains turn up with a naan bread that's about the same size as a private island owned by Richard Branson. It almost covers the entire table and is called, funnily enough, a 'table naan'.

My balti chicken jalfrezi appears in a half-globe of blackened iron, pockmarked around the edges of the sauce from where the liquid was sizzling against the iron until a few moments ago. With its juicy chunks of chicken, peppers and onions, it really does look fresh compared to the overcooked, dry cubes of meat served in slurry you get in so many restaurant curries. The bread is thin and crisp and somehow draws out a citrusy zest from the balti. Charles's 'Balti Meat' is pure class: just tender, slow-cooked lamb falling apart in its rich gravy.

Watching the four of us tear chunks from our half-acre of bread, I'm struck by how many of our favourite meals boil down to a union of bread and meat. Burgers, kebabs, bacon sandwiches and pepperoni pizzas are all iterations of the same idea, and so is the balti with its Sahara of naan. Bread has always been the staff of life in its many different forms. Along with beer, which also requires the modification of grain before it can be successfully fermented, there's a good argument that bread is the root cause of civilization, of permanent settlements and specialization rather than nomadic subsistence. And meat has always been prized as a superior and not always available source of protein that has greater spiritual significance than other foods, particularly among men, which we can see in everything from ancient sacrifices to the gods through to the manly ritual of the barbecue grill, and statistics which show that men eat an average of 86 grams of red meat a day compared to women, who average 56 grams, and that vegans are twice as likely to identify as female (63 per cent) than male (37 per cent).

Curry goes one step further than the other meat/bread meals in its appeal, by pulling off a perfect union of meat, bread and *gravy*. British curries are wetter than Indian ones and the proportion of sauce to rice or bread tends to be higher. Bread and gravy is the most British thing in the world, and now I remember one of my favourite parts of Sunday roast as a child was mopping the plate dry with a slice of bread, or even getting more gravy to pour on it. Add spices to the gravy – a hint of exoticism – and you're in a whole new world of flavour that's comforting and thrilling at the same time. Modern Anglo-Indian curry was tailor-made to shoot deep into the culinary heart of the British. This is the true Anglicization of curry: wheat and meat, these western staples, pushing rice and vegetables – the cuisine of most of India – into supporting roles.

It's a spectacular meal. As I finally admit defeat against what's left of the table naan and lean back to contemplate a shirt that is now definitely much tighter around the middle than it was a few months ago, I have just one misgiving. It's *too good*. It's not typical of a high-street curry in its quality, composition or character.

We're staying with Charles and his wife, Sylvia, for a few

days. It looks like we're just going to have to go for curry tomorrow night as well. Looking at him now, I realize this is what Charles had in mind all along.

4.

Like most of my friends, I'm now a competent cook who can follow recipes reasonably well, season a dish and spot if something's missing. I doubt I'll ever be able to spontaneously create a recipe from a bunch of random ingredients thrust in my direction, but I know what I'm doing in the kitchen, and Indian food has become my particular obsession. Whenever Liz is stuck for a birthday or Christmas present, she knows that yet another course with an Indian housewife trying to teach me how to cook the perfect rice or make my own naan is always a safe bet. I read and study my Indian cookbooks rather than just following the recipes. I love both the simplicity and the complexity of it, the deep satisfaction of grinding fresh, whole spices and filling the kitchen with their musk, the long, slow courtship of sautéing onions, twenty minutes during which you must simply focus, Zen-like, on the task in hand, until they're almost dissolving and Liz comes into the kitchen and says, 'Wow, this all smells gorgeous. What is it?' and I reply, 'Just onions,' and then the meditative satisfaction of building flavour in layers until, almost regretfully, there's nothing left to do apart from let it simmer.

Of course, cooking Indian recipes from books gets results that are very different from what you're served in a typical curry house in Britain. Most work with huge vats of a few base sauces and, depending on what you order, different vegetables, varying amounts of chilli and a few finishing spices will be added to it. Often when I'm with a group and we all order different things, when our meals arrive they look identical, their ingredients indistinct, varying only in the intensity of their heat.

After spending more years than I care to mention learning tricks and techniques that qualify me as a curry nerd, I often ask myself why I bother going out for a curry at all. My food actually tastes nicer than anything in a typical high-street curry house, as well as being healthier and much cheaper. But all the talk of delicate construction of heat and spice in layers misses the real point of 'going for an Indian'. If someone suggests that we might go for a curry this evening, I immediately begin to fixate upon it. I can't get rid of the craving for sharp, tangy pickles, buttery naan and the mild disappointment of dishes that claim to be vindaloo and never are. There are times when we've decided to go for a curry and then there's a change of plan. When this happens the desire remains stuck, immovable, even if it's several days before the excitement in my stomach and the longing in my brain are finally satisfied.

We arrive around 9 p.m., laughing, a little flushed, after a few beers but still a respectable distance away from being drunk. The music soars and swoops softly in the background. Once again, a new-looking laminate floor and some indecipherable modern art give the curry house the mid-nineties home-improvement-programme feel that so many casual dining places seem to be going mad for in the second decade of the twenty-first century. But this place obviously has a wry sense of humour: behind the bar, one wall is covered in flock wallpaper, serving the same function here as an audio sample of a camera shutter clicking or a rotary telephone ringtone on your smartphone.

Inside the front window are a few plush seats where couples and individuals sit alert, waiting for their take-out orders. They also look a little self-conscious, but then I realize that their heightened awareness is anticipation, because I feel it too. As soon as I catch that first dense whiff of spice from the kitchen and hear the first beat of the tabla, my pulse quickens. All of us here, at this point, are thinking that we're in for a real treat.

Almost everything about the experience of dining in a decent Indian restaurant is elevated above other cuisines in the same price bracket. There are table cloths, thick and white and heavily starched, which are then covered with a smaller, softer central runner, usually a shade of deep crimson or regal purple, laid diagonally to create a diamond. The cutlery is weightier, the napkins of heavy linen. It's the ritual of the place that binds this cuisine to us. Ritual is in the arrival of the menus, and with them the immediate suggestion and acknowledgement of poppadoms and pickles and in the speediness of the drinks order (Cobras all round, obviously). It's in the swift efficiency with which we're swept to our table by one person, handed menus by another and served our beers by a third. It's in every customer in a place like this being addressed as 'Sir' or 'Madam' rather than 'Guys', 'Mate' or 'Buddy'. And I love it.

There's a concern among some that service like this is obsequious and echoes unpalatable aspects of our colonial past. I understand this, and there is an unsavoury tradition of casual racism in the post-pub curry that makes the apocryphal 1957 major and his scuffed shoes seem almost innocent by comparison. But there's nothing wrong with a bit of formality when you're out for a special occasion, so long as you're equally polite and respectful in return. We all have our own hang-ups when it comes to service and etiquette. Mine is that whenever a barman or waiter calls me 'Buddy' I instantly want to punch him in the face really hard. But I deal with it.

The poppadoms and pickles arrive right after the beers, like one hand following the other in a sweeping dance move. One of the most important aspects of a satisfying meal out is the certainty that you couldn't cook a meal like this at home. I may be able to cook tastier, healthier, sub-tler curries than those served to English people in a high-street curry house, but the curry house still wins on the first go because no one I know has one of those revolv-ing, three- or four-dish relish trays that the restaurants have, and half an hour's searching online doesn't come up with anything remotely comparable. Pickles such as these are disappointing if served from anything else; in their proper vessel they seem to heighten the sensory experience of perusing the menu.

The front cover of the menu is another masterclass in subtle seduction. There's a diagonal slash across the mid-dle with the name of the restaurant in it. Above the slash, there's a stylish photo of an enticing array of spices in dif-ferent hues, mortars and pestles, grains, powders and leaves, like you might see on the cover of an upmarket Indian cookbook. Below the slash, a close-up of a juicy, oily chicken curry that makes you want to dig into it lustily. Refinement and naked desire – two fundamental aspects of cuisine which often resolve themselves into a feast or banquet – face each other across the page. I really don't want to, but as I open the menu I know that, for the purpose of my mission, I need to order chicken tikka masala.

Robin Cook's famous speech about chicken tikka masala is often quoted out of context and frequently misunderstood. In 2001, when he was Foreign Secretary, he meditated upon the theme of Britishness, exploring what it meant in the twenty-first century and arguing the case 'why we can be confident about the strength and the future of British identity'. He took immigration, membership of the European Union and the devolution of power – three issues which had been identified as threats to the strength, even the very idea, of British sovereignty – and made a case for how each one would instead 'strengthen and renew British identity'.

On the issue of immigration, he spoke about how '[t]he British are not a race, but a gathering of countless different races and communities, the vast majority of which were not indigenous to these islands,' and argued that the continuation of this enhances British life and British identity rather than diminishing it:

> And it isn't just our economy that has been enriched by the arrival of new communities. Our lifestyles and cultural horizons have also been broadened in the process . . . it reaches into every aspect of our national life. Chicken tikka masala is now a true British national dish, not only because it is the most

popular, but because it is a perfect illustration of the way Britain absorbs and adapts external influences. Chicken tikka is an Indian dish. The masala sauce was added to satisfy the desire of British people to have their meat served in gravy.

The true origin story is murky, but Cook's version is the one most often quoted. Chicken tikka has a long heritage, stretching back to the start of the Mughal Empire, when the first emperor, Babur, was so paranoid about choking on chicken bones that he ordered his chefs to chop meat into bite-sized pieces before cooking it in the tandoor oven.

One version of how tikka got its sauce is that it emerged gradually with the Bangladeshi cooks who arrived in the 1950s and 1960s and adapted their cuisine for a country that has always enjoyed its roast meat with gravy. Ahmed Aslam Ali, who ran the Shish Mahal restaurant in Glasgow, then apparently laid a personal claim to the legend. According to his son, who later took over the restaurant, in the early 1970s a customer complained his chicken tikka was too dry. Ahmed, who was suffering from a stomach ulcer, just happened to be eating a bowl of tomato soup at the time. He added some of his soup and some spices to the tikka, and the dish referred to in the restaurant industry as CTM was born.

The story became so well known that, in 2009, Mohammad Sarwar, Labour MP for Glasgow Govan and the UK's first Muslim MP, tabled an early-day motion in the House of Commons requesting that parliament recognize Glasgow as the home of CTM and support an application for PGI status.

Sarwar's total lack of success in this endeavour hints at CTM's broader origins as well as the difficulty in establishing its true story. Its bastard parentage has been used by some Brits to self-flagellate once again: in 2001, Jonathan Meades argued in *The Times* that, rather than demonstrating multiculturalism, chicken tikka masala was an example of the British facility for reducing all foreign foods to their most unappetizing and inedible form.

So it's rather awkward that the most vociferous objection to Glasgow's claim over CTM comes from India itself. When Zaeemuddin Ahmad, a chef at a Delhi hotel that was established by the last chef of the last Mughal emperor, Bahadur Shah Zafar, heard of Sarwar's attempt to claim the dish, he protested that the recipe had been passed down through the generations in his family: 'Chicken tikka masala is an authentic Mughlai recipe prepared by our forefathers, who were royal chefs in the Mughal period.'

Hemanshu Kumar, the founder of Eating Out in Delhi, a food group which celebrates Delhi's culinary heritage, agreed: 'Patenting the name "chicken tikka masala" is out of the question. It has been prepared in India for generations. You can't patent the name, it's preposterous.'

The plot thickened when American journalist Mark Hay interviewed the late Peter Grove, food historian and founder of National Curry Week, in 2014. 'Along with Iqbal Wahhab [founder of the Cinnamon Club restaurant] . . . I started the urban myth of CTM being tikka with added Campbell's tomato soup and spices for a joke,' he claimed. 'We were continually being asked by journalists from all over the world just what CTM was and they did not seem happy with the truth. I have to admit a couple of bottles of wine urged us on.'

If a restaurant in Glasgow claims to be the location of an event a food writer says he made up, at least one of them must be lying. Either way, those decrying CTM for its lack of authenticity seem to be complaining needlessly. Google 'authentic chicken tikka masala' and you get page after page of recipes, all slightly different, all claiming to be the true, accurate, original version of a dish that has no definitive origin at all. The most likely explanation is that marinated chicken in a rich, creamy sauce is such a damn good idea that it evolved in many different places at different times, adapting to suit local tastes and ingredients wherever it occurred. But the search for authenticity, even where it doesn't exist, shows no sign of abating.

'Authenticity is a big bugbear for us, and for Indian cooking generally,' Iqbal Wahhab told the *Guardian* in 2002. 'In France, no one's conditioned by Escoffier any more, so why are we so concerned that this is how a dish was made 200 years ago by some old git who's been passing the recipe down through one Lucknowi family? People say to me, "Is your food authentic?" And my response is, "Do you mean good?" What does authenticity mean anyway? Flies in your food, cholera, dysentery? It could mean any of those.'

Sitting staring at my menu, I no longer have any idea whether I'm guilty of cultural appropriation, colluding in the destruction of a great culinary tradition or falling for a massive hoax. All I know is that I'm really very hungry.

I've always loved the language of the Indian-restaurant menu. Before choosing, I always make sure to read the 'Chef's Recommendations' or 'House Specialities', to whet my appetite, if nothing else. I always look for the dishes that have the longest descriptions. These are either the ones with the highest margin for the restaurant or those the chef is proudest of. Even if I don't end up ordering one, and I rarely do, simply lingering over the menu is a feast itself. Any one of them is likely to be described as 'an exquisite dish'. The meat they contain is always 'succulent', the spices always 'aromatic' and the sauces 'rich and creamy', 'comforting and warm', or perhaps, in between, 'gently tempered with onions and spices', which invariably makes them 'tantalizing' or 'mouthwatering'. To read the menu in even a half-decent Indian restaurant is the literary equivalent of being given a tender foot massage. No other cuisine sets out its food offering as such elegant courtship.

I decide the chicken tikka masala should be shared by the table and order something else for myself. Business concluded, I take another look around.

On one long table a few yards away another booking has necessitated a slight rearrangement of the furniture and, therefore, an automatic imposition of the otherwise optional service charge. Ten men in their late thirties, all wearing the Saturday-night uniform of long, untucked checked shirts broken up by the occasional fleece, sit nursing their beers. From experience, I recognize them as a stag night for one of their number's second marriage. They've either been clay-pigeon shooting or quad-bike riding this afternoon – or both – before going back to the hotel to get changed before coming out again. Right now, they have the jovial but sedate air of people who have all been in this situation before and have an unspoken agreement that no one is interested in getting too crazy because, if they're honest, none of them was that keen on getting shit-faced, dressing up as comedy koalas and trying to seduce strippers the first time around. As I watch, they give a half-hearted 'Wheeeyyyy . . .' as another round of Cobras arrives on a silver tray, and then get back to their low hubbub of gentle conversation.

As I watch them tear into their naans, share side dishes and pass bowls of pickles and rice, I feel that the communality of this meal – what food studies refer to as 'commensality' – is often overlooked. Are there any other meals in our national cuisine as sociable as this? There's something wonderful about everyone digging in, and that particular phrase feels more apt here than anywhere else, as spoons dive and bread scoops. This is food that brings people together – especially men, who are not as good at being open with each other as women are and need excuses and props. It's not just the willingness of the restaurants to stay open late that makes curry such perfect post-pub food. Sure, the beer drinkers of the 1970s and 1980s may have been attracted initially by the promise of alcohol sales continuing after hours but, when they got here, they found a culture, an atmosphere, a way of eating, that suited them. When Liz and I got married I thought the idea of serving an Indian meal at the wedding reception would have been perfect – what better way to get to know the people you've been seated with than passing and sharing, spooning and tearing dishes of rice and curry and plates of naan and poppadoms? It was only a mutual, back-and-forth roll-call of older family members and relatives who would have been incensed, alarmed, terrified or disgusted by the idea that brought us back from the brink.

Whatever the authenticity or otherwise of the dishes, and whether or not that concept has any meaning or relevance, it's the cultural moment of sharing a curry that makes it so meaningful in a British sense. That's why I come to places like this even when I can cook better (more authentic?) food at home. We need this moment.

How tragic it is then that, just like old-fashioned fish-and-chip shops, we're in danger of losing the Anglo-Indian restaurant.

The generation of Bangladeshis who came to Britain and opened restaurants in the 1970s were fleeing war and famine and searching for a better life for themselves and their families. They succeeded, and their success enabled their children to have higher aspirations. Many descendants of curry-house cooks would rather be doctors, lawyers or bankers than curry cooks.

For those still running the restaurants, this leaves the problem of how to get new staff. The simple solution is to send home for more friends and relatives who can do the job in a way no one born in Britain can. This requires registering for a work permit. For many years, this was a pretty straightforward process, but recently it has become much more difficult, as successive governments seek to appear tough on immigration.

Now, in order to come to Britain, you need to prove that you already have a job. If an employer wants to offer you that job, they must advertise it for twenty-eight days before offering it to you and you must prove that you aren't taking that job from anyone in Britain.

The trouble is, British people tend not to want jobs in curry-house kitchens. In 2011, the Communities Secretary

Eric Pickles – a big fan of curries himself, who believes that 'tikka masala is more British than fish and chips' – announced plans for a 'curry college' that would train British-born people from all backgrounds to cook British curries for British people, but the idea was laughed at so hard by pretty much everyone outside the government that, £1.75 million later, the scheme was quietly shelved.

Nevertheless, the idea that British people rather than Bangladeshis should be cooking in Bangladeshi-owned restaurants is not going away. In late 2015, George Osborne stood up in the House of Commons and said, 'We all enjoy a Great British curry, and what we want is the curry chefs trained here in Britain so we're providing jobs for people here in this country, and that's what our immigration controls provide.' In her long-read article 'Who Killed the Curry House?', written for the *Guardian* in January 2017, Bee Wilson notes the echo in these words of a comedy sketch from the early 1980s. On YouTube, Red Cubed has edited footage of Osborne's speech to fade into the sketch from *Not the Nine o'Clock News* in which a young Rowan Atkinson plays a racist politician telling the 1982 Conservative Party Conference, 'A lot of immigrants are Indians and Pakistanis for instance, and I like curry, I do, but now we've got the recipe, is there really any reason for them to stay?'

This logic takes Robin Cook's assertion of tikka masala as a British dish and twists it to mean the opposite of what Cook intended. The Conservative argument seems to be that, if chicken tikka masala is indeed a British dish, we don't need bloody foreigners to cook it for us. Curry is British; you're not, so bugger off.

Since April 2016, restaurants must pay a £2,000 fee for each skilled labourer they wish to bring into the country, as well as £1,500 for a licence that gives them the privilege to do so; this must be renewed every five years. The applicant must also pay a fee of £1,000 per person and has to guarantee that they will be able to earn at least £29,750 a year, which is well above what even a head chef in a London curry restaurant can earn. The alternative is to hire people without proper work permits, but this has become too risky. The Border Force raids Indian restaurants without warning every week and, for each worker they find without a valid work permit, they fine the restaurant £20,000, effectively closing it down.

There were 14,000 arrests of illegal immigrants in 2015, compared to 7,500 in 2011. James Brokenshire, former Minister for Security and Immigration, stated in a letter to another MP that 'the restaurant industry, like others, needs to move away from an unsustainable reliance on migrant workers'. Why he considered an industry built entirely on the labour and talent of migrant workers to be 'unsustainable' if it continued to rely on migrant workers from the same place, he didn't explain.

This all means that two or three curry restaurants are closing down every week. Brick Lane has lost more than half its curry houses, most of them replaced by the same generic, branded chains that are colonizing high streets, old market squares, Cardiff's Chip Alley and everywhere else. Meanwhile, the government says British people can cook curry instead, but British people don't want to, and the government that claims to want to create British curry jobs for British people has pulled funding from any scheme that attempts to do so. Even if they hadn't done that, whether you're a middle-class food lover or a working-class footie fan out on the lash, let's imagine that the government's scheme of British curry cooked by British people did come to pass: if you wanted a really great Anglo-Asian meal, and you had the choice between having it cooked by Dazza from Kent and Pete from Barnsley, or Shamim and Nayeem from Bangladesh, which would you choose?

Finally, with a flourish and clatter of silver bowls and the show-stopping sizzle of a cast-iron karahi, our food arrives. 'Very hot' dish stands appear and plates are wiped clean and dry as they're placed in front of us. It's like watching a stop-frame animation of a town being built on our virgin-tablecloth territory, new arrivals still appearing long after we thought everything we'd ordered was there and accounted for.

Our lamb kebabs are violently red. Reassuringly, the salad that garnishes them is totally anaemic, which is exactly how it should be: there's no room for natural colours on this table. The chicken tikka masala is . . . *purple*, its violent hue made all the more vivid by a slash of yoghurt across its middle that's so white it hurts my eyes.

I spoon a couple of big chunks on to my plate, along with sauce that's as thick and sluggish as hot tar. The first flavour I get is almonds – all the almonds. I never had this down as a nut curry. It's not inconceivable that a few might be scattered across the top as a garnish, but almond is by far the most dominant flavour. Behind it, there's an intense sweetness. The chicken is as succulent as the menu poet promised and a lot of credit must be given for that. Then there's some nice heat that creeps up at the back of the palate.

But honestly? I can't really bring myself to eat much of it. I can well believe it was made with a can of Campbell's condensed tomato soup. I can't have this buttery, creamy thing as my main course. It would have been too much of a sacrifice, a missed opportunity. I couldn't come to a restaurant that offers all these flavours and wimp out with something so sweet and bland.

No, I'm here for the vindaloo.

Ever since the fiery hit of that first pathia, I've been one of those people who chases the chilli. I love the endorphin rush as it builds on the palate. It brings you into the moment, opening up the synapses and the links between brain and mouth. When I've been lucky enough to taste hot dishes or even chutneys made by an Indian family cook, there's a mastery to the way it builds: a deep, red fruitiness at first, with the suggestion of heat coming afterwards, like a reverse echo that grows louder with each mouthful, building to a slow crescendo. A perfect hot dish is one where the heat is just about becoming unbearable as you clear your plate. A poor one is where there's a one-dimensional flash of chilli heat on the first mouthful, separate and distinct from the rest of the spicing, assaulting the palate with brute force and then going nowhere, developing into nothing else.

This vindaloo is darker and duller than the tikka masala – it would be impossible for it not to be, really. It's muddy in both texture and colour, solemn and broody next to the cartoonish CTM.

Unsurprisingly, here in the Midlands, just like everywhere else, this is not a true vindaloo – there's no interplay of vinegary sharpness and aggressively pungent garlic, no more than there is in any other curry. But on this occasion the fulsome menu description – 'very hot' – is complete and accurate and tells you all you need to know.

I nod approvingly when people around the table ask if it's hot enough, and then again, a few minutes later, when they start asking me if I'm OK. I give a thumbs-up, because I can no longer speak. Charles, who does this kind of thing for a living, calls over one of the waiters giggling at my plight and asks what they think a vindaloo is.

'It's pan number three with extra chillis,' replies the waiter. 'It's not a vindaloo, but it's what British people want vindaloos to be.'

It's a motherfucker is what it is.

'What we eat is medium,' says the waiter. 'Hardly any Asians go above a madras, because it's all about the flavours as well as the heat.'

I nod in agreement and start dribbling from the corners of my mouth because my jaw muscles have gone numb.

For as long as curry restaurants have been a go-to destination after a busy night in the pub – if not longer – the heat of a dish has been another important factor in its close relationship with British ideas about masculinity. Now, seeing the distress I refuse to hide, one of Charles's friends leans over and scoops up a big spoonful of my vindaloo. 'Huh, it's not that hot,' he says, as his eyes bulge and a sheen of sweat breaks out instantly across his bald scalp.

I try to reply but, as I do so, the lava in my mouth burns through the last sinews surrounding it and my jaw falls off, uselessly, and disintegrates as it hits the table. My mouth may have melted, and I may be full, but I want to keep eating. I'm weeping hot tears, because I can't help it. But they're happy tears. Because I'm alive. Everything is opened up. Every sinew is awake. Anything is possible. Apart from losing the ability to speak, or chew, I'm so glad I finally got a vindaloo that's so full on. I shall live to regret this, but it happens so seldom. I really don't care whether this meal is authentic or not. I feel happy and wired, and that's not just the endorphin rush from the capsaicin.

It's not only governmental racism that's hurting the curry house: Wetherspoon's is now the biggest curry-restaurant chain in the UK, and we can heat up a ready-meal at home in minutes. We've adopted and assimilated curry just as much as we did the potato, but I reject any assertion that 'we' somehow ruined authentic Indian food in the process. Once upon a time, we welcomed people to this country and they changed their food to make it more appealing to us, because in its original form it was so different from what we were used to at the time that we would not have eaten it and their businesses would have failed. As we become more familiar with the cuisine and its flavours, our ideas of what 'curry' is are expanding and broadening.

But in an Anglo-Asian curry house we find more than just the food. How the meal is served, the manner in which diners are treated, the way we eat it, all evoke a forgotten memory of meals served as they were before we ended up with our degraded version of service *à la Russe* – the relatively recent principle of a complete plate of food being put in front of you rather than helping yourself from an array of serving dishes. Great houses used to sit down to meals similar to this – they were brought to you and consisted of many different dishes from which you could take a portion and then pass on – and some of them were curries. The working classes never got to experience them, and now they do. And while there might be some misguided worry that we're equating the servers in Indian restaurants now with the servants we had at the height of empire, the children and grandchildren of many of these immigrants are demonstrating a far greater level of social mobility than many of their peers, thanks in no small part to our enduring love for this cuisine.

But as well as linking back to the Georgian or Victorian dinner party, a meal like this also echoes the feasts of the great Mughal emperors. Elements such as biryani have survived intact, albeit customized, over hundreds of years and thousands of miles of displacement. Other elements have been bastardized, but there's a standard of service and opulence – everything from the table cloths to the menu descriptions to the silver serving dishes – that feels more special than any other routine night out.

When you order more than you intended and it's still within your budget and you leave the restaurant with a doggie bag of takeaway foil containers, you're a prince among men – a laddish, working-class phrase that was once popular and is now clichéd. But, here, it feels entirely appropriate. This style of eating evokes the idea of a banquet. Subliminally, thanks to the slow, trance-like rhythm of the music, the cold fizz of the lager, the warm reassurance of the curry, all punctuated by the occasional high notes of chilli or fresh herbs, we think of this whole experience as celebratory even when it's not very good. We are all princes and princesses, even if just for an evening.

There aren't many meals that can make you feel like that.

7.

The Full English

'It takes some skill to spoil a breakfast – even the
English can't do it.'

– John Kenneth Galbraith

1.

'I'm sorry, what did you say?'

'Can I have the full English, please, but with no egg?'

'*No egg?* Did you say, "No egg"?'

'Yes, that's right.'

'You want a *breakfast*, but with *no egg*?'

'Yes.'

'Are you sure?'

'Yes.'

'You realize you can't have any substitutions?'

'No, that's fine. And I'm perfectly happy to pay the full
price for the meal. I just don't really fancy an egg. If you
put one on my plate, I'll leave it and you'll have to throw it
away, and that would be a waste of an egg.'

'You're absolutely sure?'

'Yes.'

'Um . . . would you like scrambled eggs instead?'

About fifteen years ago, I realized that whenever I ate breakfast in a café, B&B or hotel I usually left the fried egg untouched on my plate. It's not that I 'didn't like' eggs – not as such – it's just that this was a hearty meal that I seldom finished, and the rubbery egg, slick and shiny like a murder suspect about to crack, would be the last thing to go. So, not being a fan of needless waste, I began to ask for breakfast with no egg.

I had no idea what I was letting myself in for.

The most common response is denial. The waitress gives a nervous little laugh when taking the order or, if she's from another part of Europe, her native accent suddenly becomes thicker and she starts asking you to repeat things more slowly when, a minute ago, she had no trouble at all with the language. Then, when your plate comes back, the egg is there. Because the egg has to be there. The establishment simply cannot conceive of a world where they serve some people breakfast with no eggs. The fabric of the universe would tear. I simply couldn't have asked for no eggs. She must have imagined it. Even if you see the waitress write, 'No egg!?' on her notepad, the plate usually comes back with eggs – the cook naturally assuming that the new girl must have got it wrong.

More than once in a B&B or hotel, after the order had been submitted the person in charge would come over to the table, introduce themselves and ask, 'Are you the No Egg People?' before nervously enquiring whether there was a problem with anything else about our stay. In one country house hotel, minutes after I'd ordered, the chef stomped angrily out of the kitchen in his greasy whites and asked the waitress something. She pointed at me and they both stared, shocked, before he disappeared back into the kitchen to plate me up an eggless breakfast.

When I ate in cafés, as opposed to hotels and restaurants, I began looking for eggless options in the set breakfasts and discovered that there were none. Anywhere. Go – if you really have to – to Burger King, where you can have an egg muffin, a sausage-and-egg muffin, a bacon-and-egg muffin, or a bacon, sausage and egg muffin. Once, when I was in a rush, I ordered a sausage-and-egg muffin, planning on taking out the egg once I was sitting down, and was told I would have to wait because they'd briefly run out of eggs. Delighted, I said I'd just take the sausage muffin. But they refused and made me wait for the egg so that I could throw it away.

Liz and I have simply given in now. We don't want any trouble. But my friend Chris really doesn't like eggs and, to this day, breakfast for him is a source of anxiety and conflict. We once shared a flat in Battersea and, not long after we moved in, we decided to check out our local café. We went through the usual rigmarole of attempting to convince the staff to serve us breakfast with no eggs and, amid an atmosphere of increasing hostility, we eventually succeeded. But when Chris got his plate it was also missing the slice of fried bread he'd been looking forward to.

'Excuse me, there's no fried slice!' he called over to the kitchen.

The tension that had been building since we first uttered the words 'No egg' reached flashpoint.

'BUT YOU SAID YOU DIDN'T *WANT* AN EGG!' roared the cook.

'I don't. But I do want a fried slice. What's the problem with that?' asked Chris.

The problem, we figured out, is that the speciality of this café was to serve the fried egg on top of the fried slice. The cook could just about cope with the idea of someone sullying his breakfast plate by asking for no egg. But the idea of the fried egg and fried slice being two separate components, able to exist and be enjoyed individually, was too much for him. We were lucky to get out of there without being physically attacked, and never dared go back. We moved out of the area as soon as our lease permitted. I think it was that experience which finally broke my no-egg resistance. Fine, let them throw their precious egg in the bin after they collected my plate. Chris now fights alone, the last man standing in an eggy *Invasion of the Body Snatchers*-style dystopia.

I can't be convinced it's because the nation adores eggs more than any other ingredient. And yet we eat an estimated 35 million eggs in Britain every day. They can't all be being forced on people who don't want them. So why do they dominate the breakfast menu to such an extraordinary extent?

Until the middle of the twentieth century, it was common for households in Britain to keep a few chickens. During the Second World War, animal feed became much scarcer and there was a dramatic reduction in the number of chickens being kept for laying. Numbers took so long to recover that egg rationing stayed in place until 1953. When rationing ended the market failed to pick up – people had got out of the egg habit. So, in 1956, the British government set up the Egg Marketing Board. Over the next few decades, the board ran (with the help of a young advertising executive called Fay Weldon) a multimillion-pound advertising campaign with the strapline 'Go to work on an egg', which ran on TV from 1967 until 1971 and instilled in the British consciousness the facts that eggs were cheap, easy to prepare, infinitely flexible and full of protein. The slogan survived in some form or other until 2007, when British advertising authorities banned it for failing to promote a balanced diet – which may seem a curious decision when the alternative of sugary cereal was being advertised directly to children, but the cereal adverts always said, 'When enjoyed as part of a balanced diet' at the end, which magically stops them from being bad for children, so that's OK.

More than that, eggs have always been important to us. In prehistory, we took them from the nests of the red junglefowl, the wild bird that was later bred and domesticated to give us the chicken. We first domesticated chickens not for their flesh but for their eggs, and for the enormous entertainment of making cockerels fight each other to the death. Throughout history, wherever they've been enjoyed, the male chicken – or 'cock' – has been associated with strength, virility and masculine aggression, while the eggs laid by the female have taken on a vital symbolism. As eggs are so obviously a stage in new life, they've been associated with fertility, rebirth, immortality and even divining the future, for at least as long as chickens have been domesticated. There's a Hindu creation myth that the world itself was born from an egg. Within the Christian tradition eggs are associated with Easter as a symbol of rebirth, with Christ's emergence from the tomb supposedly being like a chick breaking its thin shell, according to certain evangelical corners of the internet. On a practical level, their consumption was forbidden during Lent, so Easter was a time to joyfully reintroduce them to the diet. There's a widespread belief that the word 'Easter' derives from the celebration of a pagan goddess called Ēostre or Ostara, who was associated with both eggs and hares (hence the bunnies), but there's little, if any, evidence of such a deity being worshipped. More likely, the egg as a symbol of new life would always have had great significance around the time of year when the days are getting longer and the sun returns in the east.

Whether or not we solidify our sentiments towards eggs into a coherent religious belief – like so much egg white emerging into corporeality from something runny and transparent – we do all carry these latent feelings around with us. Eggs attained magical symbolism wherever they were produced, independently of anywhere else. Like any other religious or spiritual belief, people only have to think it in large enough numbers for it to become 'true'. So it's tempting to suggest that eggs are such an important breakfast food because each new morning is a sort of rebirth, the bright yellow yolk of a fried egg symbolizing the sun climbing in its pale, greasy sky – at least if you have it 'sunny side up'.

But the more likely answer is their practical usefulness. Mornings are all about speed and eggs are quick and easy to cook in a whole number of different ways. We have settled on fried, poached, scrambled or boiled where breakfast is concerned – the latter even being a breakfast all on its own, or perhaps flanked by a regiment of soldiers.

But still, when you think of the English breakfast it's not

defined by eggs but by their other half: the horse to their carriage, the yin to their yang, the PJ to their Duncan – the Vegetarian Killer.

Pigs have been widely kept throughout Britain since Roman times. The French may refer to us as *les Rosbifs*, but if they were going to be historically accurate, they should be calling us *les Porcbouillis*. Pigs were easier and cheaper to keep than cows because they could be herded in the forests that once covered Britain and fed on acorns to give their flesh a fine flavour. Or if there were no acorns, they could be fed cheaply on refuse rather than needing rich pasture. Pigs were reared throughout the year and slaughtered at the onset of winter, in a festive orgy of eating, slicing, curing and smoking that ensured 'everything except the squeak' was used. Big sides or 'flitches' of ham were smoked and salted, the blood was boiled into black pudding and whatever couldn't be preserved whole was ground and encased in intestines to make sausages. The word 'bacon' originally referred to pork in general but eventually came to be associated specifically with the back or belly of the animal when salted, smoked or both. In *Henry IV, Part 1*, during a robbery Falstaff refers to the villains as 'bacon-fed knaves' and urges them into action with a cry of 'On, bacons, on!' – another example of food being used as a derogatory identifying nickname. Later, pigs such as the Tamworth, Large White and Oxford Sandy and Black were bred to produce superior bacon, all of which made it mystifying to me that we've spent a long time being convinced by supermarkets and advertisers that we should be buying Danish bacon – until I found out why.

Danish bacon imports stretch back to the mid-nineteenth

century. The Danes have long had an efficient, centralized pig-farming industry (today, the number of pigs slaughtered every year is five times higher than the Danish population) and used to export most of it to Germany. After the Germans erected trade barriers in 1879 and then banned imports of live pigs altogether in 1887, the Danes desperately looked for an alternative market and found Britain ready and waiting. Population growth following the Industrial Revolution meant Britain was no longer self-sufficient in food, and urbanization had separated most people from the means to produce their own, so the family pig became a distant memory on the smog-filled city streets. Danish bacon imports made bacon so affordable that a working-class family on average wages could eat it two to three times a week.

And so, bacon and eggs became a British national dish. We've adorned the plate with other stuff, but this is the heart of the great British breakfast, the foundation that gets us through the day.

It is, without doubt, a successful combination. But each works on its own. On one side, you have omelettes and boiled eggs with soldiers. On the other, you have the mighty bacon sandwich – the distillation of the English breakfast, the best thing on the plate, so perfect, so unimpeachable, that it often makes those lists of favourite meals and national icons all on its own.

Ever since Lurpak butter ran an advertising campaign in the noughties that used heroic, hyperbolic language to celebrate home cooking (that used a lot of butter), every two-bit railway-station forecourt franchise has started spewing out posters along the lines of 'There is no morning the bacon roll cannot conquer', like photocopies losing definition with each generation.

It's the combination of simplicity and flavour that makes the bacon roll, sandwich or buttie so perfect. If you can slice bread and fry strips of meat in a pan till they're done to your liking, you can make one of the best meals in the world.

But even the simplest meal can be rendered more complex. In 2007, the Danish Bacon and Meat Council commissioned researchers at Leeds University to work out the formula for the perfect bacon sandwich. The researchers spent more than 1,000 hours testing 700 variants before literally delivering the formula for the one buttie to rule them all. And here it is:

$$N = C + \{fb(cm) \cdot fb(tc)\} + fb(Ts) + fc \cdot ta$$

(where N is force in newtons; C is the breaking strain in newtons of uncooked bacon; fb is the function of the bacon type; cm is the cooking method; tc is the cooking time; Ts is the serving temperature; fc is the function of the condiment or filling effect; and ta is the time taken to insert the condiment or filling).

'We often think that it's the taste and smell of bacon that consumers find most attractive,' said Dr Graham Clayton, who led the research. 'But our research proves that texture and sound is just, if not more, important.'

Fine. But your perfect bacon sandwich might be my idea of hell, with radically different values for tc, fc and especially fb. For example, you might mistakenly believe that bacon should be served crispy or, worse, you might be one of those bizarre freaks who prefers sandwich bacon to be streaky rather than back. But the biggest omission – after all those hours of research – is that the role of the bread hasn't even been considered.

For me, there are two legitimate approaches to the perfect bacon sandwich. Option 1: a soft, fluffy white roll, sliced in half, with two or three rashers of thick-cut smoked back bacon placed in the middle, seasoned generously with brown sauce. The roll doesn't even need to be buttered (sorry, Lurpak) if the bacon has been left pink and pliant rather than burnt to death and the brown sauce has been applied liberally up to and not beyond the point where it will squirt out and run down your fingers when you take a bite. Nothing compares. Nothing could be simpler.

Option 2: still pretty damn fine, is the toasted bacon sandwich, with slices of white bread. This tends to be my modern-day café version, because café bread rolls in London can be disappointing, whereas you know what you're getting with toasted white industrial bread. I suppose the untoasted version is acceptable at a push, if the bread is white and pillowy and the sauce bountiful, but the toasted version is better. The bread should be crispier than the bacon but should still retain a little chewiness.

The fresh, fluffy bacon roll is cheerful and gregarious. The toasted bacon sandwich is somehow a little more thoughtful and serious. And these are the only options you need. Neither option is difficult to achieve even for someone on their first day in the job. There doesn't have to be any complication.

And yet chain cafés still somehow manage to screw it up, because they feel they have to be different, for the sake of it. This is just one example of Britain's food-identity crisis, the sense that anything British must somehow be inferior to something foreign, even when this is evidently not true. At the time of writing, Pret A Manger's 'bacon roll' is in fact a 'bacon brioche', served 'with a dab of unmistakably French butter'. Why would anyone do that? The French don't do bacon rolls. The English do. So who on earth would think a French-style bacon roll would be an improvement on the original, apart from someone who hates this country and everyone who lives in it, possibly including themselves? I have no idea what your issues are, and I wish you well in resolving them, but for all our sakes, don't bring the bacon roll into it.

I always used to think that my ardour for the bacon buttie was in line with that of the nation as a whole. But over recent years I've noticed that they're a bit of a compulsion. When I judge beer and cider competitions we tend to start first thing in the morning, when the palate is still fresh. Sometimes the organizers will put out platters of bacon sandwiches, with bowls of ketchup and brown sauce on the side. The sight of them sends me crazy. I always eat as many as I can, stopping only when I think other people might notice. If I'm travelling mid-morning and I pass a place that looks like it might do a half-decent one, I'll grab one even if I've already had breakfast, even if I'm not remotely hungry, even if my original breakfast was also a bacon roll! Until I started writing this book I had always supposed I just really, really liked bacon sandwiches. And then I remembered something that had been buried away for a very long time.

We never had bacon at home when I was young. If you're eating bacon regularly, you're almost certainly having it for breakfast, which means cooking first thing in the morning, and no one in our house ever did that. Every single morning throughout my childhood was either cereal or toast, eaten alone – except for when we went on holiday.

For most of my childhood my dad worked nights and we didn't see much of him. The regular shift was 10 p.m. till 6 a.m. and, if he could get the overtime, it would be 6 p.m. to 6 a.m. I'd be woken every morning by the sound of Dad's Skoda pulling into the drive at around six twenty and then hear him potter for a bit before getting me up for my paper round at seven. He'd get us ready for school and, once we were out of the door and my mum was at work, he'd go to bed. We'd see him again for about forty-five minutes in the evening, when he got up and ate dinner before going back to work. If he could, he'd work weekends as well, switching to the day shift and doing 10 a.m. till 6 p.m. or, if he could, 10 a.m. to 10 p.m. Somehow, it seemed we always needed the money. But as a kid, it also felt like he didn't really want to be with us. The only time we got to see him properly was on our holidays – but these also stopped some time in my mid-teens, amid excuses that seemed to make sense at the time.

For a few years before then we owned a static caravan at the Lincolnshire coastal resort of Mablethorpe, which is a bit like neighbouring Cleethorpes, only without the glamour. Every morning, around seven o'clock, my dad would wake me just like he did for my paper round, so that we could walk the dog together.* He would wake me as quietly as possible – just me – and we wouldn't speak until we were outside the caravan, so as not to wake my mum or my brother. Even when we were on our way, we still didn't say much. We just

* I won't entertain any lazy, stereotypical jokes about whippets at this juncture. Mitzi was a whippet-Manchester terrier cross, which is entirely different.

walked a mile or so up the beach and got to a little food van just as it was opening up for the day. Dad bought us white, fluffy bacon rolls – the type I still regard as superior today – and Styrofoam cups of tea and we'd walk back down the flat, wet beach, not saying much, just enjoying breakfast and watching the dog on her intrepid adventures.

My dad died when I was twenty-seven. About ten years later, I had one of those rare, lucid dreams where you're clearly inside the dream but you feel fully awake and can act and move freely rather than being controlled by dream logic. I was my grown-up self, wearing the clothes I'd worn that day, and next to me was my dad. He looked to be in his late fifties, around the age he was when he died, but with no signs of illness other than the habitual stoop from his eternally bad back. We were walking down that beach at Mablethorpe with Mitzi at our feet and bacon rolls in our hands. This time, we talked. We talked for a long time.

I said all the things I hadn't been able to say to him as he lay dying, as my mum tearfully begged me to say something, anything, just in case he could still hear us, just in case simply letting him know we were there might give him some comfort. I said everything I couldn't say to him six months previously, when he told me he always guessed the fags would get him eventually but he'd hoped for a few more years. We spoke openly and freely, like mates. We even laughed together, somehow sharing the same understanding, worldview and sense of humour, in a way we never did when he was alive. I could smell the ozone and hear the invisible sea beyond the mist. And I could *taste* the bacon roll.

So yeah, maybe I like bacon rolls a little more than most people.

2.

Last time I was in Amsterdam I decided to go to a café for an 'English breakfast' to see what it was like. I came to regret this decision. They must have seen a photo of a real English breakfast and tried to re-create it from that alone, without any real-life experience of what it entailed, like some kind of Dutch Anglophile cargo cult. It consisted of a large mound of very pink, very cold shavings of streaky bacon, two sinister-looking cocktail sausages, a pulverized fried egg with green bits in it, a quarter of a raw tomato, some mushrooms and half an acre of lukewarm baked beans. We might complain that our curries and spag bol are travesties of the originals, but it works both ways: if this is what our European neighbours think an English breakfast is, no wonder British food has such a dire reputation.

Bacon and eggs (and sausages and black pudding, if you've slaughtered your pig properly) have been *food* since at least Anglo-Saxon times. But they only became breakfast *cuisine* in the nineteenth century. And even more curiously, while bacon and eggs are freely available across Europe, they only became cooked breakfast – in the way we know it – in Britain (and, in the early twentieth century, thanks to a focused advertising campaign, in North America). Cold cuts of ham may be common across Europe, but that's different. And while eggs appear in many Mediterranean breakfast dishes, they manifest in completely different ways. In *The English Breakfast*, Kaori O'Connor suggests that cuisines don't recognize national borders. This is why the continental breakfast is, with a few tweaks here and there, 'continental' rather than simply 'French'. It's why a break-fast dish based on a pan of cooked tomatoes (and sometimes peppers) with eggs cracked into it spreads around the entire coastline of the Mediterranean with minimal variations, even if it's called menemen in Turkey, shakshuka in Tunisia and huevos a la flamenca in Spain. But Britain and Japan, as islands, retain a separateness. The full English breakfast is triumphant at home, a national icon, but it hasn't pros-pered elsewhere in anything like the same form. There are few better examples of the difference between the biological reality of 'food' and the ideological construct of 'cuisine'. The story of how these food items became a national break-fast unique to Britain is one that's linked more directly and explicitly to the definition of our national identity than any meal we've looked at so far.

The traditional full English in all its stodgy glory is today a distinctly working-class meal, associated with labourers eating in 'greasy spoon' cafés, while office workers nibble pastries in continental-style cafés next door. While build-ers and scaffolders are scoffing calorific breakfasts to fuel them for the physical work that lies ahead, washing them down with the beverage middle-class people refer to as 'builder's tea', the office worker is doing something similar with their coffee – stockpiling alertness and mental energy to cope with whatever the day is about to throw at them.

Builders just refer to builder's tea as 'tea'. But middle-class people offer it and ask for it in tones of cheeky irony. By calling it builder's tea, we're acknowledging that we're familiar with and often drink a whole array of different teas, unlike builders, who only drink one kind because that's all they know. But we're also saying that, right now, we're feeling kinda unpretentious and down to earth, just regular guys.

So it's satisfying to discover that of all the different blends of tea available, the full-bodied, black, tea-heavy blend that came to dominate British working-class culture originated in Scotland and found its popularity when Queen Victoria declared it her favourite.

In the eighteenth century, when tea was still an expensive luxury available only to the wealthy, it changed the shape of a typical society day in more ways than one. As well as afternoon tea, some ladies began to hold breakfast parties, offering tea along with bread, butter, jam and, later, two more exotic new imports: coffee and chocolate. This did come with some practical headaches. Great houses would often be very cold overnight and it would take time in the mornings for fires to be lit and for everything to warm up. Butter – another luxury – was therefore often far too cold to spread properly at breakfast. The delightfully sociable solution was to huddle around the freshly lit fire with toasting forks. The German traveller Carl Philip Moritz was thrilled to discover this innovation during a walking tour of England in 1782: 'There is a way of roasting slices of buttered bread before the fire which is incomparable,' he wrote. 'One slice after another is taken and held to the fire with a fork till the butter soaks through the whole pile of slices. This is called toast.'

Before this point, breakfast simply hadn't been a thing. The earliest English cookbooks are full of recipes for large main meals later in the day but offer none for breakfast. It starts to get a few mentions in the fifteenth century but, in 1478, the household ordinances of King Edward IV stipulated that only members of the royal household down to the rank of squire could eat it and, even then, it was a simple affair of bread, cheese and ale, boiled meat or fish and eggs (obviously) on meat-free days. It was essentially a primitive version of the 'continental breakfast' that's still eaten today across the rest of Europe. But in the nineteenth century that would change.

The Industrial Revolution altered the way time was perceived. Work had been tied to the rhythms of nature, happened when things needed doing and largely depended on natural light. The employment of machines meant that people moved from the land to towns and cities and working hours were straightened out and extended.

For centuries, the landed gentry of England had been the voice and tone of the nation. Peasants worked on their land and, between the gentry and the peasants, free yeomen, who enjoyed decent home comforts and perhaps a little land of their own, kept everything running. Food was hearty and unpretentious, the bounty of the land, and therefore an indicator of the status and standards of the gentry who owned that land. The social order of England was fixed, changing little over the years.

Then, suddenly, the peasants were moving off the land and into factories and mills. In towns and cities a new, commercially minded middle class was aspiring to the status of the gentry. The gentry had always been suspicious of cities, especially the capital. Ever since Charles II returned from his exile in the French court of his first cousin Louis XIV, French habits and tastes were slavishly followed by large sections of the nobility. The gentry had always stood for what they regarded as stolid, plain Englishness. Now, with their land emptying and its value falling, the balance of power was moving to the cosmopolitan city. They feared that foreign influences and imported goods – especially foreign food, which was invariably referred to as 'French food', regardless of where it had come from – was threatening the moral fibre of the nation itself. When England lost its American colonies and the French Revolution raged, there arose a nostalgia for a more secure and knowable past, a yearning for tradition – a desire to Take Back Control and Make Britain Great Again, if you can imagine such a thing.

The answer lay in the land itself and in the produce that came from it. Old Anglo-Saxon was regarded as the 'true' version of Englishness – before the Normans came over here and ruined everything – and a huge part of Anglo-Saxon culture had been the notion of feasting and hospitality. Rural landowners welcomed house guests to parties that were several days long and breakfast became a defining feature of these events. French cookbooks were full of recipes for lunch and dinner that had come to dominate upper-class English cuisine too. But as a means of class and national expression, breakfast was virgin territory.

Served between nine and eleven, breakfast was the only meal of the day where people helped themselves, without servants in attendance. Guests were free to stop by whenever they felt like it and it was customary to go out walking or hunting first to work up an appetite. This was the most informal meal of the day. A plethora of hot and cold dishes was arrayed on the sideboard and guests served themselves. They could choose eggs, bacon, sausages, devilled kidneys and fish such as haddock from the hot selection, shored up with ham, tongue, beef and cold roast partridge, pheasant or grouse (when they were in season) from the cold table. Forget the Lurpak ads and their derivatives: this truly was the breakfast of champions – even if, today, we would call it brunch.

Part of the appeal of the great country-house sideboard breakfast was what it said about you if you could attend. The lower and middle classes had to rise early and go to work, grabbing whatever they could along the way. The gentry and their guests were demonstrating that they had the wherewithal to lay on a sumptuous feast first thing in the morning (which, in reality, meant they had servants rising at 5 a.m. to prepare it), as well as the leisure to sit and graze all morning, because there was nothing urgent to be done.

But as the swing towards urbanization continued, for most, this lifestyle couldn't last. As the gentry joined the aspiring urban middle classes in going out to work each morning, a good breakfast was seen as essential preparation for the day. Even in a much-reduced form, both practically and symbolically breakfast echoed the age of the great country houses and became a standard of morally upstanding Englishness. In 1861, the first edition of Isabella Beeton's *Book of Household Management* contained a mere two sentences on the subject of breakfast. The next edition, in 1888, had an entire chapter, including menus and table settings. It was competing against a slew of books full of breakfast recipes, aimed at people who knew they needed to keep up with fashion but had no idea how to prepare a meal that, as far as most were concerned, hadn't really existed a few years before.

The country-house breakfast sideboard survives today, much reduced, as the most expensive and, often, the most disappointing iteration of the English breakfast you're likely to find.

As part of my job, there's rarely a week goes by without my spending at least one night in a hotel or B&B somewhere around the UK. On the morning I'm writing this, I'm in a chain business hotel in a large English city. The restaurant is busy for breakfast and, as is often the case, once I've been seated and asked whether I'd like tea or coffee, I'm invited to help myself to the buffet.

The principle is exactly the same as the Victorian country-house sideboard but the contents are quite different. There are no fish rissoles, kidneys or game pie. There aren't even pears or oranges. There are, of course, little packets of Kellogg's breakfast cereal, pots of fruity yoghurt and a variety of continental pastries. But taking up most of the space is a line of silver tureens and white serving dishes containing the makings of the traditional cooked breakfast.

Sometimes, hotels like this have great reputations. The rooms are stylishly designed and full of plump pillows and pampering toiletries, maybe even fluffy white robes and slippers and the temptation of a well-stocked mini-bar. Other times there are a few teabags and sachets of Nescafé and a kettle that won't fit under the bathroom tap and therefore has to be filled with water one flimsy plastic tumbler at a time. But whatever the rest of the hotel is like, nine times out of ten, the cooked breakfast is remarkably consistent.

Like today, no matter what time you arrive, the tureens and serving plates are almost empty, their puddles of grease reflecting the 'hot' lamps that gaze down like baleful, yellow eyes without actually doing anything. There are a few strips of emaciated bacon flecked with congealed white, greasy water, sweaty sausages with the consistency and mouthfeel of cold mashed potato, rubbery eggs, mushrooms from a tin, hash browns out of a packet from the local branch of Iceland, tomatoes that seem not so much cooked as mummified and baked beans that have simply surrendered. All of it sits waiting, flaccid and melancholic, causing even the hungriest soul to be suddenly struck with an overwhelming sense of ennui. You ask yourself if you can be *bothered* to eat this. Wouldn't it just be less hassle to die of starvation? Why are you even looking at it when, if you were at home today, you'd probably just have yoghurt and fruit and a cup of tea, maybe a slice of toast? And then you remember that, whatever you choose to eat, this breakfast is going to cost you EIGHTEEN FUCKING QUID, so you fill a plate and smother the whole lot in brown sauce to try to make it edible.

This parody of the English breakfast reflects perfectly a peculiar and depressing quirk of British commerce. Business travellers have put up with this soulless version of breakfast for years. And then, in the 1990s, one new hotel chain changed the game. Malmaison, the first British 'design hotel', did something no other mid-market hotel chain had thought of doing for decades: they decided to make everything just a little bit nicer than it absolutely had to be for the prices they were charging. The rooms were stylishly designed, the staff were friendlier, the beds were more comfortable.

And the breakfast was amazing.

Thick, proper butcher's sausages, your choice of fresh eggs, succulent mushrooms and juicy tomatoes, all cooked fresh to order rather than slowly expiring on a lukewarm buffet counter. It was the first time I'd really looked at a cooked hotel breakfast and thought properly about what was on the plate. Until then, sausages had been Wall's bangers, pale and wan, sticky rather than greasy. Bacon was just bacon. Now, each ingredient had a story to tell.

You paid extra for it, of course: the first time I stayed in a Malmaison, around 1995, a typical hotel buffet breakfast was about £8. Malmaison, in line with its superior quality, charged closer to £12. But you didn't mind because the quality was so much better.

Other hotel chains could have reacted to this by looking at their own breakfasts and saying, 'Hmm . . . we really could do better than this. I wonder where the Mal sources its lovely sausages from?' Instead, they seem to have said, 'Hey, Malmaison is charging twelve quid for their breakfast and we're only charging eight. Obviously, our breakfast is awful compared to theirs, so there's no way we could charge the same as them. But we could bump up the price to a tenner without doing anything else and we'd still be cheaper.' So the tide of all breakfast prices rises, brands like Malmaison realize they can charge even more because they're still so much better, the other chains raise their prices to match, and suddenly you're paying nearly twenty quid for a bowl of cornflakes and a cup of tea and breakfast has become the most expensive dish the restaurant serves.

It's a common pattern. Around the same time Malmaison shook up hotel dining, the gastropub arrived in affluent urban areas to give traditional pub grub a kicking. Instead of offering a limp, frozen burger patty served with oven chips for a fiver, the gastropub introduced burgers that were home-made, thick and juicy, with chunky chips that were no doubt hand-cut and triple-fried, served it on a massive white plate with a sprinkle of parsley and charged a tenner. The traditional boozer knew what to do: serve the same old, limp burger and oven chips on a big new white plate with a sprinkle of parsley and put the price up to eight quid.

It doesn't have to be like this. We don't have to sit back and accept it. But in corporate Britain we march in time and force it down, without enthusiasm or enjoyment, never stopping to ask why.

4.

There's no such thing as the full *British* breakfast. While the English have always had a tendency to conflate 'English' and 'British', this is still strange because, by the time the English breakfast came on the scene, England was part of the United Kingdom of Great Britain and Northern Ireland. The cooked breakfast is eaten in every part of the United Kingdom, but the English have always claimed it as theirs alone.

It's therefore unsurprising – and entirely fair – that the

other home nations insist on defining their own specific alternatives to the English breakfast, which are, naturally, very different. All variations tend to have bacon and some other ingredients in common – of course they do – and all must be accompanied by breakfast tea. These are the essentials.

Building on this foundation, the Welsh breakfast takes a creative turn. Tea washes down a plate of bacon, cockles, laverbread and fried bread. Wales has 1,200 miles of coastline and, at its industrial peak, women and children would forage for cockles and laver, a type of seaweed that's boiled and minced to create laverbread, a gooey substance that Richard Burton dubbed 'Welshman's caviar'. This cheap, highly nutritious food was vital sustenance for miners and factory workers in the nineteenth century.

Scotland also enhanced its breakfast by looking to the sea, building a reputation that prompted Samuel Johnson to declare, 'If an epicure could move by a wish in quest of sensual gratification, wherever he had supped, he would breakfast in Scotland.' Ayrshire bacon and Stornoway black pudding gives a solid meaty core, but this is supported by the option of smoked fish such as Finnan haddock or kippered herring, as well as tattie scones, oatcakes and porridge. Scotland's facility with cereals such as oats also helped Stornoway black pudding become widely regarded as the best in the world. In May 2013, it was granted PGI status by the European Union; now, only black pudding made with specific proportions of beef suet, oatmeal, onion and blood on the Isle of Lewis or in the surrounding Stornoway Trust area can be called Stornoway black pudding.

Johnson aside, the Scottish and Welsh breakfasts really don't get the recognition they deserve as entities in their own right rather than slight variations on the English breakfast. But they each get a lot more than the poor old Ulster fry.

If you don't know Northern Ireland well, it's impossible to appreciate just how widespread the effect of the conflict known so euphemistically as 'The Troubles' was. Fear, suspicion and division affected every aspect of daily life, from the brand of crisps you bought to whether it was a good idea to go to the pub or not. To the outside world, the conflict was Northern Ireland's identity, and in England we rarely heard anything else about the place or its people.

Now, twenty years after the Good Friday Agreement came into effect, Northern Ireland is finding its voice and flexing its muscles. I first became aware of it while judging the Great Taste Awards and learning that a disproportionate number of the ciders we blind-tasted and gave the highest marks to were from Northern Irish producers. I then learned that their fellow butchers and bakers were sweeping the board too. I ended up touring the province for a long weekend, during which I ate and drink so much wonderful stuff I started to answer to the name Mr Creosote.

The Ulster fry at Newforge House, County Armagh, is considered to be the best in Northern Ireland. When I was staying here after visiting the cider-makers I had to leave for the airport before breakfast was served, and I wouldn't have been able to touch it anyway because dinner the night before had ensured I didn't feel hungry again until the following Wednesday. So I've come back again specially to try it.

The composition of the plate is visually stunning, so elegant you have to do a double-take to check that this really is a fried breakfast. That might make it sound pretentious, but it's beauty is its simple elegance. A single thick-cut rasher of back bacon and a fat pork sausage lie spooning each other, like giant, meaty quotation marks, at the top of my plate – at twelve o'clock from where I'm sitting. Between two and six o'clock a soda farl, a Scotch pancake and a slice of potato bread lie fanned like a magician's cards. A perfect poached egg, fluffy like a dollop of freshly made cream cheese, glows at seven o'clock and completing the clock face are two elegant discs of black and white pudding. Three roasted cherry tomatoes, still on the vine, sit on top of this, a concession to vegetables that's little more than a garnish.

As I'm photographing my breakfast and scribbling notes, the Irish brewers I'm breakfasting with nod at their plates approvingly. Then one of them leans over to me and says in a low voice, 'I hear the English have beans on their breakfasts. What's going on there? And sometimes even *mushrooms*?' I nod, suddenly apologetic, as he stares back at his plate, trying to imagine such horrors upon it.

John Mathers is the owner of Newforge House and the creator of our breakfast. I'm sure he could afford to hire a talented cook but breakfast is the signature of the place and he loves doing it himself.

'It's straightforward, really, it's just about good ingredients,' he says. 'Take sausages. I don't want a silly sausage, just pork – nicely spiced, but simple. I do one slice of bacon, but there's no rubbish in it, no injections, so it crisps up nicely. If it's this good, you don't need more than one slice. Then there's the black pudding, which should be dry and spicy but not crumbly. But in Northern Ireland it's all about the breads. There's a great tradition of non-yeast baking here. I get my breads from a local bakery, lightly butter them and fry them in a dry pan. We have our own chickens and we offer a choice of scrambled or poached eggs. I prefer poached, because it gives you a bit of sauce. The only controversial thing for me is you've got tomato, but you've got to be healthy.'

John leaves us to enjoy our food. The potato bread is smooth, creamy and addictive. The bacon tastes of bacon or, rather, like bacon used to taste. It's the taste of bacon at Mablethorpe in 1981, a taste that's missing from all the bacon sandwiches I now compulsively eat. The sausage is juicy and sweet. The white pudding is grainy and surprisingly light. It's a substantial plate of food, but one that encourages you to finish it in business-like fashion. When I do, I feel full, but not bloated.

'It's good, but it's not rarefied,' says John, as he scoops up our empty plates. 'People call the Ulster fry a heart attack on a plate, but it doesn't have to be. Only if it's bad.'

John's Ulster fry, as well as Stornoway black pudding, smoked Finnan haddock and Welsh cockles and laverbread, show that the cooked breakfast has always been about making the best of what's available nearby. The cooked breakfast can be a celebration of local produce and it can be a really good-quality meal. This is not a gentrified breakfast or a breakfast done 'with a twist' – no builder would turn up his nose at this plate of food and think it pretentious. It's just really well done, like the Malmaison breakfast, better than it absolutely needs to be but exactly as good as it should be.

Back in my days working in advertising, I spent a few years at an agency in Dean Street, in the heart of Soho. It was a work-hard, play-hard culture, if your idea of play was to go out drinking until the small hours with people you've already spent all day with and stay awake by doing fat lines of cocaine in the toilets. There was a macho culture of presenteeism, where the person who spent the longest time in the office was obviously the best at their job, and anyone who left before 8 p.m. was greeted with a chorus of 'Cheers, mate! Thanks for popping in.' It wasn't unusual to spend eighty hours a week in a building that had no air conditioning and where, if you left the windows open all night, in the morning your desk would be covered by a fine layer of what looked like soot.

Breakfast was provided courtesy of the agency – each floor had a tiny kitchen with a kettle and a toaster, and cheap teabags, white bread, margarine and Nutella. With a sandwich from a nearby shop at lunchtime and pizza ordered in when we worked past 9 p.m., it was often possible to eat every single meal at your desk for almost a week.

Sometimes, shooting out of the Tube into the insanity of Oxford Street at 7.30 a.m., having got home at midnight the night before, I would fantasize about spending a day's holiday (or 'annual leave', as office workers are now supposed to call it, as if they're in the army or something) taking my usual Tube into town and, instead of going to the office, buying a paper and sitting by the window in a greasy-spoon café, eating breakfast and just watching people barge their way to work. I'd wonder about their stories, study their expressions and congratulate myself on being outside their world, even if just for a day. Then, as the pace slackened, when everyone was at their desks I'd lean back, stretch and plan a day of walking around the city, visiting museums and galleries. Or something. Anything that provided the greatest contrast I could find to sitting in that office for fourteen hours.

I never did this – not once in the twelve years I worked full time in central London offices. I suppose, when I did take holiday days, Soho was the last place I wanted to be. I began working freelance in 2003, gradually shifting the weight of my career from advertising to writing. I write full time these days, but I've still never lived out my rush-hour greasy-spoon fantasy. Now, I have to do it. I have to go to a greasy spoon in Soho and enjoy a leisurely breakfast. It's essential work.

The 'greasy spoon' is much loved, especially by the kind of people who drink 'builder's tea'. It's as much a part of our urban fabric as the chippie, curry house or backstreet boozer. In the 1950s, young people began leaving home to find clerical work in cities and would often live in bedsits without the means or knowledge to cook for themselves. Soho in particular was renowned for its bedsit culture and the streets teemed with cheap cafés to cater for it.

Once meant in a derogatory way, the term 'greasy spoon', since the kind of café it applies to has started disappearing in the face of soaring rents and chain brand dominance, has been repurposed as a term of affection. Across class barriers, fans who don't perhaps fit the typical profile of the clientele seem all the more passionate, adoring these places for their architecture, decor and atmosphere as much as the food, and for the unchanging routine they represent, the idea of time out from an increasingly hectic world. The Formica tables, plastic bottles of ketchup and brown sauce, salt and pepper shakers and Pyrex cups and saucers keep alive a mid-twentieth-century image of a Britain that's as comforting to us today as the ideal of the country-house breakfast was to the nineteenth-century middle classes. There's been a spate of lovingly written and photographed guides to old-school cafés and many of them mention the Star Café in Soho as a perfect example. Just around the corner from my old work, it's the obvious choice for my archetypal full English breakfast.

The Star has a reputation for being patronized by film people, including the director Mike Leigh, and as well as the usual set breakfasts it has a massive breakfast known as 'The Terminator'. A good greasy spoon invariably acquires regulars, just like a pub, and some of them pass into the folklore of the establishment. These are people with sufficient status to ask for something special, whose individual creations are not only tolerated but celebrated. Usually, the named breakfast will be a tribute to a superhuman appetite: Jim's Special or Bill's Big Breakfast usually entails at least two of everything.

But not always.

The Star's menu includes the Tim Mellors Special. Tim Mellors was the creative director at the ad agency around the corner when I worked there. While I was dreaming of my stolen morning watching the world go by, he was in here so often he had his favourite option named after him. The Tim Mellors Special is in fact the Star's name for smoked salmon and scrambled eggs. Discovering that my former boss was a regular at a greasy-spoon café, keeping it real with the man in the street, but insisted on having smoked salmon and scrambled eggs when he got there, says more about the advertising industry in the 1990s than all the drugs, shit designer clothes and Conran restaurants put together.

Almost twenty years after I last worked with its favoured patron, the Star Café doesn't seem to be where it's supposed to be. I find the street no problem, but one side of it and most of the middle has disappeared into a large hole. Walking down the narrow gap left by the hoardings for the interminable Crossrail project, I turn and retrace my steps. There's obviously no café along this street. I check the street numbers and, when I find 22 Great Chapel Street, I'm saddened but not surprised to discover that what was until recently the Star Café is now the London Gin Club. There's still a pub-style hanging sign above the door with a Christmas-like star and the words 'established 1933', but there's no other evidence that the Star Café was ever here.

Later, I learn that the Soho Gin Club was founded by Julia, daughter of the Star's owner, Mario Forte. The Star was founded by Mario's father in 1933, and Mario worked there from 1958 until he passed away in 2014, when he was sent off with a star-studded Soho funeral. Mario's final years were blighted by the Crossrail project, which he claimed resulted in a 40 per cent drop in trade. 'I don't know how long we'll be able to continue,' he said shortly before he died. Julia had launched The Star at Night, a bar upstairs from the café, in the evenings eleven years previously. It makes grim sense that this would be the business to carry on following Mario's passing.

Thankfully, a short bus ride across town, Andrew's Café at the bottom of Gray's Inn Road is still very much open for business. It's one of three businesses occupying the ground floor of an elegant but shabby 1920s building, the other two being a gift card and printer's shop and a twenty-four-hour grocery. The building is overshadowed by its more imposing neighbours, and just up the road is the Pentagon-like mass of ITV and Channel 4's main offices and studios. Andrew's is famous for counting most of the Channel 4 news team among its regulars, as well as celebrities such as Nigella Lawson and David Walliams.

Inside, the rippled wallpaper seems to retain the memory of decades of nicotine stains. It's plastered with theatre posters and artful photography of London buses and taxis. Formica-topped tables and chairs with red-padded vinyl seats are welcoming and reassuring. There's no irony here, no self-mythologizing. It feels like it hasn't changed since the eponymous Andrew and his brother Lorenzo opened the place in the 1950s. Like Mario Forte's father and many other entrepreneurs who founded the best of these restaurants, Andrew and Lorenzo were first-generation immigrants from Italy. Opening and working in a restaurant is a relatively easy thing to do for immigrants in a new country, and the Italians were followed by Greeks, Turks and, more recently, Eastern Europeans. The great English breakfast in the celebrated greasy-spoon café is largely the work of 'foreigners' and their children.

Like any legendary café, Andrew's walls boast photos of its famous clientele. But when I look closer, Jon Snow and

Krishnan Guru-Murthy don't look as happy in the pictures as you might expect. I look closer. These press clippings aren't celebrating the cafe and its patrons. They're part of a campaign to try to save it from destruction.

The owners of the land want to tear down everything but the façade of this old building and replace it with a much bigger modern complex that will comprise 60,000 square feet of office space, 6,000 square feet of retail space and 15 residential apartments. The café's current owner, Erdogan Garip, who took over from Andrew in 2003, has organized a petition against the development, which, thanks to his famous customers, garnered widespread press coverage. But at the time of writing, despite this petition, as well as strong objections from Historic England and a grassroots campaign from local residents, Camden Council approved the development plans for this astonishingly ugly and, residents argue, entirely unnecessary development.

A spokesman for developers Dukelease claims, 'The development is focused on providing flexible space and we do envisage that there will be a café or restaurant included in the proposals. However, our plans haven't yet been considered by Camden and rental levels are therefore still to be determined.' In other words, by the time you read this, Andrew's will probably have been replaced by yet another branch of Costa Coffee.

I've always felt more at home in a greasy spoon than I do in a Costa or a Starbucks. I love the sounds of classic-hits radio stations playing over tinny speakers quietly enough so that everyone can still hear themselves speak and the surgically filleted copies of the *Sun* and the *Star* lying draped across tables and chairs. If I'm in a place like this early in the morning, every single customer will be male. Apart from me, they'll all have close-cropped hair and will be wearing jeans, sweatshirts and hoodies. Some of them will sport hi-vis bibs, while others will have slung theirs, along with their hard hats, across the backs of chairs or on the floor beneath the tables. They sit, and read, and eat, with an air of solemnity that always surprises me. These are the lads who are stereotyped in popular culture as wolf-whistling, cat-calling boors when they're up on the scaffolding. But here in the café, they speak softly and are almost ostentatiously polite to the heavy-accented Turkish or Eastern European women serving their meals. When one of the younger guys attempts a bit of levity, he'll be gently but firmly silenced by one of the older men. This is a time for preparing for the day ahead. This is breakfast as sacrament.

Andrew's is open all day, and does roast dinners for £5.90, fresh, filled rolls for less than half the price of their cellophane-wrapped, factory-produced counterparts in big chains and jacket potatoes for under a fiver. A blackboard on one wall offers syrup pudding, sultana pudding, apple pie, cherry pie, jam roll served with custard or ice cream and – on Thursdays only – apple crumble. But the breakfasts are the star, dominating the huge blackboard above the counter. The available options cover most of the board with dense writing that looks more like the workings of a Nobel physicist than a restaurant menu but, to the trained eye, it's fairly navigable.

There are four main set breakfasts. Set One consists of egg, bacon, sausage, baked beans or tomato, two slices of toast or bread and tea or coffee for £5.20. Set Two removes the option of baked beans – you're only allowed tomato – and otherwise differs from Set One only in that it also has mushrooms, and for that it's 70 pence more expensive. Set Three goes the other way, getting rid of the tomato and switching out the mushrooms for chips, while Set Four tears up convention and freestyles, controversially opting for two eggs instead of one, allowing you mushrooms *and* baked beans, adding black pudding and swapping the toast for a fried slice. The extra egg comes at an extra cost – Set Four is £6.50.

These may be the chosen sets. But none of them, as far as Andrews is concerned, counts as the full English. Maybe they are *a* full English but they're not *the* full English, which has its own separate listing. The same price as Set Four, you get hash browns, mushrooms and beans shoring up the core, and we're back to two slices of toast or bread.

As if that's not enough to choose from, there's also 'Andrew's Breakfast', which loses the hash brown from the full English and adds an extra egg and an extra sausage.

To any of these you can add extra items: £1.50 for extra bacon or sausage, or £1 for extra anything else. But you are rewarded for staying within the prescribed sets. Upgrade from one set to the next and you pay an extra 60 pence or 70 pence. Go off piste, and it'll cost you at least £1 extra. There are also two vegetarian set breakfasts and a series of 'toast combinations'. These are clearly aimed at the gullible: Baked Beans on 2 Toast costs £2.70, but '2 Toast' on its own is 90 pence, and baked beans as an extra is, as we've established, £1. I wasn't born yesterday.

To the uninitiated, the menu is a work of daunting

complexity in the guise of simple, honest food. Why and how do cafés go to such extraordinary bureaucratic lengths? The answer, as I discovered when I started talking to people about whether an egg was necessary or obligatory, and about whether mushrooms or beans had any rightful place on a breakfast plate, is the simple truth that everyone has their own favourite breakfast items, and that these preferences are hard-wired. This, remember, began life as a meal where people served themselves from platters on a sideboard. Even if we're unaware of the history of the great country-house breakfast, its legacy means the modern greasy spoon needs to offer as much choice – or illusion of choice – as possible. And from the café's perspective, it needs to do so while minimizing the dreaded possibility of customer substitutions.

If you're some noob who orders Set One and asks if you can have mushrooms instead of the sausage, you have no idea of the forces you are playing with. You might think it's a straightforward request. You might even think you're being helpful by saying you don't mind paying the full price for Set One even though, according to the extras list, mushrooms are 50 pence cheaper than the sausage. But you're ruining everything. The café has gone to Herculean lengths to create its own permutations, which will vary slightly from those offered by any other café, if you look closely enough. The establishment has exhausted itself working out the Byzantine economics of Sets, Deals and Extras. Don't believe me? Think it's simple? OK, come on, let's look at this menu in a little more detail.

Close scrutiny of the various boards and menus at Andrew's reveals that they have a total of thirteen different ingredients that they use across all their breakfasts. They are: egg, bacon, sausage, beans, mushrooms, black pudding, hash brown, chips, tomato, fried slice, bubble and squeak, onions and burger. Is a burger a legitimate breakfast item? As for chips, we'll deal with those later. But we are where we are, in Andrew's, and we're playing by Andrew's rules.

Each of the set breakfasts consists of five or six of these ingredients, which seems like a reasonable number. So how do you work out what to put on each plate? Well, the number of potential different five-ingredient breakfasts that can be made from a list of thirteen ingredients can be calculated using the mathematical formula for combinations. For a set S, where the number of possible breakfast elements is expressed as n, and the subset – the number of ingredients on our breakfast plate – is k, we can work out how many different five-item breakfasts it's possible to create by using the formula:

$$\left(\frac{n}{k}\right) = \frac{n(n-1)\cdots(n-k+1)}{k(k-1)\cdots1}$$

This may look complicated, but it's a neater way of writing down what you actually have to do to work out the answer, which – with thirteen possible ingredients going on to a five-item plate – is:

$$\frac{13 \times 12 \times 11 \times 10 \times 9}{5 \times 4 \times 3 \times 2 \times 1}$$

This works out as:

$$\frac{154,440}{120}$$

which gives you a possible 1,287 different five-ingredient set-breakfast combinations from those seemingly harmless thirteen ingredients. That means you could have a different breakfast every single day for over three and a half years and still not quite get through them all.

This is before you even get into multiples of each individual ingredient or consider that there's another big number of possible six- or seven-ingredient breakfasts (1,716 each) to throw into the mix.

And so, finally, I have my answer to why eggs are so ubiquitous. Forget convenience. Forget religious symbolism. If you simply decree that every single five-ingredient breakfast must contain a fried egg, at a stroke you reduce the number of possible combinations from 1,287 to (roughly, give or take) 495 – less than one and a half years' worth of different breakfast combos.

Problem solved. But this is only the first level of complexity, just one portion of the necessary maths. To run a successful business, you need to consider that not all these ingredients cost the same to buy, so you would need to somehow give each combination a profit weighting, which would also be influenced by the popularity of each ingredient, the economies of scale in which it can be ordered and the likelihood of wastage. To get all of this down to a list of four of five different sets, with the odd personalized special thrown in, involves a complex web of invisible, delicate golden threads. When you *dare* to ask to substitute even mushrooms for beans, because you're one of those people who doesn't really like mushrooms because they're a bit slimy, you might think you're substituting one vegetable for another, a simple operation because both are on the same stove top and both are the same price on the extras menu. You fool! Don't you realize you're upsetting the balance of the universe itself?

And to think I used to assume it was just because the waitress didn't want to complicate her order pad or the cook was lazy.

Of course, you're now thinking that it would all be much easier if restaurants like Andrew's simply listed all possible breakfast ingredients and assigned a price to each individually so you could build your own breakfast. Well, it's funny you should say that. Because, aside from all the combinations on the boards above the counter, on another wall Andrew's boldly innovates with its All Day Choice Breakfasts menu. Twelve separate ingredients are listed (if you want a fried slice with your All Day Choice Breakfast, you can forget it, but this is where the burger makes its entrance) and you can select any two of these for £2.60. You can then add more ingredients and the total price goes up. I try to fathom how this has been worked out, what the economics are, and quickly realize I need to plot it as a graph to make sense of it.

Chart One shows what seems to be a roughly linear and commonsensical progression: the more items you have, the more your breakfast costs. But look more closely and the relationship isn't as linear as it seems. To make this clearer, I crunched the numbers to show the additional cost of each ingredient added.

Chart Two shows that it costs 70 pence to add a third item, then 90 pence to add a fourth. As we've established,

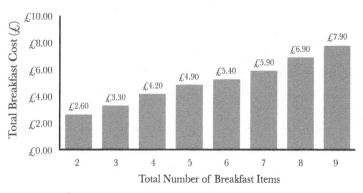

Chart One: Total Breakfast Cost by Total Number of Items

four-ingredient breakfasts are terrifying, so you're then financially incentivized to add a fifth, sixth and seventh ingredient, before being punished for getting greedy.

We can therefore now use this data to work out the best breakfast deal when building your own by working out the average cost per item at each level.

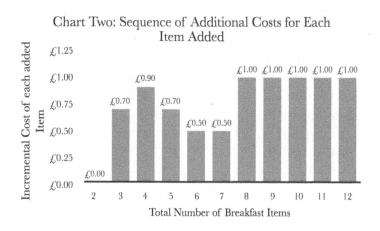

Chart Two: Sequence of Additional Costs for Each Item Added

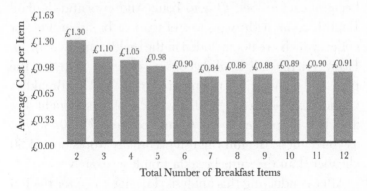

Chart Three: Average Cost Per Item by Total Number of Items

As fans of Chart One will have realized already, Chart Three confirms that the two-item breakfast is a complete rip-off. But who orders a two-item breakfast anyway? If you do, you deserve what you get. The economics gradually improve, but not in a totally linear way, until the value peaks at a seven-item breakfast, which costs just 84 pence per ingredient, compared with £1.30 per ingredient for the two-item breakfast. The greediness tax of £1 for each additional item then kicks in, but such is the improvement in value leading up to seven, and because you're progressively dividing the additional cost per ingredient between an ever-greater total number of ingredients to get the average, even when you get up to twelve the price per ingredient has only reached the same level it was at six.

I'm sure you're now thinking, 'Well, this is compelling stuff, Pete, but I'm dying to know – how does this build-your-own scenario compare with the value of the set breakfasts? As established, well-worn combinations, are they financially incentivized?'

I'm glad you asked. A direct comparison is difficult because each of Sets One to Four, Andrew's and the Full English come with two slices of toast or bread and tea or coffee, which are not included in the build-your-own menu. However: the full English consists of seven items on the plate and it costs £6.50, compared to an All Day Breakfast Choice seven-item at £5.90. Two slices of toast bought separately is 90 pence. Tea is £1 and coffee is £1.50. So yes, as you'd guess, the full English eventually works out £1.30 cheaper than the same breakfast built separately.

After conducting this analysis, I decide to go for the full English breakfast. I was always going to anyway.

Like every breakfast, bacon and eggs are at its heart. The sausage in addition to the bacon makes it luxurious, while the mushrooms – which appeared on the working-class breakfast plate only in the late twentieth century, when dedicated farming made them more affordable – give the whole plate a healthier hue. I enjoy the crunch of a cheap, nasty hash brown, the American import that gives the plate a cosmopolitan air. And the baked beans give it its conversation points: we call them baked when in fact they are stewed and, while we now think of them as the most mundane workers' café staple, when they were first imported from the United States they were a luxury item, available only from Fortnum & Mason until the end of the 1920s.

Andrew's full English appeals because of what's *not* on the plate as well as what is. I like the idea of tomatoes with breakfast, but they only ever seem to be half cooked unless you get a posh version with juicy, sweet, bursting, baked cherry tomatoes. I'm not over-fond of black pudding, and

I've yet to find bubble and squeak in a café that's anywhere near as good as what Liz makes at home.

And then there are chips.

The addition of chips to the roster of acceptable ingredients for a full English breakfast troubles me. It's a southern thing. In the north, we love chips more than anything, but there's something vulgar about adding them to the breakfast plate. It's like having dessert before the main course, or pouring gravy on a cheese sandwich. Justine, one of my closest friends, doesn't eat chips very often and isn't even from the north, but she encapsulated my unease perfectly when we were discussing the issue and she said, 'But if you have chips with breakfast, what are you going to have for the rest of the day?'

Exactly.

I order at the counter, find an empty table and sit down. Seconds later, a waitress places a mug of tea on the table in front of me. It's served exactly as it should be, milk already in, teabag still in the bottom of the mug, leaning against the bowl of a teaspoon, like a happy drunk against a lamp post. The tea is the colour of He-Man's skin, already so dark and tannic the spoon seems capable of standing upright, given a bit of encouragement. A minute later, my '2 Toast' arrive, white bread gently browned and crisped, the crusts still soft, the margarine melted and fully absorbed, a light golden haze in the middle of the lightly tanned bread.

The main meal arrives just as I'm starting to wonder if I'll need more toast. It's presented on a white oval plate – the specialist equipment you only get in cafés like this. The surface area is undoubtedly greater than that of a standard dinner plate but the only way everything can be fitted on is by piling it up. Dominating the east wing of the plate, about a quarter of the total area, is a reservoir of baked beans. A single sausage, glistening brown, has been deployed as a makeshift dam to keep some room for other ingredients, but it's only half as long as it needs to be and the beans seep around its edges. To the south they pour into a mountain of fried mushrooms, halved vertically through their stem and then sliced chunkily to form a pile of thick 'J' and 'L' shapes which here and there sport the tan of caramelization rather than simply the slickness of sautéing. Two crispy hash browns dominate the west side of the plate, half obscuring a fried egg whose yolk peeks out from under the potato, squished slightly by its weight, without quite breaking. The yolk is adroitly cooked, a compromise between two schools of thought on the perfect fried egg: the outer edges are cataract-misted by the fat, the centre still shining bright yellow, ready for piercing and dipping. There's no room left for the bacon, so two rashers are laid like extra blankets atop the northernmost hash brown, putting further gentle pressure on the egg. The bacon, too, is perfectly judged – the edges crispy, the start of some browning on the flesh, but still succulent and juicy.

And it tastes exactly how I wanted it to taste. It's good. It's not outstanding. Erdogan Garip was not down at Smithfield Market this morning sourcing these ingredients directly from celebrated livestock farmers, and rightly so. I strongly suspect that the beans are Heinz and the hash browns were in a frozen packet until ten minutes ago. That's exactly what we want from this meal. Churches don't use Château Margaux and artisanal sourdough for their sacrament of communion, and neither does the English café. The mushrooms taste like mushrooms and the bacon is a bit salty and has some body to it. The baked beans are sweet and the hash browns are hot and soothing like baby food inside their crispy crunch. The sausage has the deep satisfaction that you get from a bit of filler along with the meat, the kind that, if you grew up eating them, means that you can only ever admire a free-range, rare-breed 95 per cent meat sausage rather than truly loving it.

What do you mean, 'What about the egg?'

It's a fried egg. Fried eggs are all the same. I wish I'd dared ask for poached. But that would have been too posh and would have spoiled everything.

Andrew's full English breakfast is no better and no worse than I'd expect from an authentic café with a good reputation. It's honest, reasonably priced and hasn't been mucked about with. It's not Newforge House, nor even Malmaison. So why do all these celebrities come here to eat? The workers come looking for calories to fuel them through the day, but the newsreaders? The old lady with her granddaughter at the next table? *Nigella bloody Lawson?* They're here for something else. They're looking for simplicity, satisfaction and a connection to something bigger, something real. As sales of bacon and sausages plummet in value every year thanks to misguided and misleading scare stories about cancer, and while 'developers' destroy our culture and replace it with monotone corporate brown, eating here is a political act.

Andrew's will serve you breakfast at any time of day, and there's something transgressive about that. It's not as wrong as chips with breakfast, obviously, but it still feels naughty. There comes a time that must mark a cut-off point for breakfast and we must finally accept that the day is well and truly, irreversibly, under way. McDonald's famously declares this moment to be ten thirty, but what do they know? For many establishments, this magical beat is at noon. Whenever it is, afterwards, the fixings for breakfast are still there, like they've always been, but it would be wrong to have them now. So when a café or pub announces that its breakfast is available all day, it's an illicit thrill. Imagine eating a cooked breakfast in the evening!

Here in Andrew's, the clock hands reach eleven and a change comes over the place. There's no alarm, bong or announcement, because we don't need it. The volume of conversation drops. Half the tables empty, all at once. The timing, like the composition of set meals and strict rules around substitutions, like apple crumble being available only on Thursdays, reveals that, when it comes to our favourite meals, we like to be bound by rules and conventions. We British are quite comfortable with a bit of light authoritarianism, with being told what we can and can't do. No matter how long it's available, you shouldn't be needing breakfast after eleven. There's work to be done. Whether you're reading the news or digging the road, it's time to get on with the day. Keep calm, and carry on.

8.

The Main Event

'The art of cooking as practised by Englishmen does not extend much beyond roast beef and plum pudding.'

– Pehr Kalm, Swedish visitor to England (1748)

1.

I wanted to do it differently. Properly.

When I used to watch Nigella or Nigel on TV advising us all to 'ask your butcher' to prepare something in a certain way, my reaction was always, 'Yeah, it's all right for you lot with your fancy butchers who know you by name and banter with you 'cos money's no object and you know your topside from your silverside and you're off the telly. The rest of us don't live in your little world. Most of us buy pre-packed, pre-priced parcels from supermarkets. We buy what we can afford and what we feel comfortable with.'

And then, a few years ago, because I live in a part of London that's gentrifying even more rapidly than the rest, an upmarket butcher's shop opened around the corner on the main shopping street. Their meat costs far more than anything you can get in the local supermarket and yet there's often a queue out of the door. Liz and I are trying to eat less meat for both health and ethical reasons. If you've read this far, you'll have correctly surmised that I could never become vegetarian (you can prise my bacon buttie from my cold, dead hand), but my new compromise is to only eat very good-quality meat and not too often. By buying our meat from the new posh butcher's, we greatly increase our chances of succeeding in this, not only because of their excellent sourcing and butchering practices but also because at the prices they charge we can only afford to eat any kind of meat once or twice a week.

And then I realized that this was the kind of butcher's where, because I was spending so much, I could start asking questions I'd never felt comfortable asking bored teenagers in Tesco's in places like Mold. I could try buying my meat the same way Nigella and Nigel do, just to see what it was like.

For an average middle-class bloke in our foodie age, going to a proper butcher's has joined shopping at a local hardware store as a trial that must be passed. Men are supposed to know what cut of meat they want, just as we're supposed to know what kind of screws we need. Real men *do* know these things, or so we imagine. We see ourselves as frauds, failures, so preoccupied with our lily-livered media or office jobs that we have lost essential skills, and we're terrified of anyone finding out. So you do your research beforehand, rehearse saying, 'Can I have a dozen Phillips head three-quarter-inch screws' as casually as possible, and they rumble you instantly, asking, 'Counter sunk or pan head?' just for the pleasure of watching you crumble. If you look particularly useless, they'll bypass the toying phase, sigh deeply and simply ask, 'What do you want them for?' before listening to your mumbled explanation and then telling you you don't want Phillips screws for that at all but slotted cheese heads, as any fool knows.

These people see me coming, and I've long abandoned any pretence of knowing more than I do. When I started thinking about making my best-ever Sunday roast, I didn't even bother looking up what cut of meat I thought I needed. The financial risk was too great.

'Yeah, I want to make a really good roast beef,' I said to the butcher when it was finally my turn. He took one look at me, smiled and reached for a boneless rolled joint – the foolproof one that everyone cooks because it's quick and, more importantly, easy to carve.

'No.' I shook my head, hardly able to believe my own defiance. 'If I was going to make the *very best* roast beef, what's the best cut of the animal I should go for?'

Now his smile suggested that I had either passed a test of discernment or failed a test of gullibility – I wasn't sure which.

'You want the fore rib,' he said, reaching for something that still looked a lot more like part of a dead animal than the neatly trussed rolled joint. It was a very heavy set of ribs, the meat browning because it had been hung for a while. On one side was a thick layer of subcutaneous fat that was obviously still feeling separation anxiety from the skin that had recently been attached to it. The bones on the other side were still recognizable as part of a sizeable ribcage. The butcher stroked it, pointed out the quality of the marbling, invited me to smell it. It smelled rich and warm and wholesome.

'How many people?' he asked.

'Just the two of us – with some left over,' I said.

'You'll just need one rib, then,' he said.

'No.'

I'd just said no to a proper butcher for the second time. I was feeling bold.

'Make it two.'

Later that day, following a carving experience from which I emerged with dignity if not honour, I served what was without doubt the best roast beef I've ever cooked. It was buttery and rich and soft and caramelly and fresh and vibrant. Nigel Slater gives a recipe for roast beef in *Appetite* in which he insists that, if you de-glaze the pan with some red wine, you need do nothing else to produce perfect gravy. I try this every time I cook roast beef and, without fail, I end up having to supplement my meagre, greasy offerings with boiling water and stock cubes. But this time I finally prove him right. The gravy is silky and seductive, not just smothering the meat but *dancing* with it. I'll remember that roast dinner for ever. Which is good, because I doubt I'll ever be able to afford to buy it again.

I had no great plan when I spent sixty quid on a piece of beef – we didn't have anyone round for dinner or anything like that. It was just an ordinary Sunday. Normally, if we do cook a roast dinner at home for the two of us, we just bung a chicken in the oven, like most people, do a bit of mash, steam a few vegetables and, if we can be bothered, make a quick gravy. But I was curious. I'd started my research for this book and I'd been reading about the historical significance of roast beef in defining Englishness and thinking about the meal as I'd grown up with it. And slowly, over a period of months, I realized there was more to my extravagant purchase from the butcher than first met the eye.

The Sunday roast is a meal that unites us – as families, as a class and as a nation, and when asked by YouGov in October 2018, more of us still cited beef as our favourite roast than any other option. It's the one meal in this book that has given us a national nickname. The French started referring to English merchants and traders working on the Continent as Rosbifs in the 1730s, and were using the term to describe the English more generally by the 1770s. Even today – when it has arguably been replaced by fish and chips as our national meal – there's no other meal that unites us all in quite the same way: we all have a roughly similar idea of what it consists of, we all eat it at roughly the same time and we all associate it with home and family. As Ben Rogers argues in the introduction to *Beef and Liberty*, this is how national traditions of cookery provide reassurance, in that we know we're part of a much bigger group all eating the same thing.

These ideas, even if we don't articulate them openly, give us comfort as well as sustenance. Comfort feeds belonging, and belonging feeds identity. Perhaps that's why our favourite foods are invariably rich and stodgy comfort foods, and perhaps these strong associations are also why we insist these meals are still our favourites, even when market data suggests they're a generation behind our actual behaviour.* We are what we ate.

But when something unites us as powerfully as this it's in our nature to look for status and difference within it, to be

---

* In the YouGov survey, while beef is the preference of 41 per cent of over-sixty-five-year-olds, with chicken coming a distant second at 23 per cent, eighteen-twenty-four-year-olds are twice as likely to prefer chicken as they are beef.

more equal than others or, as the American art-punk band King Missile once put it, 'I wanna be different, just like all the different people I wanna be like.' There's lots of leeway within the meal we all prepare to express our differences from some parts of society and similarity with others.

By the time I was in my teens, Sunday roast was the only meal we sat down to together as a family. My dad would get home from work on Sunday at 6 p.m., so that's when we'd have it, the only time 'dinner' in our family ever meant an evening rather than middle-of-the-day meal.

It was the only meal my mum would cook for the whole family together, and it followed the traditional northern, working-class template. The meat had to be surly and grey – if there was any redness, that meant it wasn't done yet. Greens had to be boiled until their very defining green-ness had been leached away – any sign of crunchiness, again, meant they weren't done. Both my parents had full dentures, so there was practicality as well as tradition in the insistence that the toughness of the meat be balanced by a watery softness in everything else. The perfect Sunday roast was essentially leather accompanied by baby food.

And I loved it.

Sure, I didn't know any better but, apart from the occa-sional lump of gristle, I devoured everything on my plate and then, following my dad, asked for a slice of bread and more gravy so I could leave the plate with only a greasy smear to suggest it had had anything on it since it was last washed. I loved the chewiness of the meat, the squishiness of the mash and the crunch of the Yorkshire pudding and tolerated the dutiful consumption of carrots and cabbage between the highlights. More than that, by my mid-teens it was the final thing that held us together and made us feel like a family, just for an hour or so.

Cooking meat until it's leather and boiling vegetables to mush are seen, outside the homes that do it, as signs of a lack of sophistication. Squeamishness around beef still being red and juicy is considered to be a lack of education or refined taste or both rather than a simple preference. Restaurants have a reputation for being particularly snooty with anyone who asks for their steak well done, but I have friends from various backgrounds who simply prefer it that way.

I like a lively crunch to my vegetables now, even if I had to learn to love them that way. I have to admit that I made myself, because I saw it as a sign of being middle class, the other foot falling after taking that first step and cutting my sandwiches diagonally instead of straight across. In Barnsley, we used to refer to the blended mix of leftover potato and veg the following day as a 'fry-up', not to be confused with the full English breakfast (which we never had at home.) Now, I call it bubble and squeak – a term that, once upon a time, struck me as nauseatingly middle class. And I love my roast beef red. Genuinely.

So when I bought my fore rib I think it was more than curiosity. I think I wanted to make a Sunday roast that was as different from my mum's as possible, not because I hated the way she did it but to show to myself that I now have more in common with Nigel and Nigella, that I can appreciate the sweet freshness of my vegetables, nod approvingly at the marbling of the beef and pay sixty quid for it without exploding in the traditional Yorkshire battle-cry of 'OOOOOOWWWWWWWW MUCH?!'

2.

I once went to a pub on my own that was advertising 'Sunday Roast', with no elaboration. I think the barman was new, and I'm guessing he wasn't sure where my accent was from.

'What's your Sunday roast?' I asked him.

'Well, it's like, meat. Roast meat. On a plate, served with roast potatoes and lots of different vegetables,' he replied helpfully. 'And gravy.'

'Yes, I know,' I said. 'What I meant was, what *kind* of meat is it?'

'BEEF?' he said very loudly and slowly, suddenly looking at me as if I were some kind of idiot, as if it were perfectly ordinary for someone to be entirely unfamiliar with the concept of a roast dinner but the notion of any meat on the plate other than beef would be obscene. I looked at the regular menu: burger and chips, chilli con carne, spag bol, lasagne, steak-and-kidney pie. Fair enough.

A few months later, the BSE or 'Mad Cow Disease' epidemic saw exports of British beef banned in Europe. Sales of beef at home fell off a cliff and have never fully recovered. Any decent pub now offers a choice of chicken, pork, lamb or nut roast as well as beef and, in terms of sheer numbers, chicken is now by far the most popular meat we eat, in the Sunday roast and everywhere else. But that doesn't matter: when we think of a roast dinner, we think of beef, even if we eventually choose chicken. That barman's reaction may have been a little over the top, but if the pub was only serving one meat option as its roast dinner, of course it was going to be beef. It's what we are and who we are. When Jacques Chirac joked about mad-cow disease at Gleneagles in 2005, he wasn't just attacking British cooking, he was saying that our very moral fibre was diseased.

I've always thought there must be a hint of contempt in the idea of *Les Rosbifs*, that it perhaps implies a lack of art-istry or subtlety in our cuisine. But from a historic point of view it's a badge we've worn with pride in our eternal sib-ling rivalry with the French, turning what they see as a lack of culinary sophistication into a triumph of the super-iority of our country – of our strength and prosperity and of the land itself.

The ability to afford meat has always been a sign of sta-tus. Around the world even today, when previously poor countries start to become more affluent the amount of meat they eat increases dramatically. And in Britain we've always eaten more meat than our neighbours, even when that really wasn't very often. In southern Europe olive oil has always been plentiful and has defined the Mediterra-nean diet for 2,000 years. In northern Europe we can't grow olives but we do have pasture for livestock, so we've always relied much more on meat and animal fats.

The kind of meat available varied very much according to your status in society and, for most, it was a rare treat. In Tudor and Stuart times, the nobility looked down on beef, lamb and pork as farmed meat and valued game that had been shot while out hunting. The poor kept pigs if they had any meat at all and mainly ate pork and bacon, or rab-bit or poultry when they could get it. But from the fifteenth century onwards, one result of the enclosures was that more land was given over to livestock, with a large increase in the number of sheep and cows. At this point, sheep were more popular, providing the basis for Britain's world-leading wool industry.

The pasture in Wales, Scotland and the north of England favoured both cows and sheep and Britain was quick to establish markets and a relatively joined-up system of food supply. By the late seventeenth century, it was common to see large herds of cattle being driven down to markets such as London's Smithfield and visitors from abroad began to marvel at what they saw as an abundance of meat. As early as 1562, an Italian merchant called Alessandro Magno visiting London observed:

> It is extraordinary to see the great quantity and quality of meat – beef and mutton – that comes every day from the slaughter-houses in this city, let alone the meat that is sold at a special market held every Wednesday for meat brought in from outside the city . . . The beef is not expensive, and they roast it whole, in large pieces.

If game was the preserve of the nobility and pork the lot of the poor, the people who turned beef into a national icon were those between the two. Yeomen were descendants of the free tenant rather than the serf. They had the right to vote and owned solid houses and, as the feudal system receded, they gained in power and influence. Writing at the outbreak of the English Civil War, Thomas Fuller, a moderate royalist preacher, described the yeomanry as 'an estate of people almost peculiar to England' who would welcome you with a well-stocked table of 'as many joints as fishes: no meats disguised with strange sauces . . . but solid substantial food'. The Yeomen of the Guard – founded by Henry VII in 1485 as a permanent bodyguard to the king – became known under the Stuarts as Beefeaters. As late as 1813, the thirty yeomen on duty at St James's Palace enjoyed between them a ration of 24lbs of beef a day, washed down with 37 gallons of beer.

Apart from the availability of the meat itself, the way it was cooked was also a symbol of status. Since Anglo-Saxon times, the standard method of British cooking was a bubbling cauldron over a fire, with whatever scraps of meat, vegetables and roots you could find being thrown into a gradually evolving stew, much like we had in our flat when I was a student. Roasting took longer, required more fuel and was therefore more expensive. As Claude Lévi-Strauss pointed out, roasting also involves the meat shrinking in volume, which only the upper classes could afford to happen. Boiling means that, whether it's still in the flesh or not, all the fat and moisture from the animal is still in the pot somewhere, rather than spitting on the coals and going up in smoke.

When we say we roast our beef today most of us are technically incorrect: in a gas or electric oven, technically, we're baking it. But we still call it roasting as a hangover from when the meat was hung from a spit by the fire, slowly turned by a servant or a child and later by ingenious contraptions such as a dog inside a running wheel – a bigger version of what you'd see in a hamster's cage. Later still, roasting jacks would use the smoke passing up the chimney to rotate fan blades that powered the jacks. Long after the French had started cooking in enclosed ovens, the roasting jack was still a typical feature of an English kitchen, leading some food historians to speculate that our fondness for the roast helped inhibit our development as cooks more broadly.

The result would have been quite different from our 'baked' beef today. Ben Rogers describes how the 'outside would have been puffy and crisp, the inside tender and pink'. Roast beef became a dish for which the English gained a reputation for doing particularly well. Visiting England in 1784, Pehr Kalm wrote:

> Englishmen understand almost better than any other people the art of properly roasting a joint which also is not to be wondered at; because the art of cooking as practised by most Englishmen does not extend much beyond roast beef and plum pudding.

It's typical of attitudes to British food that, when checking this reference, I found several versions where the first part is omitted, as I did at the top of this chapter, giving the second part a much sharper sting than Kalm perhaps intended.

When the royal court returned from its French exile with the coronation of Charles II, their newfound habits and preferences started to harden the divisions between the rural yeomen and the fashionable, cosmopolitan London elite. In the years that followed, stock emerged as the founding principle of a new kind of French cookery, giving birth to a novel style of ragouts and fricassees that were aped and literally devoured by the Quality in town and viewed with increasing suspicion by the yeomen in the country. In France, as the tensions that would ultimately lead to the Revolution gathered heat, food was used actively to reinforce class divisions. The French style of cooking favoured small dishes with more intense flavours that were more expensive and time-consuming to produce. The more this style developed, the more the English nobility copied it, setting themselves apart from the rest of the country – a metropolitan elite, if you will.

In the rest of England the yeomen and their rising urban counterparts – the artisans, industrialists and merchants – were seen as the poster boys for a more unified nation. The Swiss traveller Béat Louis de Muralt noted, 'The pleasures of the table in this happy nation may be put in the same rank as the ordinary, everyone is accustomed to good eating . . . Roast beef . . . is the favourite dish as well at the king's table as at a tradesman's.'

Religion surely played its part in the schism, the puritanical rump of Britain's Protestantism being at odds with the ornate ways of the Catholic French. This contrast was right there in the way the food looked – chop things up small enough and cover them in enough sauce to create an ornate, beautiful dish and you can forget where it came from. The English, with their freeholds full of pasture and prize-breed cattle, luxuriated in the quality of the beast on their plate and cooked and presented it in a basic, unfussy fashion that wouldn't let you forget that it was a bit of an animal – preferably a very big bit of a very large animal.

When the Revolution finally happened, there was suddenly a lot less work in France for the superstar chefs who had made their names and fortunes catering for the *Ancien Régime*. Many fled to England, which may technically have been at war with France but still had a noble class who were in thrall to classic French style. Newspaper advertisements showed that a trained French chef could earn up to £60 a year, whereas a 'good, plain' English cook was more likely to be earning between £6 and £10.

Resentment simmered. The figure of John Bull, originally created as a criticism of traditional British boorishness, was reinvented as a national hero, depicted as stocky and fierce, sometimes even as the bull he so enjoyed eating. Meanwhile, satirists such as Hogarth would portray his French counterpart as weedy and malnourished from his weak broths. In 1731, Henry Fielding penned 'The Roast Beef of Old England' for his play *The Grub Street Opera*. The play was never performed – possibly thanks to pressure from the government – but the song took on a life of its own, expanding in length over the years and increasing in popularity until it was routinely sung by theatre audiences before, after and even during any new play, becoming an unofficial English anthem that went like this:

When mighty Roast Beef was the Englishman's food,
It ennobled our brains and enriched our blood.
Our soldiers were brave and our courtiers were good
Oh! the Roast Beef of old England,
And old English Roast Beef!

But since we have learnt from all-vapouring France
To eat their ragouts as well as to dance,
We're fed up with nothing but vain complaisance
Oh! the Roast Beef of Old England,
And old English Roast Beef!

Our fathers of old were robust, stout, and strong,
And kept open house, with good cheer all day long,
Which made their plump tenants rejoice in this song –
Oh! the Roast Beef of old England,
And old English Roast Beef!

But now we are dwindled to, what shall I name?
A sneaking poor race, half-begotten and tame,
Who sully the honours that once shone in fame.
Oh! the Roast Beef of Old England,
And old English Roast Beef!

When good Queen Elizabeth sat on the throne,
Ere coffee, or tea, or such slip-slops were known,
The world was in terror if e'er she did frown.
Oh! the Roast Beef of old England,
And old English Roast Beef!

In those days, if Fleets did presume on the Main,
They seldom, or never, return'd back again,
As witness, the Vaunting Armada of Spain.
Oh! the Roast Beef of Old England,
And old English Roast Beef!

Oh then we had stomachs to eat and to fight
And when wrongs were cooking to do ourselves right.
But now we're a . . . I could, but goodnight!
Oh! the Roast Beef of Old England,
And old English Roast Beef!

It's worth quoting at length because it tells us as much
about the fears and obsessions of 1730s England as a *Daily*

Mail front page does today. In an age when Britain was unprecedentedly wealthy and well on its way to building the largest empire the world had ever seen, we're presented with a picture of a country in some kind of moral decline, and it's the foreigners and their dirty muck that are to blame. The good old days were a generation or two beyond living memory, as distant but as tantalizingly close as the Victorian era is to us now. Foreign products such as tea and coffee – which aren't French but might as well be – are sapping our strength and moral fibre. And all we need to do to reverse the trend is take back control and resist the creeping influence of Europe, make things better, like they were in the old days. Nearly 300 years later, when Tetley's 'Britishness audit' puts 'a British cup of tea' at number six in the list of British icons, 'Making a cup of tea in response to a crisis' as the fourth most British thing you could possibly do, and suggests more Brits think our national emblem should be a cuppa than think it would be better to have Big Ben or even the Queen, it's impossible to imagine what it must have been like to live through such bitter, xenophobic paranoia that our culture and prosperity were under threat from Europe.

Plainness and bounteousness were attributes to be actively celebrated in food, not apologized for. When you had meat and produce that was as good as the British had, it didn't need to be 'disguis'd'. This attitude, born of opposition to the French, would set a course for British food that would dominate until the end of the twentieth century, by which time it had become horrifically mangled and misunderstood.

3.

If there's one phrase that sums up traditional British cooking in both content and tone, it's 'meat and two veg'.

In a literal sense, this is a stripped-down version of the roast dinner, adapted to the pace of the working week. Meat is always the star, either leftovers from the weekend baked into a pie or substituted by cheaper cuts such as chops or sausages. One of the 'veg' will almost certainly be some form of potato, with peas, cabbage, carrots or whatever boiled and piled on the side.

I'll admit it doesn't sound too thrilling when presented so baldly. But a well-made steak-and-kidney pie and a satisfying mound of bangers and mash almost made the cut as chapters of this book in their own right, such is the ardour many of us feel for them.

But beyond a literal description of a meal, 'meat and two veg' has become a signifier of a plain-speaking, unpretentious kind of person or attitude, the type embodied by John Bull himself. It carries a value judgement which – depending on your age and class – either makes a virtue of plainness or suggests a lack of sophistication. It is also – like so many phrases in the English language – slang for male genitalia. As such, it sums up what the British traditionally eat, at the same time as giving a useful insight into how our minds work.

And then we get to Sunday and say, 'To hell with meat and *two* veg – it's the main event, why not have five or six? And some other stuff besides?'

When the barman explained to me what was served

with my Sunday roast, I thought it was absurd because, obviously, everyone knows what it comes with. The main attractions still, of course, come from the oven, whether we call them baked or roast. The most important accompaniment to the meat itself is without doubt Yorkshire pudding, a national icon in its own right that again is capable of topping polls of our favourite foods without the help of the rest of the roast dinner. As well as its roast beef, Britain has also had a long reputation for the excellence of its puddings, even if they are generally hearty and stodgy compared to the light delicacies of the French and the Italians. Batter-and-dripping pudding had its origin as a partly cooked pancake that was placed beneath the turning spit of beef to catch its juices as it roasted, an idea that makes me want to stop writing and start building a roasting jack this very second. The first recipe for 'a dripping pudding' appeared in *The Whole Duty of a Woman*, written, perhaps inevitably, by a man (Sir Alexander William George Cassey) in 1737. Ten years later, Hannah Glasse included a recipe in *The Art of Cookery Made Plain and Easy*, renaming it Yorkshire pudding. Like any other dish, it has evolved over time: in the north it was traditionally eaten doused in gravy on its own as a first course, especially if there wasn't quite enough of the more expensive meat to go around. It's doubtful that any early Yorkshire pudding would have risen much in front of an open fire in a draughty kitchen, but the lightness of a perfect Yorkshire pudding today is taken so seriously that in 2008 the Royal Society of Chemistry ruled that, to be considered worthy, a Yorkshire pudding must rise to no less than four inches in height.

Very close behind in the league of importance come

roast potatoes and, while you're peeling them, you might as well do some for mash too. What could be more traditional than that? Well, pretty much everything else on your plate, actually, given that potatoes found favour in polite society only about the same time curry did, around the late eighteenth century. With the meat on, potatoes, too, were originally cooked by catching the fat from the dripping spit.

So the trinity of roast beef, Yorkshire pudding and roast potatoes were done by the fire. Everything else that went with it really began life as an afterthought. The British have never had a great reputation for the cooking of vegetables. We seem almost pre-programmed to dislike them, with many children having to be forced to eat them. Hannah Glasse wrote that 'most people spoil garden Things by over boiling them'. Regency-era cooks boiled vegetables until they were soft, believing that, if they didn't, the veg would be 'tremendously indigestible, and much more troublesome to the stomach than underdone meats'. When your mum puts the sprouts on for Christmas dinner sometime in late October, she's upholding a long tradition of patriotic suspicion about our five a day that we seem to have overcome only recently. To people who grew up in homes like mine the idea that vegetables can be flavoursome and attractive in their own right rather than something you have to insist is eaten still feels like an exciting novelty.

Even so, you probably have what chefs now like to refer to as 'potatoes done two ways', as well as three, or maybe even four, vegetables, plus a batter pudding, as well as the meat itself, with a gravy and maybe one or two extra sauces or condiments. Each is simple and straightforward in its own right:

traditionally, there's not much seasoning or 'disguising'; you're just cooking the whole lot through. What could be easier?

The preparation of a roast dinner starts off deceptively simple: you heat the oven, season the meat and bung it in. This was the whole point of the traditional Sunday roast: you could stick it in the oven (or on the spit) and go to church and it would be done by the time you got back. Take church out of the equation and it's even easier – hey, you can do this! Sure, you still have the potatoes to peel, but you zone out while doing that, maybe pour yourself an early glass of red wine. You've got ages yet to get the rest ready. But gradually, imperceptibly, more pans appear and you start to worry that there might be an element you've forgotten about. You can't put the greens on yet because the roasties have only just gone in but, hang on, isn't the meat nearly ready? The table isn't set. THE YORKSHIRES! You forgot about the Yorkshires! So, you take the meat out to rest and slam in the Yorkshire-pudding batter. Like freshly baked bread or coffee, the dream of Yorkshire puddings is always superior to the reality, at least when *you* make them. There's an air of science fiction about them: once they're in, you know it would be a disaster to open the door again, even if – especially if – you can see them failing to rise. All you can do is watch helplessly through the glass, like Kirk watching Spock die at the end of *Star Trek II: The Wrath of Khan*. And while you've been preoccupied with that, you've forgotten about the draining, mashing, stirring, pouring, all of which have to be done at exactly the same time, and once again you realize you're not going to be able to pre-heat the plates, and you're trying to keep everything warm even as you're taking it all off the heat, so you end up half pissed as more red wine goes into your stress-relieving glass than into your bravely improvized gravy recipe and you end up staggering to the table with plates and serving dishes, screaming, 'EAT IT QUICKLY BEFORE IT GOES COLD!' before collapsing into your seat and sobbing.

But it's not over yet. Some poor bastard has to carve. The clock is ticking and the dishes are cooling and the carver has to attempt to produce thin, even, smooth slices like you see on the adverts, using a knife that was last sharpened so long ago it's only useful now for tearing and hacking and you end up producing chunks instead of slices. Even in an age of sexual equality, this is yet another failed, arcane test of masculinity. The handing of the carving knife and fork by a father to his eldest son has been used more than once to depict a tense, dramatic coming of age. I seem to have blocked out the traumatic memory of it happening to me. I once went to someone's house for roast dinner where the man had cooked the dinner and another man present jumped up and insisted on carving the meat for him. No one said a word – none of the usual cooing over how appetizing the meat looked. Everyone looked away – the humiliation was too painful to watch.

This is an incredibly complex meal to serve. It would be a challenge even for a professional chef to prepare it in a domestic kitchen without the help of a brigade of staff. And yet I know several people whose only attempt at cooking is the roast dinner and don't fancy the idea of trying to cook anything else because of the trauma it caused them. We look at how easy it is to bung a piece of meat in the oven or bring a pan of spuds to the boil and we don't appreciate the astonishing logistical challenge until – sometimes literally – our repeated failures have scarred us. And we attempt all this on our supposed day of rest.

There's clearly more at stake here than simply providing a meal to feed a family. There's an idea at the heart of it that's about feasting, even if we'd never use that word. A proper British meal – be it the roast dinner, its inferior weekday counterparts or the full English breakfast – has to have its constituent different parts on the plate. Therefore, the more parts you have, the better a meal it must be, and there can't be any meal better than your Sunday lunch – that would be wrong. When we sit down the experience of eating is not just a coming together over a meal, it's an uncommon celebration of the food itself.

People can then choose what order to eat the different parts in, and we all have our own rituals. Some eat the bits they don't like first (i.e. vegetables) and save the best till last. Some of us have to assemble a bit of everything on the fork, while others go around the plate in strict rotation. Philip Larkin once said, 'I like spaghetti because you don't have to take your eyes off the book to pick about among it, it's all the same.' The roast dinner demands your full attention – put that book down! Larkin was unusual: I've heard many older people dismiss meals like curry or spag bol because they're 'one thing the whole way through' and therefore dull and boring to eat, compared with the excitement of trying to decide whether your next mouthful is going to be a slice of meat or another forkful of peas. Even when we have stews and casseroles, we expect them to be accompanied by something even if, on paper, they contain everything necessary for a full, balanced meal. Never mind the flavour, it's the logistics you're meant to enjoy. Plainness is subverted.

The meal that trumps all others in this respect, the paragon of the roast dinner in its complexity, its feasting and the meaning it has, is the Christmas dinner. The number of different components goes off the scale and we love it for that. And we love it because, even more than the year-round Sunday roast, it unites us in a shared identity because we're all together as families, all doing the same thing at the same time. Those of us who hate it tend to do so for exactly the same reason. We know that most households in the country are doing something very similar to us and, for me, that's a significant chunk of the magic of Christmas, a powerful reminder of that which unites us being stronger than that which divides us. In his 2006 book *Imagined Communities: Reflections on the Origin and Spread of Nationalism*, Benedict Anderson wrote that we need to 'imagine' the idea of a nation because 'the members of even the smallest nations will never know most of their fellow-members, meet them, or even hear of them, yet in the minds of each lives the image of their communion'. The media reinforces this. For weeks before Christmas Day, every cookery show and supermarket ad talks about 'the big day' and dinner as 'the main event'. As Peri Bradley argues, 'The media reinforces this imagined community through representation and repetition, presenting Britain with what appears to be a cohesive and unified national identity.' That sounds sinister when presented in the flat, redbrick language of the social sciences but, in the case of Christmas dinner, I don't think it is. It fosters a warm sense of belonging and safety. 'It is through food, rather than political rhetoric, that people experience the nation in everyday life,' wrote Catherine Palmer, author of a 1998 academic paper exploring the concept of 'banal nationalism', and I believe she's right. Even people belonging to other religions and those from a wide range of ethnic backgrounds often indulge in Christmas dinner because, above all else, it's about belonging.

For those of us who don't want to feel like we're doing exactly the same as our neighbours or our competitive cousins, Christmas dinner turns the social jockeying of the roast dinner into an art form, one that's enshrined in our popular culture and repeated every year, evolving slowly with our changing tastes. Get a load of how middle class I am: I spend nearly a hundred quid on an organic turkey far bigger than I need – from the posh butcher's, of course – and I brine it in a bucket on Christmas Eve, just like Nigella says. Of course, this makes me aspiring lower middle class, because that's what Mick does on *Gavin and Stacey*, repeated on Gold every December. Both Mick and I are socially superior to the strictly working-class Denise from *The Royle Family*, who battles with trying to defrost her turkey in the bath before every imaginable thing goes wrong and she breaks down, sobbing that she just wanted Christmas to be perfect, just like Nigella's, unaware that she's chasing an impossible fantasy. But neither Mick nor I are as middle class as the switched-on people who go against type and know that, actually, Lidl's turkeys are perfectly good and just as ethically reared as those from Waitrose and half the price. And of course, all of us are in the shadow of those who sniff at the very thought of turkey and cook goose instead, because that's the traditional Christmas roast, or didn't you know?

Such is the totemic power of Christmas dinner that, despite its astonishing complexity and difficulty, despite the fact that you can spend the first two days of the 'holiday season' working on it, it would be a sign of failure both as a cook and a family member to say, 'Bugger this, let's go to the pub instead.' An increasing number of pubs serve Christmas dinner and they fill an important gap for those of us not lucky enough to be able to spend Christmas morning in a warm, spacious family home. But for the rest of us, going out for Christmas dinner would be an admission of defeat.

When it comes to the typical working week, though, an increasingly cash-rich, time-poor (or even cash-poor, time-poor) population has acknowledged the insanity of trying to prepare such an insanely complicated meal on the day we aspire to making as little effort as possible and has shifted the Sunday roast from the home to the pub.

For pubs themselves, this is a welcome tonic. Over the past forty years, there's been a general shift away from pubs. Once the absolute focus of English life, the pub now competes with restaurants, cinemas and shopping malls for our precious leisure time and our homes have become much nicer places to live in than they were a century ago. Against plasma screens showing hundreds of channels and more programmes than we can ever watch on demand, high-speed internet, social media and quick home delivery of anything we can imagine wanting to buy, the pub has lost much of its allure. It's still the centre of the community, which is why it remains the focus of any successful soap opera. But the pubs in soaps – like the lists of our favourite meals – seem to belong to a previous age. In reality, around twenty pubs are closing every week. Twenty years ago, the typical Brit visited the pub once a week. Now, we go once a month.

When we do go to the pub, a majority of us now do so to eat rather than just to drink. Food has become more important financially to pubs than beer, and the food pubs serve is generally hearty comfort food: fish and chips, burgers, pies and, above all, the Sunday roast.

I don't know how pub kitchens do it, but they manage to turn out as many as a couple of hundred roasts every Sunday. They may not be perfect. They may not be like Mum used to make (and for some, this might be a relief) but, on the whole, they're acceptable, a rare example of something that hasn't been dumbed down and ruined after having been taken out of the domestic kitchen and put into commercial hands.

As well as relieving us of the logistical insanity of preparing it and allowing us to relax on a Sunday, the pub reinterprets the Sunday roast for modern times. When children grow up to have different values or even find themselves in a different social class from their parents, the pub on a Sunday lunchtime is neutral ground where no mother-in-law can politely chide you for not doing the gravy the way she would and no son or daughter can scare you by putting some unholy new vegetable on the plate that you've never seen before. Here, in this neutral environment, a roast dinner reconnects us with the past, with family, with a stability and safety we've lost.

When Liz and I used to go to visit her dad, Eddie, in

South Wales, Sunday dinner would be the highlight as well as a bone of contention. Abergavenny was orbited by countless pubs in the hills offering good food, as well as having some great places in the town itself, but we'd have to book a table no later than Thursday to avoid disappointment. For months at a time, Eddie would book the same pub every visit without consulting us and then, one month, he'd abruptly change. When questioned, he would simply say he had 'heard reports', either about underhand practice or marital strife among the owners of the pub we used to visit, or about the quality of the meal at the pub we were switching to. After he died, we felt disloyal trying pubs he would never countenance and finding them fault-free and wonderful. In these pubs – both Eddie's favourites and our later alternatives – the landlord could tell you the herd and breed of the cow on your plate and the name of the farmer, not because this was a new-fangled gastropub but because they'd always done it that way.

While it may be a big production, Sunday roast is an intimate family meal. Some meals we have with mere acquaintances, but you have to know someone pretty well to have Sunday lunch with them. Many of us don't live near our families any more, and so we make our 'families' our closest networks of people we love and trust. In cities many people live in apartments that are too small to cook and serve a roast dinner in, even if the will was there. So these manufactured families all go to the pub and eat the same meal, together. An Italian brewer now living in London recently told me, 'I've made some of my closest friendships so far over roast dinner. It's the one thing I love about this country more than anything else.'

5.

'Pint of cider, please.'

'Certainly, sir, which one would you like?'

'Er, just an ordinary cider.'

'There is no ordinary cider here, sir, just good, and out-standing, which is made on the premises and has more apples in it.'

'Oh. Well. I'll have a pint of outstanding, then, please.'

Matt Slocombe is a natural. A modern equivalent of the country yeoman, he shares the stocky physique of John Bull himself, but John Bull was never pictured with such a warm, welcoming grin. Matt is behind the bar serving drinks because there's nowhere else he'd rather be just now. He could be supervising the kitchen, walking the floor and chatting to customers or checking his latest batch of cider to see how it's coming along. He doesn't even have to be here at all if he doesn't want to be, because he has enough staff on to cope even when, like today, his pub is packed to the rafters. But where else would he go?

All through this journey I've tried to order the *typical* version of each of the meals I've tried rather than the best. There's little point trying to tell you who does the best full English breakfast or chicken balti because you'd almost certainly disagree. If I choose a typical place, it's one you will at least recognize as being representative. But Sunday roast had to be in a country pub and, goddammit, if I'm going to do that, I'm going to the best one I know. This meal is too important to mess around with.

When a country pub has an outstanding reputation for

food it undergoes a subtle change in the way we refer to it. My current local is The Axe in Stoke Newington. The first pub I drank in was The Talbot in Mapplewell. Both do good food. But when I was growing up, the food pub the adults talked about in hushed tones was the Black Bull at Midgeley, a small village near Wakefield. I never made it there myself, but that substitution of 'in' for 'at' made it sound unbearably important and glamorous. The first episode of Michael Winterbottom's *The Trip* saw Steve Coogan and Rob Brydon dining at the Michelin-starred Inn *at* Whitewell. Number one in the list of the UK's Top Fifty Gastropubs in 2017 was The Star *at* Harome. Winning an 'at' instead of an 'in' is an important step in being recognized as one of the best food pubs in the country, and The Crown is most definitely known to be *at* Woolhope rather than *in* it.

As Orwell captured perfectly in 'The Moon under Water', his 1946 essay on what makes the ideal pub, as a general rule it's pretty much impossible to find a pub that has everything: if the food is great, the beer is poor; if both beer and food are great, the service is surly or the place is overpriced, and so on. Orwell talked about the most important thing being 'atmosphere' and, in a good pub, the atmosphere is an extension of the landlord's personality.

Orwell was very clear that he was describing the ideal urban pub: the criteria for a perfect country pub are slightly different, although the point about the publican and the atmosphere they create is as important as ever. Matt Slocombe seems to have all bases covered: he combines a natural, easy-going charisma with rigorous standards and a genuine passion for hospitality. I first met him when I was working on a book about cider. Woolhope is in the heart of Herefordshire, one valley over from the villages of the Marcle Ridge, which for me are the centre of the world as far as cider is concerned. The Crown ticks every box for what you want from a country pub. In my mind, after visiting many times, it has a thatched roof, even though a quick look at photos confirms the roof is slate. There's a generous beer garden and a big car park. Inside, the menus are packed with locally sourced food and drink. Tables and chairs are wooden and simple but not artfully mismatched. An open fire burns in the grate. The white walls reflect the afternoon sun. It's economically furnished but somehow still cosy and welcoming. The way good pubs are decorated – like a typical bed & breakfast – often telegraphs the owner's personality, and this is a pub that screams I LIKE CRICKET from walls full of framed newspaper clippings recording England Ashes triumphs, framed autographed cricket bats and signed photos of cricket teams. This is a pub that represents the heart of England, a median point in the variety of British pubs and what we want from them.

The qualities that make the roast dinner so daunting for the home give an ambitious pub a chance to shine: the Sunday roast is the jewel in the heart of a good pub operation. If a table can order two beef, two chicken and a nut roast and the pub can bring them all out at the same time, all hot, with the vegetables perfectly done, you can generally trust them with everything else.

'The best thing about the roast dinner is that it's the sum of all its parts,' says Matt, when he gets a spare minute. 'There are so many different elements on the plate and the trick is to get them all perfect. The gravy should be good enough to eat as soup. But it's always "The meat is good but the horseradish wasn't quite doing it," or "The potatoes were perfectly crispy but the meat was a bit dry." You're building a pyramid and, when you've got to the point where you're saying, "Even the purple sprouting broccoli was good," you know you've made it.'

Matt is unusual for an English food-and-drink provider in that he manages to brag shamelessly in a way that's virtually American yet makes it somehow sound like perfectly understated Englishness at the same time. It's just a Sunday roast, right? We all know what that entails. But the menu, seemingly harmless at first sight, is where Matt gets to show he's not messing around. The descriptions are capable of creating awe, excitement, consternation, even panic. It's not that simple dishes have been messed around with – they haven't – it's that the *quality* of the ingredients has been so carefully explained. I'm not just ordering roast beef here, I'm ordering the roast sirloin of Ledbury beef from Vineyard Farm – served pink – with hot horseradish and Rioja gravy. Liz normally has beef whenever we go out for a Sunday, but she always has to have something different from me and the tyranny of choice is building.

'I don't know whether to have roast leg of Ludlow lamb with mint sauce and rosé gravy, or roast loin of Cotswold orchard pork, King's cider gravy and apple sauce!' she says (albeit maybe without describing the options as fully as I just did).

All options are served with roast potatoes, parsnips, Cornish cauliflower cheese, Yorkshire pudding, stuffing and a selection from butternut squash, leeks, Chantenay carrots and purple sprouting broccoli. Matt's own pyramid seems to be built particularly high.

This generous array of supporting acts highlights another curious change that's happened since the Sunday roast moved from the home to the pub. For me, last Christmas seemed to mark a tipping point on a specific issue: from Christmas Eve till about 28 December, my social-media feeds were full of arguments about whether or not Yorkshire pudding was a legitimate, acceptable component of the Christmas turkey dinner. My own reaction was one of confusion, as if I were suffering from amnesia: I think it is, but why do I think it is? Did we have it growing up? I can't remember.

Yorkshire pudding – nightmare that it is to make well – is an accompaniment to beef in the same way mint sauce is an accompaniment to lamb. If you're cooking roast beef at home, you'd be committing a crime if you didn't do Yorkshire puddings. With other meats, not so much. You wouldn't be a freak if you *did* have Yorkshires with lamb or chicken, but they aren't a necessary part of the deal. When the roast first moved to the pub, if you ordered beef, it would obviously come with Yorkshire puddings. If you ordered lamb, pork or especially chicken, you might not get a Yorkshire. But now, instead of the family table where everyone was eating the same roast, you have a pub table where everyone is ordering a roast but, within it, they're demanding something slightly different and often paying the same price. In this situation, if the beef comes with Yorkshire pudding and the other meals do not, there are howls of outrage. Therefore, a side-effect of the roast moving to the pub is the evolution of 'roast beef and Yorkshire pudding' into 'roast meat (or nut roast) and Yorkshire pudding'.

'And what would Sir like to drink with that?' asks Matt, arching an eyebrow, after I place our food order.

There's only one possible answer, and it's not claret.

Beer has always been the natural accompaniment to roast beef. In the sixteenth century, John Coke wrote to a French correspondent:

> For your wyne, we have good-ale, bere, metheghelen, sydre and perry, being more wholesome beverages for us than your wynes, which maketh your people drunken, also prone and apte to all filthy pleasures and lustes.

The Duke of Marlborough, who led the British and their allies to victory at the Battle of Blenheim, insisted, 'No soldier can fight unless he is properly fed on beef and beer' and, later, the Prince Regent proclaimed, 'Beer and beef have made us who we are.'

Butty Bach is more than a beer: in these parts it's an institution. It's one of those special, localized beers that drinkers switch pubs for – or would if they had to, but around here it's sold in every single pub. It's brewed by Hereford's Wye Valley Brewery, which was founded in 1985 and now feels as though it has been part of the local landscape for ever. 'It's more ale than bitter,' says Matt. 'A nice and nutty, foaming pint.'

At least, it is when it's cask-conditioned, perfectly cellared and drawn from a traditional hand pump. Cask-conditioned ale is not quite unique to Britain, but as good as, and it's possibly the most perfect example of how adept we are as a nation at talking down our excellence in food and drink. There's no other beer in the world quite like cask ale. It's still alive and conditioning as it sits in the pub cellar, that secondary fermentation giving it a subtlety and depth that other beers of the same alcohol level don't have. Like sourdough bread or cheese cultures, the live yeast in the barrel responds to its environment, and a regime of tapping, venting and spiling a cask that might work perfectly in one cellar may not work quite as well in another, or even with a different beer in the same cellar. Many pubs can serve a pint of cask that falls within the parameters of acceptability – it's not 'off' in any way – but relatively few publicans can make it truly shine. A pint of Butty in the Crown will likely taste very different from a pint you find in a corporately run pub in central London. If this were a French product, we'd be hailing it as one of the gastronomic marvels of the world of drink. As it is, it's dismissed by many as boring, old-fashioned real ale which is drunk only by the constituency *Viz* lovingly refers to as 'real ale twats'. Even within the revolution that is craft beer, it's overlooked by many beer geeks who would much rather be drinking bright, hoppy American-style pale ales, even as the founders of the breweries who created those beers cite British cask ale as their main inspiration.

With our order placed, the anticipation starts to build. To relieve the tension, I take a good look around the pub. I notice for the first time certificates declaring that the Crown was shortlisted for the Best Roast Dinner Award (sponsored by Knorr and Coleman's) in 2015 and was highly commended as Flavours of Herefordshire's Pub of the Year in 2010 and 2011 – an award that celebrates the use of local ingredients. Behind the bar is a poster that looks as though it dates from the 1970s. Above a cartoon of farmers drinking cider while painting a Union Jack on the side of a cow the headline reads, 'When you've seen Herefordshire, you've seen England (and a bit of Wales too.)' My old bosses in advertising would suggest that, as memorable slogans go, this one still needs a bit of work. A line across the bottom reads, 'Herefordshire – the friendly county'. I always think friendliness is one of those attributes that, if people feel the need to tell you they have it, you become suspicious that they probably don't, but on this occasion, I'm not going to disagree.

The certificates and poster prompt the realization that, unwittingly, I've chosen to eat my Sunday roast beef in a county that's famous for its cows. Over the eighteenth and nineteenth centuries, the breeding of cattle became something of an obsession for progressive British landowners. The principles of selective breeding had been understood and used by racehorse owners since Stuart times but weren't used for other livestock until the 1740s, when Leicestershire landowner Robert Bakewell developed breeds of sheep and cows that fattened quickly. By the end of that century, some animals were double the size they had been in the Middle Ages.

Hereford cattle were never quite as celebrated as the Scottish Highland, Galloway and Aberdeen Angus breeds, but they were remarkably successful. Once originally strong, hardy oxen able to forage for themselves, Herefords were used mainly for pulling carts. They were carefully bred to enhance their stocky build, grazed on pasture and developed as beef cattle. Hereford cows have a red-brown colouring with distinctive white faces that make them instantly recognizable. In Victorian illustrations they're the cows that are depicted as massive rectangles with a head at one end and tail at the other. They were first exported to the United States in 1817 and, by the 1840s, the first breeding herd in New York State had been established. The breed's hardiness was celebrated in 1940 when a ship carrying Herefords to the US was torpedoed in the North Atlantic and two cows swam ashore safely in Ireland. Herefords have now been exported to over fifty countries and form the basis of herds on almost every continent, from Australia to Canada to the Russian Steppe and the great beef-raising countries of South America.

'Herefordshire cows are world famous,' says Matt, when I ask him about the breed. 'It's a stocky, well-built, fat-laden animal, so it could travel around the world when no other animal could. It's very dense and slow-growing. Most of what you see in Hereford now is crossed out with something else to make it more economical.'

This is an astonishing success story for British agriculture and food production and one I had absolutely no idea about until now. In 300 years, we've gone from lauding beef and beer as the twin pillars that built a nation and an empire to celebrating neither.

Vineyard Farm is near Ledbury, just a few miles away, and has been in the same family since the 1850s. All their beef is twenty-eight-day dry-aged and not vacuum-packed, so it develops 'bark' – the buttery, yellow fat that's a good indication that it's been grass-fed.

'We cut it crossways so there's always a good bit of fat on the end,' says Matt. 'The sirloin presents really well. You still have to tell people that animals don't come as pure lumps of protein – you have to chew on them for a bit.'

So how does Matt make sure he gets the best quality?

'It's about building relationships with your butcher. You've got to be able to say, "I'm not quite happy with this sirloin, can you get me another?" Once you've done that a couple of times, it doesn't happen again. And the farmer eats in here, so that helps.'

It's particularly comforting that our meals take so long to arrive. It's always unnerving when a plate of food that is so complex to prepare appears at your table five minutes after you've ordered it, like it was ready and waiting outside, smoking a fag, waiting to be called. I take another look around the pub. Liz and I are on a small table for two by the bar. The rest of the room is dominated by big tables of six or eight. All are occupied by families and, at each, there are at least three generations. Mum (or Dad, but here I'm guessing it's mostly Mum) is liberated from the kitchen, and everyone is relaxed. There are red-trousered Audi drivers – Matt's shooting set – next to nervous young couples. Some of the men wear shirt collars and jackets, but there are no ties, and there are more fleeces, casual stripy tops and untucked checked shirts than there are blazers. Everyone looks perfectly comfortable being here. All are experiencing the pub in the same way, descendants of yeomen and peasants, children and grandchildren of miners and of minor aristocracy. This pub, like so many at this time of the week, is a cross-section of British society. We may have our differences in how we think the perfect version should be cooked and served but, right now, we all want the same meal at the same time. This is a very democratic feast.

By the time our food arrives, I've had to order another pint of Butty Bach to keep it company. The sirloin does indeed present very well: three slices, each half an inch thick, brown at the edges but a rusty red throughout, with a thick layer of seasoned fat down one side. They almost fill a surprisingly modest-sized plate, leaving just enough room for parsnip, roast potatoes and stuffing, the whole array crowned with a perfect Yorkshire pudding, towering and confident.

Next comes a chunky board carrying cauliflower cheese, horseradish, a bowl of chopped carrots, halved lengthways, gleaming and fresh, and deep green and purple broccoli, and two separate jugs of gravy. The Rioja gravy for the beef is next to the horseradish, while Liz's rosé gravy is placed next to her mint sauce.

Gravy is another overlooked element of British cooking. Too often we take it for granted and, in its powdered, instant form, it's much abused but still more than edible. In *Taste: The Story of Britain through Its Cooking*, Kate Colquhoun writes, '[S]o sacred was gravy to nineteenth-century diners that the Empire might have been founded on it.' Gravy was considered by some to be the very essence of meat, the best part of it. So it's nice to see it being treated with due reverence here.

I feel like I need a plan, but I don't have one. Stunned into indecision, I have no idea where to start. I'm desperate to try the beef but my plate is now so loaded up with everything else I can't get to it. I'm going to have to work my way through its outer defences.

The parsnips have an initial crispness that provides momentary resistance before yielding and bursting in a soft mush. A mouthful of beer and carrot together is sweet and earthy and buttery. Christ, I almost forgot about the roast potatoes and the stuffing. Like the parsnip, the potatoes are a perfect balance of alert crispness and embracing softness. There's some asparagus, too, here because it's in season and perfect. Pert, green and bursting, along with the purple sprouting broccoli (yes, which Matt has nailed), it elevates the whole dish, contrasting brilliantly, when I finally get to it, with the sleazy, sweet bitterness of beef fat.

The condiments served with roast beef disprove once again the notion that the British affection for spicy food is a recent development. The mustard plant is native to Europe and has been used in kitchens dating back to Roman times, and horseradish was a common feature in medieval kitchens. But the English always wanted them to be stronger and more powerful than those of their European neighbours – think of the difference between English and French mustard today. It only required the gravy made from the meat's own juices to finish it off – a habit which led Voltaire to quip that the difference between England and France was that '[w]e have a hundred sauces, and only one religion; whereas, you have a hundred religions, and only one sauce.' But I honestly can't think of any other sauce or condiment that would improve the meal before me now. It's perfect. And as for the Rioja in the gravy? Well, given how good the beer is, it's nice that the wine has something to do.

Above all, the meat is the star. Everything tastes good but the meat is special. When roast beef tastes like this it's as sophisticated a dish as any other. It has depth and complexity to rival that of any cuisine: it's rounded and complex and I can taste hints of butter, iron and crispy caramelization. It delivers all this on the first mouthful and, instead of fading with familiarity, it somehow continues to deliver everything on every last bite. The Rioja gravy is a smooth, almost impossibly elegant accompaniment. And if that's not enough, here's the horseradish: rich and creamy and ever so slightly sharp on the palate with a retro-nasal kick of heat that clears the sinuses and makes the eyes water without having ripped up the palate first. It now makes sense why the most passionate advocates of this meal were also quite fond of snuff.

The Butty Bach tastes like the meat's other half, its best buddy, good cop–good cop. It's not just the way the roast and caramel flavours present in both beef and beer marry and wrap around one another, it's the way the pairing creates a sweetness and fullness that's not there in either one alone. Somehow sensible, the beer unites any stray elements and rounds them up.

I seem to have forgotten about the Yorkshire pudding. More air than batter, it's an ambassador for the gravy and horseradish and meat juices that are commingling on the plate and becoming even more satisfying now the meal is losing its shape and visual elegance.

My brain whites out and I swear I'm hearing traditional brass-band music, reverting to some childhood pit-village memory, and then I realize it's real. There's a brass band outside playing 'Bat out of Hell' and, somehow, it's the perfect accompaniment. As they switch into 'Bohemian Rhapsody', the last forkfuls of cooling, congealing gravy, horseradish, batter and vegetable fragments disappear, leaving a clean plate.

I wonder again about the difference between a meal and a feast. When does one become the other? Is it about the amount of food you consume? The number of different dishes on the table? Or is it just about the amount of pleasure it gives you? The dictionary defines a feast as 'any rich or abundant meal', but we probably think of the term mainly in its secondary definition: 'a sumptuous entertainment or meal for many guests'. Served in a good pub with care and heart, the Sunday roast easily meets both definitions.

I've broken my self-imposed rule and gone for the very best example I could find of this iconic meal, rather than seeking out a typical version. I should feel bad about this, but I don't. Because dammit, this *should* be the typical version of this dish! Sunday roast is a summation of what it means to be British, of our land, our history, our outlook and attitudes and our eternally weird relationship with the French. It should always be this good, for everyone.

As we finish the perfect Sunday roast and I think again about Matt's pride in how it's put together, it strikes me that the success of this meal is all about solid English efficiency rather than 'Continental' creativity. It's about being a technically skilled cook rather than a creative chef. That's what defined it in its history during our interminable wars with the French and it's a tradition that's still intact today. It's a display of skill and competence rather than flair and imagination. It suddenly strikes me that when people come to our house for a meal and I'm cooking, no matter what I have in mind, Liz always says something like, 'Just don't fancy-Dan it. Don't waste your time in the kitchen when we should both be chatting with our friends. No one's really bothered about the food. Just do something simple.'

Unless it's a Sunday lunchtime, of course, and we've agreed on a roast dinner. Then, all I get is, 'Best of luck. Make sure the gravy's hot.'

This unlocks our relationship with our national cuisine in general. If British food *is* rubbish, it's not because we aren't being as *imaginative* as we should be, it's because we aren't being as *skilful* as we should be, whether that's serving everything hot at the right time, getting pastry bang on or knowing just when to take the chips out of the fryer. This is a practical, industrious country, not an artistic one. These are skills every good cook should possess because, if you care about what you're doing, there's no excuse not to. All those components on the plate together, all hot, with nothing under- or over-cooked, is an extraordinary feat of cooking skill – something we expect and demand from anyone who attempts it.

9.

Crumble

'British food is a celebration of comfort eating. Our traditional savoury recipes are all about warmth and sustenance, our puddings a roll call of sweet jollity, our cakes are deep and cosy. We appear to be a nation in need of a big, warm hug.'

– Nigel Slater

Liz and I both love cooking, but we're very different cooks. I'm experimental and adventurous, ambitious in scope, whereas Liz is more practical, one of those people who can open the fridge to find nothing but a bendy carrot, an old potato and some lard and still somehow create a delicious meal from it. I regularly cook beautiful meals from the cookbook of a Michelin-starred Indian restaurant, taking six hours and using every pan and utensil, and then fall down on my simple and enduring inability to cook rice properly.

It was slightly depressing to read a report on cooking by market researchers Mintel and learn that this makes us absolutely stereotypical of British households. As a rule, men overreach and make everything into a huge production, while women can somehow get a tasty old favourite on to the table in twenty minutes.

When I ask Liz when she first made crumble, she said, 'I've always known how to make it.' When Felicity Cloake did rhubarb crumble for her long-running 'How to make the perfect . . .' series in the *Guardian* and asked around for different recipes, someone responded, 'Who uses a recipe for crumble?' It's as if the knowledge of how to make a good crumble is something we're born with. Regula Ysewijn, author of *Pride and Pudding: The History of British Puddings, Savoury and Sweet*, claims it's our favourite pudding as a nation.

It's certainly the favourite pudding in our house. A few years ago, Liz found a small supermarket just round the corner that did packets of pre-prepared crumble topping and jars of stewed apples. The resulting dish wasn't up to her usual standard but it took a minute to prepare and she bought the two ingredients whenever she was passing until, one day, the woman behind the till said, 'Oh, hello! It's the crumble lady.' Liz was so embarrassed she never went back to the shop again.

Today's crumble is made from scratch. Given that I have a severe allergy to apples, we go for rhubarb. This odd, somewhat mystical vegetable is a perfect case study in British food. Like the tomato and the potato, like Danish bacon and clotted cream, rhubarb is an immigrant to our shores. It was originally found growing along the banks of the River Volga in Siberia and was allegedly introduced to Britain by Marco Polo. Go back far enough in time and almost everything in our diet has transcended international borders.

Accustomed to cold, wet, wintry weather, rhubarb thrived in Yorkshire. I remember my dad growing huge bunches of it on his allotment but I rarely ate it because the way it was prepared at home meant it was sour enough to turn your face in on itself. I had absolutely no idea that we were living just eight miles outside the famous 'Rhubarb Triangle'. It wasn't famous to us. I'd never heard of it until I was an adult living in London. Just like our fish and chips and pork pies, I doubt many people I grew up with were even aware that we were sitting on top of culinary treasure.

Reading about forced rhubarb now, it sounds like a product of *terroir* and skill to rival any food superstar. The land between Morley, Wakefield and Rothwell was planted extensively with rhubarb from the early 1800s and at one point the area accounted for 90 per cent of the world harvest of forced winter rhubarb. 'Forcing' is a process that was introduced in 1877 whereby rhubarb is grown for two years in fields that were once fertilized with horse manure, woollen waste from the nearby mills and 'night soil' from the nearby bustling cities. Then, when frost hits in November, the plants are taken into long, low, forcing sheds and kept in complete darkness and warm temperatures, traditionally from coal heating but now from diesel. As the leaves wither and turn yellow, the stems grow thick and strong and the carbohydrates stored by the plants in the field turn into glucose. The process creates an appealing fuchsia-pink colour, a tender texture in the stems, thanks to the lack of light for photosynthesis, and a subtler flavour than rhubarb harvested from outside. In 2010, Yorkshire Forced Rhubarb was awarded PDO status by the EU.

Forced rhubarb is harvested from January to March, the pickers doing their back-breaking work by candlelight.

Photos taken in the forcing sheds make it look otherworldly and out of time, and the Rhubarb Triangle is, perhaps inevitably, in decline: in the 1960s and 1970s, many of the forcing fields were sold off to build housing for the overspill from cities like Leeds, Bradford and Wakefield and now only twelve growers remain. They're finding the work increasingly tricky: this product of the Siberian winter needs a good period of frost and the Rhubarb Triangle is in a frost pocket created by the Pennines. Increasingly mild winters are reducing the crop.

Today, there's no indication of where our rhubarb comes from. It's labelled in the shop as 'English organic rhubarb', but we're too late in the year for forced rhubarb. Liz chops it up and spreads it on a tray, sprinkles it with water and sugar and puts it in the oven to bake for twenty minutes.

'I used to make this all the time at university,' she says. 'It was just so comforting.'

Now, she rubs some butter into plain flour and adds a mix of golden caster sugar and demerara, 'to give it a crunch', adds a pinch of salt and rubs until she has a mixture resembling breadcrumbs, with some bigger, chunkier bits. The rhubarb comes out of the oven, goes into a pie dish and has a thick layer of crumble mix spread over it, before going back in the oven for about thirty-five minutes. And that's all there is to the crumble itself.

We only started to eat crumbles during the Second World War, when a regular supply of ingredients to make pastry became difficult to obtain. A chunk of the flour can also be replaced by oats or flaked almonds. Like all the best British meals, it's adaptable to any budget. It's also a perfect union of scratch cooking and convenience. Because, to go with the crumble, we of course have Bird's custard: a tablespoon of powder from a tin, mixed with a little milk and sugar into a smooth paste then added to a pan of milk and stirred until it thickens. There are as many recipes for custard online as there are for any other meal, but all of them are howling into a void: there's simply no point making your own if you've got Bird's – one of those rare products that's better bought than made and is as good now as it's always been.

What do we mean when we say food is 'good' or 'bad', especially when we carve up different meals according to their supposed cuisine of origin?

Is Al Gittner's spag bol worse than the beef ragù linguine on the menu at Carluccio's because he serves it with the 'wrong'-shaped pasta? Is the 'invented' chicken tikka masala at your local curry house 'better' than the roast beef and Yorkshire pud at your local gastropub because it's spicier and more exotic, or worse because it's not truly authentic?

I think any of us, if we think carefully about it, would eventually conclude that, while we might think about authenticity, tradition, value and sourcing, ultimately none of that matters if it doesn't taste nice. And if traditional British dishes are made well, they're as nice as any other.

Take Liz's rhubarb crumble, for instance. The caramelization where the sugar has burned on to the sides of the dish screams simple home cooking, warmth, comfort and quality. Large portions go into white bowls and the whole lot gets smothered in bright yellow custard. The rhubarb is searingly hot and I feel the first mouthful burning its way down my chest. This has to be eaten with care, but appetite takes over and I have to force myself to hold back. As it cools a little, the rhubarb is sharp and edgy, mouth-watering without being too sour. The custard and the crumble mix sweeten it, but not overly so. It's unbelievably comforting and seems to create its own nostalgia. I can't remember ever having this dish when I was growing up, but Stoke Newington is home now, Liz and Mildred the dog are my family. Writerly necessity means that, strangely, we're eating crumble in the blazing summer heat, but it makes us yearn for winters past and eagerly anticipate those to come, when we'll huddle over our dishes, breathe in the steam and say, 'Do you remember when we ate crumble on the hottest day of the year?' Like spag bol on a rainy Tuesday, fish and chips on a sunny seaside evening after cream tea in the afternoon and curry after a few beers in the pub, our best meals remain a product of their environment, even if they aren't linked directly to the land.

Over the eighteen months I've spent researching and writing this book, my basic cooking skills have improved dramatically. Partly, this is because I've discovered new methods and techniques. But largely, I'm more mindful of the character of each meal while I'm preparing it. With spag bol, the full English breakfast and roast beef, I've learned that, with a little care and attention and some discernment about the quality of the ingredients, they can be elevated to rival the best of any cuisine. I've learned what Liz and any competent British cook has always known: simple things, done well, win hearts.

I've had some terrible meals along this journey too: breakfasts dissolving into puddles of watery grease; sandwiches that are 90 per cent mayonnaise and 10 per cent wet cloth; curries that seem to be made from perfectly neat, identical blocks of something fibrous that is supposedly chicken (but definitely isn't) served in tepid tomato soup with a sprinkle of Schwartz curry powder; and, of course, my self-inflicted spaghetti Barnsleyaise.

Most of the time they were bad simply because the people preparing them couldn't give a toss, serving a commodity they would never dream of eating themselves or exposing their own families to.

Other times, food is awful because it's gone too far the other way – an experimental mash-up of ingredients, cuisines and flavours catering to a manufactured 'lifestyle' that screams, 'I'm the kind of person who is open and adventurous.' These are the meals that reveal why certain things have never been brought together before. (We've been eating chips for 150 years. Why have we started following the Dutch and Belgian practice of putting mayonnaise on them in the last ten?)

And sometimes you get both together, the 'diffusion' of a 'concept'. A curry that claims to be meltingly hot but isn't. A TV chef's branded range of processed meals that are cynically disgusting, all aspiration with nothing behind it. A 'Mexican' meal where the restaurant proprietor patiently and patronizingly tried to tell me that he wasn't cooking Tex-Mex but authentic Mexican food and I had to say, 'Yes, I know what the difference is, thanks, but this is a microwaved chicken breast and sauce that's obviously from a jar, on a plate that doesn't even contain half the ingredients listed on the description of the dish on the menu.'

We're just as capable of ruining food from anyone else's cuisine as we are our own. But it's a peculiar kind of self-loathing that describes this as bringing foreign cuisines 'down to our level'. This can happen anywhere you go. As well as having an inedible full English in Amsterdam, in my time I've had revolting steak frîtes in Paris, terrible tapas in Andalusia and poor tagine in Marrakesh. Any country is as capable of offering sub-standard versions of its own cuisines as it is of mangling others'.

Such is crumble's simple brilliance, it's now becoming increasingly popular in France. In 2005, a book by French-woman Camille Le Foll entitled simply *Crumble* had to be hastily reprinted after it rapidly sold 200,000 copies of its first edition. Around the same time Jacques Chirac was insulting British cuisine, his country was also acquiring an appreciation of English muffins, while cheeses such as Stilton and Stinking Bishop were finding favour in Paris-ian *fromageries*. In 2017, Gordon Ramsay won a second Michelin star for his fine-dining restaurant Le Pressoir d'Argent in Bordeaux, where he combines British produce with traditional French culinary style, paired with English wines. Ramsay told the *Daily Telegraph*, 'I took a lot of shit when I brought over wines from Kent and venison from Scotland, but the French didn't turn their noses up at it. They are enjoying it. They were going to hang me upside down in the square, but they love it so much.'

For most of us, for most of history, food wasn't something you could be fussy about: you ate what you could get hold of. As food security improved around the seventeenth and eighteenth centuries (aided in no small way by the intro-duction of the potato) and ideas of national cuisines first started to emerge, Britain quickly established a preference for plainness and lack of fuss, driven by the belief that this was better in terms of quality, and even morally, than sophisticated creative cookery that was both wasteful and sought to disguise the origin of the ingredients. Our huge breakfasts and roast dinners, with generous portions of meat at their centre, were an emphatic statement of the superiority of our land, climate, breeding practices, generous hospitality and lusty appetites.

These were the meals that fuelled the architects of the world's first Industrial Revolution, which in turn further increased the nation's prosperity. But the spoils were divided unevenly. Britain industrialized first, quickest and hardest. Countries like France and Italy industrialized later and less dramatically. People there remained tied to the land more closely, for longer, and so kept in touch with a sense of the land and the food that came from it, of regional *terroir* and local delicacies and traditions, of the importance and nature of a good harvest and simply of food as a natural product. In Britain, this bond between the land and the people wasn't just stretched, it was surgically sliced. Workers in towns and cities became detached from any sense of where their food came from and had to rely entirely on shops and institutions. Britain's manufacturers and shopkeepers have always had a fondness for watering down, bulking out and using the cheapest ingredients they can find – it wasn't even illegal to adulterate food with poison until 1875 – so the expectations of what poor people were able to eat began to diminish, setting up a cycle where the ready availability of cheap food is still considered more important by many than quality or ingredients.

Add to this the snobbishness of the class system, and

even where working-class, ghetto ingenuity threw up some-thing like fish and chips, which provided hot, cheap, nutritious food at prices affordable to anyone, it was decried by people who thought they knew better. Even the most well-meaning researchers at the BBC are complicit in this. In early 2018, the otherwise brilliant programme *Back in Time for Tea* took one family through a century of northern working-class diets. When they reached the 1920s and 1930s, fish and chips were not mentioned once – even when the family in question went to Blackpool! In reality, a family such as the one featured would have been eating tasty, wholesome fish and chips two or three times a week.

At the time when the majority of the British working popu-lation were being separated from the land, this divorce must not have felt like much of a problem – in fact, it was seen as the very opposite. Britain was a powerhouse, the most advanced country in the world. Progress and perfec-tion would bring prosperity for all. Food production became scientific, mechanized and profit-driven. We invented mod-ern cheese production and gave it away free to the world. We did nothing to protect the recipes or processes that made our cheeses or our beers world famous – the commer-cial trademark was all that mattered. We happily became a nation that was utterly dependent on imported food, because we would always have superior goods and tech-nologies to sell in return – or so we thought until German U-boats came long.

But inequality prevailed. Class seems to have been the main factor in determining what British people ate between 1900 and 1945. While late-Victorian and Edwardian middle-class diets were becoming ever more varied and interesting, agricultural labourers and the city poor sub-sisted on bread, sugar, treacle, dripping and suet, bacon, milk, cheese, tea and the odd bit of meat, with fish and chips as a welcome treat.

That's why we jump too quickly to blame the parlous state of late-twentieth-century British food on rationing. The nationalization of milk- and cheese-making is evidence of how, from a discerning point of view, the Second World War flattened out the British diet and made it duller. But when you look at the same picture from the perspective of a northern industrial worker, the effect is quite different: an averaging, a flattening, brings some things down but it also lifts other parts up. While the black market ensured that those with means still ate better than their inferiors, the average diet of the working family improved greatly during the war and its immediate aftermath. Questionnaires given out in government-run Communal Feeding Centres – quickly renamed 'British Restaurants' – showed that two thirds of their clientele hoped they would continue after the war. Despite being officially disbanded in 1947, many survived well into the 1950s. Those who had enjoyed quality and variety before the war saw this destroyed by rationing. But for most of the population, bland monotony was a significant improvement on what had gone before. In 1946, Orwell was commissioned to write a long essay on 'Food in Britain' by the British Council. He painted such a glowing picture that the piece was not published at the time, because it was considered 'unfortunate and unwise' to publish it for its intended audience, 'the continental reader', given the deprivations in Europe.

The criticism that should be aimed at post-war British

food, then, is how it allowed itself to be surpassed so dramatically by continental cuisines as they gradually recovered from the effects of the war.

The new cuisines that arrived with increased immigration seemed even fresher and more exciting than they would have anyway. It's no surprise that those who could afford it quickly adopted meals like curry and spag bol. As foreign travel became more affordable, our horizons spread. When we began to compare exotic foods eaten on holiday with a diminished local cuisine at home, it's no surprise many of us started to regard British food as inferior. It rapidly became a reflexive habit.

And the stuff we ate every day did itself no favours. Yoked to desks and machines, we began to prioritize the convenience of sandwiches over the intimacy and communion of family mealtimes. Manufacturers who took pride in business and brands rather than in ingredients and *terroir* began to use technology to make things cheaper rather than making them better,* until we get tins of 'minced beef' that smell the same as dog meat, bacon sandwiches containing gossamer-thin strips of something that looks like a child's drawing of bacon they remember seeing a week ago, and fish-and-chip shops that can't even be bothered to make their own chips and buy in McCain's instead.

---

* A recent in-depth report by the *Grocer* magazine showed that consumers were increasingly switching to 'artisan' bread because they were motivated by flavour, quality, stories, natural ingredients and a variety of styles. The authors went to several of the biggest mainstream brands in the market and asked how they planned to respond to this trend. Their reply? Cut the price and increase the advertising.

Among affluent, middle-class food lovers, the link with the land is being re-established. The food revolution of the last twenty years has traceability, sustainability, naturalness and relationships with producers at its very core. This is a very big part of why, at a broad level, there's a perceived improvement in the quality of food in Britain. But the quest for 'authenticity' that often accompanies the genuine enjoyment of quality produce is also a source of 'cool hunting' that renews the class divide in the appreciation of good food. Traditional British food such as pork pie and peas or fish and chips is not cool, partly because it's old-fashioned, partly because, as we've become more sedentary, what was once seen as comforting and wholesome in our cold, damp climate now seems stodgy and unhealthy, but also because this traditional food is accessible, familiar and available. So meals are deconstructed, reinvented or done with a twist, in forms many people can't afford. Ritual and etiquette are invented and amplified to strengthen these distinctions, so we end up with people paying sixty quid for tea and scones in a fancy hotel and finding them distinctly lacking.

It's tricky, being proud to be British – more so to be proud of being English. There's a fine line between pride and jingoism and, as soon as we start to get too vocal, we can cross that line very easily. Most of us haven't done national pride for so long we've forgotten how to do it at all. When people try, it feels like a throwback to the 1950s, clinging on to the death of the empire, and we're very sensitive to that. Someone in the food industry warned me that Ben Rogers' book *Beef and Liberty*, on the history of roast beef as a British icon, was 'a bit dodgy', a little xenophobic. It isn't at all. But it tells the story of a time when many of us were, when beef was strongly linked to jingoistic nationalism. Even describing this time in a neutral manner opens the author to the risk of being tarred as some kind of Farage-esque Little Englander.

So we go too far the other way, conspicuously talking ourselves down, freely telling each other and anyone else who will listen how crap we are as a nation. In 2012, Des Lynam opened the BBC's coverage of the Euro 2012 football competition with the words, 'Let the agony begin.' Later that year, everyone agreed that the 2012 Olympics were going to be an embarrassing farce until their jaws hit the floor thirty seconds into Danny Boyle's opening ceremony. In the run-up to the 2018 World Cup, it felt like every newspaper carried jokes such as the England team bus being in the short-stay car park at Heathrow and, when they started scoring goals, no one quite knew how to cope, with many fans insisting even a 6–1 victory was entirely down to poor opposition rather than any skill on our own side. And I know of no other people in the world who are so quick to agree that their national cuisine is the worst in the world, when it patently isn't.

But there is a middle way. Beer and beef are modest, democratic pleasures. At their best – like they are at Matt Slocombe's Crown at Woolhope – they're as good as any cuisine from anywhere else in the world. Secretly, we know this, just as we know the full English breakfast is the greatest in the world and good fish and chips are worth crossing great distances for. We confess all this if someone with a clipboard asks us what the best things are about being British. When we get it right, our food doesn't have to look spectacular or taste surprising, and the thanks we get for it are quiet and perfunctory. Yes, it's good. It's great. But we're British, and we don't have to bang on about it all the time. We are subtle and understated, straightforward and democratic – just like the meals themselves.

Acknowledgements

It took seven years for this book to grow from a few disconnected observations into a fully-fledged idea that, by the end, hopefully makes some kind of sense. Thank you to my agent, Jim Gill at United, for the patience and enthusiasm that helped it grow, and to my editor at Particular Books, Cecilia Stein, first for trusting me to simply get on with it when it wasn't at all clear what it might turn into, and then for shaping my manuscript into something much more elegant and coherent than when she first read it. Thanks also to Sarah Day, Pen Vogler and to everyone else at Penguin who helps create books with such poise and class. Believe me, the book you have just read was not nearly as good when I first handed it to them.

For meals, wheels, guidance, education, inspiration, acceptance, encouragement and support, thank you to Richard Boon, Charles Campion, Sheila Dillon, Travis Elborough, Alastair Gittner, Chris Gittner, Claire Keenan, Mel McGrath and Simon Booker, Kate Manning, Andy Metcalf, Dusty Miller, Dan Saladino, Niki Segnit and Vanessa Toulmin.

As always, I couldn't have got anything done without my primary reader, sternest critic, biggest believer and the person who fed me while I was writing. Liz Vater makes me a writer. And Mildred distracts her by begging for scraps so she doesn't get bored while I'm locked in the study.

To all who proudly make, sell and enjoy traditional British food: save me some chips.

Cheers

Pete Brown

London

November 2018

Select Bibliography

Beeton, Isabella, *Mrs Beeton's Book of Household Management*, Ward Lock, London, 1888

Belasco, Warren, *Food: The Key Concepts*, Bloomsbury, London, 2008

Bentley, Amy (ed.), *A Cultural History of Food in the Modern Age*, Bloomsbury, London, 2016

Boisard, Pierre, *Camembert: A National Myth*, University of California Press, London, 2003

Bradley, Peri (ed.), *Food, Media and Contemporary Culture: The Edible Image*, Palgrave Macmillan, London, 2016

Brillat-Savarin, Jean-Anthelme, *The Physiology of Taste*, Penguin, London, 1970

Burnett, David, and Helen Saberi, *The Road to Vindaloo: Curry Books and Curry Cooks*, Prospect Books, Wiltshire, 2008

Cloake, Felicity, 'How to Make the Perfect Bolognaise', *Guardian*, November 2010, https://www.theguardian.com/lifeandstyle/wordofmouth/2010/nov/25/how-to-make-perfect-bolognese

—, 'How to Make the Perfect Rhubarb Crumble', *Guardian*, May 2018, https://www.theguardian.com/lifeandstyle/2018/may/03/how-to-make-the-perfect-rhubarb-crumble

Collingham, Lizzie, *Curry*, Vintage, London, 2006

Colquhoun, Kate, *Taste: The Story of Britain through Its Cooking*, Bloomsbury, London, 2007

Counihan, Carole, and Penny Van Esterik (eds.), *Food and Culture: A Reader*, Routledge, New York, 1997

Davies, Russell M., *Egg, Bacon, Chips and Beans: Fifty Great Cafés and the Stuff That Makes Them Great*, HarperCollins, London, 2005

Drummond, J. C., and Anne Wilbraham, *The Englishman's Food*, Jonathan Cape, London, 1939

Edgar, Gordon, *Cheddar: A Journey to the Heart of America's Most Iconic Cheese*, Chelsea Green, Vermont, 2015

Emina, Seb, and Malcolm Eggs, *The Breakfast Bible*, Bloomsbury, London, 2012

Griffiths, John, *Tea: A History of the Drink That Changed the World*, Andre Deutsch, London, 2011

Hall, Christine, James Hayes, and Jo Pratt, *The Nation's Favourite Food*, BBC Worldwide, London, 2003

Hartley, Dorothy, *Food in England*, Little Brown, London, 1954

Kindstedt, Paul, *Cheese and Culture: A History of Cheese and Its Place in Western Civilization*, Chelsea Green, Vermont, 2012

Knight, Sam, 'How the Sandwich Consumed Britain, *Guardian*, November 2017, https://www.theguardian.com/news/2017/nov/24/how-the-sandwich-consumed-britain

Laudan, Rachel, *Cuisine and Empire: Cooking in World History*, University of California Press, London, 2013

Matthews, Rupert, *The Great British Cream Tea: Recipes – Etiquette – History*, Bretwalda Books (Kindle), 2017

Montanari, Massimo, *The Culture of Food*, Blackwell, Oxford, 1994

Nosrat, Samin, *Acid, Salt, Fat, Heat: Mastering the Elements of Good Cooking*, Canongate, Edinburgh, 2017

O'Connor, Kaori, T*he English Breakfast: The Biography of a National Meal*, Bloomsbury, London, 2013

Orwell, George, 'British Cookery' (initially unpublished), 1946, https://www.orwellfoundation.com/the-orwell-foundation/orwell/essays-and-other-works/british-cookery/

—, 'In Defence of English Cooking', *Evening Standard*, 1945, http://orwell.ru/library/articles/cooking/english/e_dec

—, 'A Nice Cup of Tea', *Evening Standard*, London, 12 January 1946, https://www.orwellfoundation.com/the-orwell-foundation/orwell/essays-and-other-works/a-nice-cup-of-tea/

Panayi, Panikos, *Fish and Chips*, Reaktion Books, London, 2014

—, *Spicing Up Britain: The Multicultural History of British Food*, Reaktion Books, London, 2008

Pollan, Michael, *The Omnivore's Dilemma*, Penguin, London, 2006

Poole, Steven, *You Aren't What You Eat*, Union Books, London, 2012

Potter, Andrew, *The Authenticity Hoax: Why the 'Real' Things We Seek Don't Make Us Happy*, HarperPerennial, Canada, 2010

Rappoport, Leon, *How We Eat*, ECW, Toronto, 2003

Rogers, Ben, *Beef and Liberty*, Vintage, London, 2004

Scholliers, Peter (Ed.), *Food, Drink and Identity*, Berg, Oxford, 2001

Segnit, Niki, *The Flavour Thesaurus*, Bloomsbury, London, 2010

Silver, Katie, 'Bacon Butties, Roast Dinners and a Cuppa: 50 Things We Love Best about Britain Show We're a

Nation of Food Lovers', *Daily Mail*, February 2012, http://www.dailymail.co.uk/news/article-2095973/50-things-love-best-Britain-nation-food-lovers.html

Spencer, Colin, *British Food: An Extraordinary Thousand Years of History*, Grub Street, London, 2002

Visser, Margaret, *The Rituals of Dinner: The Origins, Evolution, Eccentricities and Meaning of Table Manners*, Penguin, London, 2017

Walton, John K., *Fish and Chips and the British Working Class*, Leicester University Press, London, 1992

Wilson, Bee, 'Who Killed the Curry House?' *Guardian*, February 2017, https://www.theguardian.com/lifeandstyle/2017/jan/12/who-killed-the-british-curry-house

Zuckerman, Larry, *The Potato*, Macmillan, London, 1999